A MIGHTY CASE AGAINST WAR

A MIGHTY CASE AGAINST WAR

What America Missed in U.S. History Class
and What We (All) Can Do Now

KATHY BECKWITH

Dignity Press
World Dignity University Press

For inquiries about author visits, in person or via the Internet, and other books by Kathy Beckwith, please contact Kathy at www.kathybeckwith.com.

Published by Dignity Press
16 Northview Ct.
Lake Oswego, OR 97035
www.dignitypress.org

Cover design by Masha Shubin | Inkwater.com
Cover image: Melting Planet © djmaksic (bigstockphoto.com)
Author photo by Ron Karten Photography

Book website: http://www.dignitypress.org/case-against-war

ISBN 978-1-937570-68-2
ePub edition: ISBN 978-1-937570-59-0
Kindle edition: ISBN 978-1-937570-71-2

Contents

With special thanks to:

Bozeb Beckwith
Tad Beckwith
Ralph Beebe
Curran Howard
Jane Kristof
Benji Lewis
Sharon Michaud
Ron Mock
Lee Nash
Phil Newman
Gretchen Olson
Uli Spalthoff
David Swanson
Yamhill Valley Peacemakers
Chuck Zickefoose

those before me who recorded the stories
and others who remain unnamed

and to my husband Wayne Beckwith

Chapter 1

Two Young Men and a Question:
"More than an end to war, we want …?"[1]

The young man spent Sunday, October 7, 2001, biking from Hyderabad, India, toward his next destination – a small village in the neighboring state of Karnataka. That night he slept behind a large pile of boulders, so as not to be visible from the road. His bike was parked beside his tent, his gear inside with him. It wasn't his usual overnight setting, but on this two-year bike journey, he couldn't easily define "usual." He had stayed in the occasional hostel, but more often his lodging was dependent upon what was found as night approached – space next to a small shop, a family home with its pig and armadillo, a church, a gurdwara, in the hollow of a huge tree trunk, behind a movie theater, or under the thatched roof of a Guatemalan forest reserve with crocodiles filling the nearby lakes. And the night the locals were quite concerned for his safety, he accepted their offer to stay inside the town jail.

As he stirred this October morning, he realized he wasn't as well-hidden as he thought. He had been spotted by three young men who were approaching.

"One of the fellows asked me what I thought about the war with Afghanistan. I had been studying Hindi/Urdu, but communication still wasn't easy. I thought they were referring to the September 11th attacks in the United States and possible US attacks on Afghanistan. 'I hope not,' I told them."[2]

He rode on that day, passing through small villages in the midst of harvest. The roadway doubled as a threshing floor for the grain, set out in the sun so that cars, buses, and lorries could roll over it, making the separating of the chaff from the grain easier. It was also a day of celebration. A little further down the road he reached the 15,000 kilometer mark on this bike journey around the world. He and three other PeaceBikers had met all kinds of people along the way, but they especially took time to visit schools and connect children and classrooms around the world with each other, through stories of the PeaceBike journey and through the children's own stories and letter exchanges. As he reflected on earlier celebrations of distances pedaled, his thoughts were of gratitude for the journey, for support from so many at home, and for the opportunity to fulfill a childhood dream to bike the world and to help build peace.

It wasn't until the next morning, however, that he realized it was war, not peace, that the three fellows had wanted to talk about. Now large crowds began to gather around him. They had the local newspaper in hand and were discussing among themselves the United States and United Kingdom bombing in Afghanistan. They had one question for him, *"Ye kya he, Amerika?"* He understood their Urdu: What is this, America?

As he heard the details, and looked at the photos in their newspapers, he desperately wanted the answer himself. He recorded his thoughts in his journal: "Now, as on September 11th, a wife discovers she is a widow; a child, an orphan." He described his disbelief, then sadness and anger as the questions welled up within him: Won't this just bring more acts of terrorism? Does my government actually believe this will be a just conclusion to the conflict?

He had been working to get visas for the next leg of the journey – the Middle East. He hoped to carry on sharing the stories that made people laugh and cry and understand that they had a lot in common with people everywhere. But his journey would be cut short by the events he had just learned of and the question that he pondered along with the people on that roadside in India. Yes, America, *ye kya he*?

Another young man, a few years later, spoke to the audience gathered at the college library. He paced up and down in front of us, yet we could see he was more passionate than nervous.

He began by describing the music blasting into the air, pumping their adrenalin, as they entered Fallujah that day. It was the same kind of music played for them back in basic training as they targeted the human images of the enemy. Now they were real, and the music was perfect for retaliation, for destroying every last ounce of resistance these insurgents could muster. He felt it rush through his whole being. He was ready for battle.

Did we remember, he asked, why they were there? After all, he understood that it was hard for people at home to keep the details fresh. Did we know about the four US contractors who had been brutally killed in Fallujah? The audience nodded, confirming that the news had been remembered. We had seen the pictures.

The Marines responded to that atrocity, and he was one of them.

But did we also know, he asked, what he had learned later, that those four Blackwater contractors were killed in retaliation for an attack a week earlier that took the lives of several Palestinians[3] – not carried out by Americans, but rather by American weaponry in the hands of Israelis? The silence of the room indicated that either the news coverage back then hadn't highlighted that detail, or we had forgotten. Did that hold significance for what was happening in Fallujah? And did we remember how things turned out for the people there?

He stopped pacing. He stood in front of us and told about the woman who came rushing out of the city toward them, begging for help. Two of her children had already been killed in the bombardment. And her baby – the baby had been crying, trapped underneath the rubble that was their home. But the crying had stopped. She needed help, before it was too late for her child. He looked into the woman's eyes, but what he remembered were the stain marks her tears had made down the side of her cheeks. Were they salt lines? How long had she cried before her tears dried into those stains?

She didn't seem to realize that she was begging help from the man who most likely launched the mortar that killed her two children and buried her baby alive. He supposed the baby was dead now, but felt compelled to at least try to help this woman. They could get her to the Red Cross, actually the Red Crescent, just a few minutes away via a route under US control. But the request was denied. He asked again. Again, denied. He watched the woman turn and walk back toward the rubble.

"People have asked me why I'm doing this," the two-tour Iraq vet said, "why I'm telling my story. 'Are you trying to make restitution, or what?' a kid asked me."

He looked out at us. "Yes. And I've got to tell you why I came to question it all."

He was a military man, like his father and grandfather before him. He had been trained and had become a trainer of others. But living it firsthand eventually tore him apart with questions. "From the Iraqi perspective," he said, "we were there solely for the oil. We Marines couldn't quite believe that, but they did."[4]

Whether or not you would have chosen the paths of either of these two young men – one biking for peace, the other battling for peace – or would have reacted as they did to the circumstances around them, you will likely concur that their experiences stirred them deeply and brought questions.

And rather than push the questions aside, they chose to face them head on, and challenged others to join them in the questioning. Asking why, against the current, can take courage. But it can also bring the beginning of change.

It can start with a biker who returns home to tell how others saw and reacted to what the US Government did, or with a Marine who comes back from war and makes the decision to tell what it was like for him. It can start with a mother of two children dead and a third silent under the rubble of her own home, who pleads for help through her tears. I am a mother too, and I must question my role in the deaths of that mother's children.

I propose that the time has come for America, and all others, to question deeply. Because, whether we realize it or not, we are a part of the story of war, a story set to keep repeating itself unless we intervene. So I invite you in to an adventure and an intensity of experience through reading about and discussing our past. It is a fascinating and, at times, disgusting story. I believe it will stir within you some new questions.

A close look at America's past and a review of alternatives now known to have been possible in those times, combined with the knowledge of how war is conducted today, offers startling information that makes questioning not only critical, but also full of potential for powerful, positive change.

I warn you in advance that this book will take you on quite a journey. It will mean re-looking at what most of us have lived and been taught our entire lives. It makes us think about something we've left to "the experts." It challenges what we've forever taken for granted. And if the answers don't mesh with what we've assumed to be so, we're left in a quandary: what do we do then?

I extend the invitation to those of homelands other than mine, yet ask that you read America's story in Chapter 2, not to condemn a people for their past, but as an acknowledgment that it is crucial for all of us to reexamine our histories, to learn, and to create together the momentum to move into a new way of living as nations and as people. Be willing to ask yourself: How was it with my government? What has been my country's story of war? I encourage you to look for similarities, for I suspect there are some. There is an "Evaluation of War" template on page 144 that you may wish to use in your extended study. Then we'll reflect on it all together beginning again with Chapter 3.

Our small town community chorus and a local big band joined together to put on an old time radio show, set in 1944. The crowd in the chairs on the high school gym floor and in the bleachers became the show's live audience. I was among them. We were prompted to take part in the "Armed Forces Salute" to come later in the program. As the band broke into the strains of the theme songs of each branch of the military, the announcer asked those present who had served in that branch to stand and be honored. The songs were still familiar to me from grade school music class, and I couldn't help but sing softly or hum along as people stood here and there in the audience.

The man behind me reminded me of my dad, who at ninety-four still told us the names and stories of his army buddies killed at Pearl Harbor and in the Philippines. Up in the bleachers a couple of guys stood that made me think of my nephews, recently back from wars in Iraq and Afghanistan. One of our kids' high school teachers stood. He's retired now, but came back to emcee our May Day programs each year, because it wouldn't be May Day without him. I looked around to make sure my brother, a career soldier, hadn't slipped in without my noticing. He wouldn't want much fanfare; he would just stand quietly while the music played. But he hadn't come. Yet in those moments I saw that our small community is home to many men and women who have devoted some part of their lives to their country in this way.

I brushed away the dampness from my eyes as the last song ended. The belief, the commitment, and the willingness of these – my neighbors, my family – to sacrifice and to serve others, was real, and I saw and felt that.

For those who have family in the military, or who have lost someone to war, or felt the deep pain of war, or spent years of their lives training to take part in war, the questions are even harder to ask. What becomes of the sacrifice, the loss, the dedication, if we learn that a war was not necessary? How do we bear the possibility that lives were needlessly lost?

We must not be silenced by the voice, even our own, that says questioning our wars desecrates the honor of those who have died in service to their country and makes their sacrifice appear unbearably meaningless. If there is anything that sacrifice deserves, it is the vigilant search for truth. If that truth raises doubt, or even certainty, that the sacrifice was made in vain or for a cause unworthy or immoral, that too must be known and true honor be shown through a determination to let knowledge bring change.

Few will deny that whatever is accomplished by war is attained through a powerfully violent happening. War kills and wounds soldiers and even more civilians. It destroys communities and homes and the labor of years, leaving survivors in the clutches of hunger, sickness, homelessness, and despair. Its power to destroy is greater than ever before in the history of the earth. War diverts funds from other uses and places debt on the future lives of our children and grandchildren. War is a highly accepted, often enthusiastically supported, deeply entrenched system of governmental violence. Is it not reasonable that something this powerful, this violent and destructive, and this costly, be scrutinized carefully?

If we believe that concerned involvement of the people is critical to the destiny of their nation, questioning and evaluating becomes a proper work for us all.

If the questions aren't being raised, we must raise them. If the answers aren't being given, we must seek them. If the powers-that-be ridicule or dismiss questioning as naive, unproductive, or even dangerous, we must seek to understand why they might react that way. Then rather than being intimidated, we must carry on, and challenge them to question with us.

Franklin Roosevelt had planned to answer the question that opens this chapter, in a radio address to the nation on April 14, 1945, in the midst of World War II: What was longed for even more than an end to that war? But he died the night before his speech, of a cerebral hemorrhage. I invite you to let that question hover, until we return to it in the concluding chapter.

In the meantime, as you read on, may this book and the many months of research behind it be a useful tool to help you look back, and then forward.

Let the adventure begin ...

Chapter 2
A Gallop Through America's Wars[5]

What does history tell us?
Who uses war and for what purposes?

Throughout time, wars have been fought to obtain or protect resources, including territory claimed as one's own. Those with enough wealth to maintain an army and weaponry were able to use war to protect their resources from intruders, use war to take resources from others or to control or intimidate people. Battles have been fought to retaliate, punish, force cooperation, and destroy people. They have been fought to protect people and uphold their rights. Wars have been fought preemptively to take advantage of the element of surprise or to draw the enemy into battle before they have had time to accumulate more weaponry. They have been fought to enforce agreements, or from fear that agreements will not be kept. Wars have been fought over religion, often with outcomes that seem later to have had more to do with territory and power than theology.[6]

When popular opinion said that land was "there for the taking" or was "destiny" to be had, and when lands were seen as fair game to conquer or to make into colonies, war was often considered a legitimate way to win land as the "spoils" of victory. Wars or near-wars have even been fanned into flame by pigs and potatoes, an ear missing for eight years, a flagpole, and a golden stool. [7]

But America does differently, we say, than those involved in the bleak past of warfare. All of that was before our time. We are still a new nation, comprised of people committed to justice, freedom, human rights and moral uprightness. We seek to enact these values in all our dealings – national and international.

Okay, we admit, we were involved with the pig and potatoes, bringing us very near war with Britain in 1859 when Lyman Cutlar, an American, went after a pig owned by a Hudson's Bay Company sheep ranch in the San Juan Islands. But that pig was eating Lyman's potatoes! So on June 15th Lyman shot and killed it. Confusion over who actually owned the Islands and had a right to settle and farm there escalated from this action to the boiling point of frustration and anger. The British threatened arrest of Cutlar and eviction of the "trespasser" Americans from the islands. Americans asked for military protection and the 9th US Infantry responded. By August 31st, 461 Americans were ready with fourteen field cannons and eight naval guns in a "potentially explosive international incident."[8] They stood against five British warships mounted with seventy guns and carrying 2,140 men.[9]

As news eventually reached Washington, and officials from both nations learned how the military buildup had proceeded, caution was advised. Investigation and negotiations began, and reason won out. The San Juan Islands were held under joint military occupation for twelve more years, and eventually things got settled without war.[10] But the "Pig War," as it's called, reminds us that America isn't entirely immune from some of those reasons that wars are conducted.

Many Americans, when asked about war, would say that it must be a last resort, after all other efforts have failed. It is to be used for defense and protection, not for aggression or dominance of others or their lands. It is there to stop evil and oppression and to protect human life and ensure freedom and justice. We have a general sense that, perhaps with a minor glitch or two, that is indeed the path our country has taken in its history of warfare.

But is that the case?

The adventure thickens …

To look at the past is a challenging task. There are libraries full of books about wars and, as with all history, there are perspectives through which the stories are told, and varying viewpoints as to what actually happened and why. Yet that must not keep us from seeking to learn.

Some of us may be relentless students of history, but for others, our last real review of US History was our junior year in high school. We may have added to that background by reading novels or watching documentaries, war movies, or seeing a war re-enactment at a park or museum. But as time goes on, we find the details of US wars growing vague, and wonder if we're mixing fiction with fact.

> We can also register the cost of the war, in both human life and resources. Watch for the boxed-in "Costs of the War" after each sub-chapter to follow.

It would do us well to check our assumptions about why our wars were fought, and what was gained or lost, against the records. We find "the records" include varying perspectives and descriptions of what opposing sides claimed. There are details and background information that seemed significant to the recorders of history, and seem important to us. We can note the perspectives, consider the claims and, based on the background information, ask if there might have been alternatives that can be seen now that the war is past.

I acknowledge having taken a closer and harder look at the American perspective, actions taken, and possible alternatives than those of the "other side" – purposefully – for it is American actions and options that we are scrutinizing in this chapter. I also admit that describing an "agreed upon perspective" as THE viewpoint of a large group of people is not possible, as there are always minority dissidents to any position. The following viewpoint summaries, however, have been carefully based on a study of each war and on what was written by and about those who held opposing views. References by endnote and in the recommended readings section give further background source information on these "commonly" held views.

So, let's begin the gallop through America's wars.

2.1 The Revolutionary War (1775 – 1783)

A commonly agreed upon American colonialist (patriot) perspective for the war

We do this to gain independence from the oppressive rule of King George III and to be out from under the unfairness of taxes and economic and political control imposed on the colonies by the British Parliament. We act soon in order to throw off such tyranny before we become a ruined, enslaved people. We have patiently and humbly brought our cause to the British for redress. Our petitions have been answered with further injury, and our rights as Citizens ignored. We can no longer bear this treatment. We don't need them, and we certainly don't need their oppressive taxes!

The perspective of the other side (Great Britain)

We are the rightful, legal government of these colonies. Yet there are among them those who would continuously challenge our governance and stir the emotions of the people to work against us. We must stop belligerent behavior by firm action. Why do they feel they have no responsibility to help pay their way? Why should they be exempt from taxes, putting even more burden on those in Britain already paying the heavy costs of the Seven Years' War? That war which began in 1754 in North America against the French and their allies was for the good of these colonies. They would never have been safe as long as the French were there, encouraging the Indians to raid their frontier settlements. Have they so quickly forgotten the days they had to flee to the east to get away from such danger? We were victorious. New France is gone; new lands are open. Yet they complain when asked to pay taxes which will assure their continued safety. Instead, they defy us, these wild and uncontrolled "sons of liberty," who act so rashly in defiance of tax and disregard of the law.

We offer them protection. We offer them wise, competent governance. We have given them what they most need, the opportunity for economic growth and a part of the richness of our history and tradition. They are our colonies. We cannot and will not allow rebellion.

Background

The North American continent was an object of desire for French, Spanish, and British conquest and control. Each was determined to hold the land and its resources for their economic progress and well-being. A war for the conquest of empire had been waged against the native population and against each other [the 1754–1760 "French and Indian War" in America and a part of "The Seven Years' War" in Europe]. Britain was victorious over France and her ally, Spain, and thus controlled the terms of peace. In North America France gave up Canada and the land it had claimed east of the Mississippi River. Spain gave up East and West Florida.

The colonists felt the impact of those years of war coming to a close:

> During the French and Indian War ... the merchants in New York City, and elsewhere in the colonies, had prospered greatly. Money had poured in not only from smuggling [with French and

Spanish West Indies sugar trade] but also from wartime profi-
teering. Then suddenly, instead of mounting prosperity there was
a postwar depression in the city.[11]

Compounding this difficulty, Britain insisted that the colonists help pay for
their own defense and the continued protection of troops kept in the colonies
to assure peace. Citizens in England were weary of heavy taxes required by
the debt incurred for distant war and protection of newly gained territory.
Parliament determined to shift some of the tax burden to the colonies, first
by the Sugar Act (primarily a tax on imported molasses) and then the Stamp
Act (a direct tax levied by requiring the purchase of stamps affixed to many
documents to make them legal). There was outrage. Colonists felt no need for
British troops to remain in the colonies, and they didn't want to pay for them.
Resistance grew. Delegates from all over the colonies came to New York and
convened their own Stamp Act Congress to determine their plan of action
against the latest British tax. Their acts included a boycott of imported British
goods and determination not to cooperate with the Stamp Act.

Massachusetts assemblymen agreed on confrontation, petitioned the King,
and then sent their Circular Letter to the other colonies encouraging them
to do the same. Britain's response came back to them via Secretary of State
for the Colonies, the Earl of Hillsborough. He ordered the royal governor
of Massachusetts to have the Assembly rescind its letter or be dissolved. The
Assembly refused, and when dissolved, the members acted quickly to establish
a Convention which simply met elsewhere and continued working to defy
British actions, including that of their governor.[12]

Resistance against the taxes eventually resulted in their repeal. Merchants
eager to reestablish trade and colonists ready to enjoy the things the long
boycott on imported goods had kept from them, let things return to normal.
The Massachusetts governor called the Assembly back into session. An
uneasy but seemingly workable "truce" had come with the pattern of protest
followed by British reconsideration and repeal of the offending legislation
over a period of several years.

However, 1773 brought passage of the Tea Act. Smoldering discontent was
fanned to flame, bringing renewed cries for freedom from British taxation
and control. That Act granted a monopoly on tea trade in the colonies to
the East India Company. This would have undercut merchants smuggling
Dutch tea and thus destroyed their profits. It also set up agents authorized to
sell the tea and reap the profits, further impacting the well-being of colonial

merchants. It retained a small duty on tea that Britain assumed the colonists would consider too insignificant to bother about. But the reaction was just the opposite. They determined that this was the time to act forcefully to break British control.

"Committees of Correspondence" defied British restrictions against political organization and created new ways of getting both news and opinion to the public. Leaflets and handbills were circulated denouncing the law, and colonists refused to unload tea brought in by British ships. In both Boston and New York imported tea was dumped into the harbors. The British Parliament took retaliatory measures, especially on Boston which had caused them such trouble before. The Boston port was to be closed and blockaded by British ships until they paid damages for the lost tea. They refused to pay.

Rather than squelch the rebellion, British actions only heightened resolve. Virginia declared that the day the Boston port was to be closed would be a day of prayer and fasting for the people of Virginia. When the Virginia assembly was dissolved, they moved into a tavern and kept meeting and working.

The colonies established a Continental Congress, wrote a "Declaration of Rights" to the King and to the people of Great Britain, declared a boycott on all trade with England, and set plans to meet again the following year. A strong voice, the Loyalists, called for non-cooperation against British policies while still remaining loyal to the Crown, as was fitting for British subjects. They believed that reason and persistence would be enough to accomplish their goals, which would also have the advantage of leaving their privileged status, economically and politically, intact. However, many others talked increasingly of revolution and of war.

Speaking out the mood of the colonies, George Mason said, "We owe to our Mother-Country the Duty of Subjects but will not pay her the Submission of Slaves."[13]

A growing concern over the possibility of armed conflict resulted in both the colonists and the British Regulars amassing arms. Militias had been well-established under the control of the royal governors, but the colonies began to form independent militias directly under their own power and leadership. When British troops stationed in Boston decided it was time to take control of the arms the colonists had stored in Concord, their plan became known. Locals were warned by nighttime riders that the troops were moving, and colonial militia came out to stop them. Fighting broke out at

Lexington and at Concord in April 1775. A move for independence through force had occurred.

A Declaration of Independence followed in July 1776.

The major debate among the colonists seemed to be whether they had the right to defy the rule of the King by asserting independence, not whether they should use war to gain that independence. Most of the revolutionaries "seem to have regarded the resort to warfare as almost a matter of course."[14] The British had encouraged the ownership of guns in order to build their strength against the French and some Indians, thus equipping men for a dual role of provider and fighter.

George Washington was appointed commander of the Continental Army in July 1775. The war was fought until 1781 and was finally concluded with a peace treaty in 1783 that recognized America's independence. Those in the war experienced increasingly dire circumstances:

> By 1780, the Continental soldiers had become discouraged and angry. They had been asked to fight but had not been paid except in the almost worthless Continental dollars being minted by the colonies. And food, clothing, and other goods supposedly sent to the troops never seemed to arrive. One private from New Jersey wrote in his journal that he saw men roasting their shoes over a fire and eating them. He also complained that he had not eaten anything in four days except for 'a little black birch bark,' which he gnawed off a small stick of wood.
>
> Things exploded in an ugly way in 1780. Troops in the Pennsylvania Line regiment began attacking civilians. They took money, food, valuables – anything that could be sold. Their officers tried to control the men, but they were beyond control. They even killed three of the officers sent to restore order. ... Washington ordered the ringleaders shot and warned the rest that they, too, were in danger. ... By the time the coldest weather [winter 1780] had passed, more than one-fourth of Washington's army had died of cold, malnutrition, or disease at Valley Forge.[15]

The slaughter of war reached civilians on both sides. Colonists' and Indian villages alike were attacked and burned. George Washington "felt it was important to destroy the Indians' farmland right at the time when their crops were close to harvest. People who were hungry and had no means of feeding themselves were less likely to wage war, he reasoned."[16]

Loyalists and Iroquois Indian fighters joined in raids, killing entire families of colonists, burning homes to the ground, and shooting livestock.

The assistance of the French, by providing war materials and then later in the war by providing thousands of ground troops and their navy, was a critical factor in the defeat of the British.

The war that began with shots in Lexington in April 1775 ended six and a half years later. There was rejoicing, and then the facing of reality:

> Physically, their new republic was in ruins. Large cities like Charleston and New York had been badly damaged in the fighting. Streets and roads were torn up, homes were gutted by fire, and rubbish lay in heaps everywhere. The countryside was no better. The lush valleys and rolling hills of New York, Virginia, Pennsylvania, and New Jersey bore the scars of the war. Homes and barns had been destroyed by fire, and livestock had been killed by Loyalist and Indian raids. … The challenges faced by the new republic were varied … like a huge war debt … which forced Congress to impose heavy taxes on the American people.[17]

Were there alternatives to war?

Yes. Further non-cooperation was one option. The colonists had become quite skilled at refusing to cooperate with taxes or practices they believed to be oppressive. Their methods were varied, creative, effective, and an astounding example of broad-based networking. When they decided to boycott British imports, they joined together in direct action. They raised flax for linen and sheep for wool, and people learned how to spin as a patriotic action. They found herbal substitutes for imported tea, promoted local industry, and established markets for homemade goods.

When the Stamp Act was passed, they refused to cooperate or use the stamp-tax on paper and documents as was required. In spite of unemployment, severe economic distress, and doing without, they held to their plans of resistance – until on the other side of the ocean, merchants trading with the colonies bombarded the British Parliament with complaints of ruined business, and the legislation was repealed.

They used pamphlets, leaflets, and "broadsides" to stir the people to action through words. They took to the streets in parades and processions, though the "street theater" they used now seems rather gross, with stuffed puppets of the devil and of the offending British administrators disposed of crudely.

Their defiance was not always without violence or counter-productive consequences. Mobs lost control and went on rampages of destruction. Crowds harassed British soldiers and administrative personnel. Correspondence to General George Washington from the British peace-making delegation was not delivered to him because his title was not written correctly on the envelope.[18] One wonders how deeply pettiness and hot-headedness impacted the course of history and how it compromised the effectiveness of boycotts and other methods of resistance.

But these many actions moved too slowly to satisfy some of those demanding change. The struggle appeared to be losing ground, or at least repeating itself in cycles. In the midst of struggle, when the end could not be seen, it was easy to lose patience.

The colonists could have refused to be drawn into war or carry out violent acts that triggered the British reaction to send troops in to regain control. They could have continued to ignore or defy the dictates they believed to be unjust and refused to cooperate with them. Their drive for self-determination and their independent spirit could have continued to foster creative responses. What if, instead of war, the voices of the "Founding Fathers" had called passionately and clearly for continued resistance? Could they have inspired the people to leave war behind and work for an independent nation birthed without violence or for a mutually beneficial renewal of citizenship under just terms? That possibility cannot be ruled out.

And what could "Founding Mothers" have done had they chosen to become vocal in leadership for justice without violence? What would have been the will of "the common people," who had no vote and were not allowed to play an active role in political doings? What if their opinions had been sought out separately from those of the wealthy merchants, landowners, and others who seemed most antagonized by the economic consequences of British legislation and were so vocal about not putting up with it? Had they been invited in and taken a role in the decision-making, would they have found a course other than war?

Though obstacles to communication were enormous in light of today's technology, open diplomatic channels could have been persistently pursued.

Change was continuous in British parliamentary leadership, and it included those sympathetic to the American requests. There was active influence on the Parliament by British merchants, providing an eventual internal check on legislation.

There was recognition of the relationship of the colonists to Great Britain and of their history not only as long-time British subjects, but as people capable of autonomy and efficiency in their decision-making over many years. The implementation and then reversal of acts of Parliament relating to the colonies had become common, showing that there was sensitivity to what was not working, even though change took time. Exercising patience rather than pushing for war was an alternative open to the colonists, had they believed there were advantages to doing so.

When political independence did finally come there was not so much concern in Great Britain over the status of the colonies, as there was for advantageous trade and economic gain. Great Britain had spread itself thin trying to control its overseas territory. Could this situation have been recognized and promoted earlier? It is entirely possible that with time, with leadership committed to action without violence, with continued willingness of the people to adapt to hard times, and above all, with patient persistence, war could have been avoided. And without the lingering residue of this war, some of the troubles that fueled both the Indian Wars and the War of 1812 would have been eliminated.

It is of interest to note that Canada did take an alternative route in gaining independence. That nation chose to work for more autonomy from Great Britain over time, through diplomacy, from the formation of the Dominion of Canada with approval of the House of Lords and House of Commons and assent of Queen Victoria in 1867, through the Constitution Act of 1982. The United States, however, chose to replace its many methods of nonviolent resistance with war. One must wonder if that part of her history, which is hailed as heroic, set the country on a trajectory that has caused untold damage and has been difficult to reset.

Costs of the War

U.S. Department of Defense (DoD) Estimated Dead
(American) = 4,435
Estimated Wounds Not Mortal (American) = 6,188;[19]
(Others estimate Americans Killed in Action [KIA]
deaths at between 6,000 and 7,000, with thousands
of additional deaths due to disease and to conditions while held as Prisoners of War, i.e., "The
prison ships killed more than 13,000 Americans
during the war. The *Old Jersey* was known as the
worst. 11,000 men – more than the total killed in
George Washington's army – died aboard that ship,
known as 'Hell Afloat.'"[20]; American Allies – French,
Spanish, Netherlands, Native American – deaths are
not included.)
Total British side KIA deaths are estimated between
5,800 and 15,000, with additional thousands of
deaths due to disease not included.[21]
American War expenditures = $101 million
($1.825 billion in 2008 dollars)[22]
Moral impact – unknown.

2.2   The War of 1812 (1812–1814)

A commonly agreed upon American perspective for the war

We must be free to conduct trade. Our livelihoods depend on it. Yet the
British make this impossible. As a neutral country not involved in the war in
Europe, we have every right to trade with whom we please. The British must
repeal their unjust laws, these Orders in Council that declare our merchant
ships illegal and blockade ports against our entry.

They must stop their cruelty to American seamen who are being taken off our ships and forced into service in the British Navy. President Jefferson tried to bring change by pressuring the British with his Embargo Acts. The Embargo was not easy to live with and punished us as much as the British. Nor has President Madison been able to stop these injustices, carried out with such arrogance and disregard of our rights.

We'll also put an end to the British encouragement of the Indian menace to our people and the resistance to our progress into the West. There are some among us who say we may even be able to take Canada and Spanish Florida. Our patience has run out. The honor of this nation is at stake. We have no option left, other than war, to accomplish what must be done now.

The perspective of the other side (Great Britain)

American merchant ships are encouraging British sailors to defect from our Navy to work on their ships. We are at war on the Continent, carrying the burden of the world against the tyrant Napoleon. We are giving our lives and our fortunes in the battle against evil, and will not allow this deceptive, immoral game you are playing, to weaken our mastery of the seas. We have a right to stop these ships and seize our own deserters, along with British citizens who put profit before duty and quickly turn themselves into Americans with forged papers in order to avoid serving their country. Yes, it is our right to stop these ships and take these men, and we will.

Our Orders in Council have clearly declared illegal the false claims of America and others crying "Neutral, neutral" in trade. You are not neutral when you bring goods into the hands of the enemy and its allies and empower them with the supplies they need, all for your own gain. We will protect our nation from such insult and practice by declaring and enforcing our laws. We do not restrict your trade with us and will issue you licenses for all trade that is legitimate. We are not seeking war with America, but we will defend ourselves.

Background

Much of the decade preceding the War of 1812 was a time of great frustration for American leadership trying to deal with policies of other nations that impacted American lives and livelihoods. War in Europe was raging, but it offered a boon economically to America by selling American goods to those who were in need and eager to buy. In 1793 and 1794 the British enacted "Orders in Council" which restricted the trade of countries claiming rights of commerce as "neutrals." The battle between England and France included a battle to control each other's access to supplies, and in a time of war, anything that provided sustenance was seen as aiding the enemy. Blockades against incoming merchant ships were set up. Adding further to difficulties for American trade, Napoleon prohibited commerce with England in all territories under his control. Britain responded by prohibiting any trade from any port refusing trade with England unless a ship was first inspected and granted a license. France said any ship holding the British license would be seized and sailors would be imprisoned.[23]

America responded in a variety of ways, both diplomatic and economic, to address what was felt to be outrageous and unjust control. Thomas Jefferson chose to pressure the British into letting up on their policies by showing them that America could help or hurt them through economic decisions. The Embargo Acts were implemented. They made it illegal for any American to export goods to foreign ports. These Acts were designed to keep America from being drawn into the war raging in Europe, clearly exhibit commitment to neutrality, and show the British how much they had to lose economically by refusing to change their unjust laws. American strength would be felt through the power to hurt their profits, and they would come around to reason.

However, the Embargo Acts were unpopular, especially in New England where American profits from trade were hit hard and unemployment soared, and in the South where agricultural exports were lost. US merchants' ships, forbidden to sail except in coastal waters serving American ports, found their ships being "blown off course" and ending up in ports in England, ready to trade their wares. Farmers found their pigs "getting out and running across the border" into waiting Canadian markets. They surely could not be blamed for strong winds and unruly hogs.

Harsher enforcement policies were implemented, resented, and again defied by American merchants. While there was some restructuring of the local economy by a move from trade and shipping to local manufacturing, it was more common that the status quo continued, along with smuggling and acts of defiance against the Embargo. Because the Embargo had the effect of increasing prices, there was even more of a temptation to ignore it and go for the high profits to be gained. Although there was some impact on Britain, it did not accomplish what was expected. Their trade policies were not rescinded. Political criticism remained strong against Jefferson, and he left office under the controversy and disappointment of a failed policy.

When Madison took office in 1809 a new plan had replaced the hated Embargo. Trade with both France and England would be prohibited, but open to all others. Little changed. Finally, in an attempt to lessen the negative impact of restrictions on American business, all trade was allowed, but came with the condition that if either France or England repealed their repressive policies, the United States would cut off all trade with the other country. Napoleon responded that he accepted the offer, so trade with England was cut. It turned out that Napoleon did not keep his word, and hopes of the new policy bringing the long sought-after change were lost, leaving things even more antagonistic.

Along with the issue of neutrality and trade restrictions, America was adamant that the practice of impressment of American sailors be stopped. Britain felt entirely justified in continuing what they had the power to do – maintain their naval strength by stopping merchant ships and returning deserters or conscripting British citizens for service in their Navy. America saw it differently, as kidnapping American citizens and challenging the sovereignty and honor of the nation and the freedom of individuals. Perspectives varied. The British held that citizenship did not change once an Englishman arrived on American soil and that responsibilities for service to the nation needed to be upheld.

The reality was that there were many cases of desertion because sailors found it much more profitable to work on the American ships. But there were also some taken who were American citizens – neither deserters nor British citizens. Even though the practice had become much less common as 1812 approached, it was still happening, and inflaming the anger and resentment of Americans. As abhorrent as this was to America and as great a slander to the nation's sovereignty, it appeared there was no movement on the part of the British to abandon the practice.

Diplomatic efforts seemed no more effective than the economic measures that were tried. Ministers of state came and went and news traveled slowly across the ocean. Further exacerbated by negotiators working outside of the bounds allowed them by their superiors, offers once given were retracted, bringing not just frustration, but embarrassment and humiliation to American leaders who had celebrated these new accomplishments with great pride and later were seen as having been fooled.[24]

As businessmen in England began to resent the restrictions on trade that impacted their profits, they became more forceful in making their positions known. Parliament began serious reconsideration of their policies. But in May of 1812, as America was stirring for war and England was moving toward peace, the British Prime Minister was assassinated, and confusion slowed down the workings of the government. At a time when a few weeks would have made a great difference to those weary of waiting for change, nothing seemed to be forthcoming from the British. There was no light at the end of this multi-year tunnel of repression.

On June 18, 1812, following seventeen days of deliberation – three days in the House and fourteen in the Senate – the US Declaration of War against Britain was signed into law by President Madison. Five days later, the British – unknown to America at the time – repealed their Orders in Council regarding commerce on the seas and neutral rights, one of America's primary reasons for going to war.[25] A fleet of ships, laden with goods to trade and with the good news of the reversal of the Orders in Council, left England headed for America. When they arrived, they were taken as the first prize of war. Thus communication of each side's impending action did not reach the other until war was officially underway. And when the news was known, nothing was done to stop the war.

Two and a half years of war passed, with the British taking and burning Washington in September of 1814. The American invasion of Canada ended in a terrible defeat for America. The war finally ended by treaty on December 24, 1814. But again, a communication lag meant that those involved in fighting didn't learn immediately that peace had been reached. Andrew Jackson went on to wage the Louisiana Campaign against the British, including the battle of New Orleans on January 8, 1815, for a total of 55 Americans killed, 185 wounded, and 99 missing, 386 British killed, 1,521 wounded, and 552 missing.[26] Andrew Jackson and the Battle of New Orleans were considered heroic, even though the battle took place after the treaty of peace and cessation of fighting had been declared, and even though it did not affect the terms of settlement.

The entire war was hailed as a grand victory in America, in spite of the fact that the major economic reasons and terms for which it was fought were no longer an issue, no other grievances were addressed in the settlement, nor had the United States gained the land some expected to be a boon of war. Things were left as they were when the war began, except for the many deaths and injuries, the destruction of property, the life impact on all those involved in the war, and diversion of funds from other causes to warfare.

Were there alternatives to war?

Yes. The US Government could have waited for news to arrive from England at the end of July. America could have been more diligent in seeking out and paying attention to the winds of change in England during the early months of 1812 when unrest was being expressed over the financial loss to British merchants caused by trade restrictions with America. They could have been forthright about their role in using British deserters on American ships, and with some humility allowed that problems are complicated and often have different perspectives. Certainly, once word was received that Parliament had reversed the Orders in Council that America had worked so hard over years to have rescinded, the government could have declared victory and refused to carry on with war.

Impatience and the belief that everything possible had been done, that nothing had made any difference, and that America had no other recourse but to go to war was shown as short-sighted and fully incorrect.

As war in Europe came to a close and the demands on the British Navy decreased, the issue of impressment was no longer the concern it had been. However, Britain's policies on the seas continued to be a source of irritation for America right through World War I. The war did not resolve that. Neither was the situation with Native Americans improved by this war. The expectations that war would "fix" everything America was frustrated about were not realistic. Recognizing this in advance could have given the government more incentive to work diplomatically and practically on these issues.

One wonders what might have happened if people had cooperated with President Jefferson, carrying out the Embargo purposefully, giving his economic experiment a better chance to accomplish its goal, or redesigning it to find ways that would impact foreign decision-makers without causing unbearable personal hardship at home. If merchants and shippers had been willing to set aside profits from international trade and focus instead on further developing local trade, and if the country had been willing to cooperate with leadership working to accomplish the goals without war, it is very possible that the change in British law may have come, say, even five months before war was declared rather than five days after.

The war of 1812 accomplished nothing it set out to do, unless it was perhaps to show that America would not wait forever. In this case, waiting – not forever, but a little longer – would have been a wise and honorable option and prevented the War of 1812.

Costs of the War

DoD Estimated Dead (American) = 2,260
Estimated Wounds Not Mortal (American) = 4,505[27]
Estimated American deaths by disease = 15,000 to
    17,000[28]
British killed, wounded, or missing = 8,600
    (acknowledged by source as difficult to calculate
    with accuracy)[29]
Direct U.S. War expenditures = $90 million
    ($1.177 billion at 2008 purchasing power)[30]
Moral impact – unknown.

2.3   The Indian Wars (1817–1898)[31]

A commonly agreed upon American-immigrant perspective

We have sacrificed so much for this new life in this new land of ours. Now we must defend ourselves from those who would cause us harm. We seek to acquire the territory we need to fulfill our Destiny as a nation and as individuals. These uncivilized people cannot block our progress. They must give way to what is to come. And we are coming.

As J. Ross Browne, sent from Washington to investigate and report on Northwest Indian affairs, said in 1857:

> "Civilization cannot be held back upon grounds of priority of possession. The question is simply one of public policy. When it becomes necessary to remove aboriginal races to some more convenient location, they must be removed...."[32]

The perspective of the other side (American Indians)

We live in this land. We are of this land. These people do not just come through to trade with us. They come to stay, to take the land for themselves, wherever they want. Their hogs and cattle destroy the roots that are our food. They steal our wives and daughters for their own pleasures. They kill us for sport, yet nothing is done. There is no justice. Those who believed the promises of these men and agreed to be removed from our lands, met with starvation, disease, and death. These men say they will give us knowledge. Our knowledge is sufficient. They will give us laws. We do not need their unjust laws. We need to be left alone. We will resist.[33]

"If your mothers were here in this country who gave you birth, and suckled you and while you were sucking some person came and took away your mother and left you alone and sold your mother, how would you feel then? This is our mother, this country...."[34]

Background

Most Americans are familiar with the story of Native Americans being driven from their traditional lands by the settlement of immigrants and their westward migration, causing conflict that sometimes erupted in war. Yet familiarity mellows, and time flattens the intensity of a story. We would do well to revisit our history. Since this history repeated itself all over the country, we can each seek out the details of what took place in the area we call our home. For me, it is Dayton, Oregon. The stories here are tragic.

Joel Palmer of Dayton was Oregon Superintendent of Indian Affairs from 1853 to 1856, and many Indians were brought through Dayton as they were taken to the reservation at Grand Ronde. Events unfolded over several years. Many settlers coming into Oregon in the 1840s and 1850s believed the land was theirs, and there was no need to honor the prior hold of Indians on it. Stephen Beckham, an historian with extensive research on Pacific Northwest Indians, writes in *Oregon Indians: Voices From Two Centuries*, "Overland emigrants carried not only their food, clothing, tools, and personal possessions in their covered wagons; they also brought a heavy load of intellectual baggage ... racism shaped their perceptions of Oregon Indians."[35] A Siuslaw Indian spoke later of what they had experienced: "What makes the whites think our people are no better than dogs.... How can the whites believe in a just God and try and drive the Indians off their land?"[36]

It was believed that Indians should be made into "civilized people" and converted to Christianity. Failing that, there were those ready to call for their extermination. Especially problematic were areas of southern Oregon where discovery of gold brought a great influx of miners, who "formed volunteer companies to make war on the Indians. They then billed the federal government for services rendered...."[37] Fear spread as some Indians responded with violence, cruelty, and burnings to their losses and to the direct attacks on their members and their villages.

"On 7 August [1853] a mass meeting was held at Jacksonville, calling for the extermination of the Southern Oregon Indians. To show that they meant business, a group of citizens hanged two Shastas along with a nine-year-old Indian boy.... 'Nits breed lice,' the miners said as they hanged the boy."[38]

In February of 1854, a white man wanting the business of a ferry operated by Indians on the Chetco River [near present day Brookings, Oregon] got men together, went to the Indian village and killed twelve Indians as they came from their lodges, burning two more to death inside the lodge, and shooting to death another coming out for breath.[39]

In August 1854 an immigrant train from Kentucky was attacked near Fort Boise by Snake Indians. Twenty were killed, with only one boy surviving. Fear of a general Indian uprising which would include local Indians increased throughout Oregon. Military and volunteer forces were called for, sometimes protecting whites from Indians, and sometimes Indians from whites.

Though there were pockets of concern for the fate of the Indians, many spoke boldly for their demise. The *Oregonian* reported:

> It [their inter-tribal hostilities] will save the whites the trouble of exterminating them. [April 15, 1854][40] ... The decapitation of every Indian in Oregon would not atone a thousandth part for the valuable lives they have destroyed during the last five years within our borders. [August 25, 1855][41]

In the same editorial, the Indians were called "red devils" and "filthy animals in the shape of men."

Indians calling for justice saw that whites were treated differently than they were. Those defying the usurping of their land by whites found their rights compromised by the white's law as it changed over time. The Northwest Ordinance of 1787 had declared in Article 3:

> The utmost good faith shall always be observed towards the Indians; their lands and property shall never be taken from them without their consent; and, in their property, rights, and liberty, they shall never be invaded or disturbed, unless in just and lawful wars authorized by Congress; but laws founded in justice and humanity, shall from time to time be made for preventing wrongs being done to them, and for preserving peace and friendship with them.[42]

Early law in Oregon territory (1843 Organic Law) incorporated this wording into its preamble.[43] The words and laws, however, began to change. The Donation Land Law of 1850 opened the very same protected Indian land to settlement by whites, intensifying their drive to move west and claim the land as their own. Indian land was to be available to settlers **after** Indian rights had been "extinguished," but that did not happen before the whites arrived to take their claims.

Terence O'Donnell, in his book, *Arrow in the Earth*, describes an Indian man settling and cultivating a tract of land, one-half of which was subsequently taken over by a settler who arrived to stake his claim. Sometime later another claim adjoining the first settler's took the Indian's house, spring, and pasture land. That man, Mr. Kennedy, said the "law" would make the land his or he'd have it anyway. Oregon Superintendent of Indian Affairs Joel Palmer became involved trying to settle the dispute, maintaining that the Indian had prior rights to the land, as granted in the Northwest Ordinance of 1787 and confirmed in the Territorial Act of 1848. He didn't stress that the Donation Land Law opened the same land to white settlement. No treaties with the Indians over that land had yet been made.

Though other white settlers, who had been in the area and knew the Indian for several years, spoke on his behalf, the situation was "resolved" when a group of whites murdered the Indian and his father-in-law and one of them moved into his cabin and took over his assets. O'Donnell continues, "Several Indians witnessed the killings, but because Indians could not testify in court, charges were never brought against the killers."[44]

Stephen Beckham describes the governmental policy succinctly: "The primary goals of federal Indian policy in Oregon between 1848 and 1877 were to reduce Indian lands, confine native peoples on reservations, and transform them into Euro-Americans."[45] The US Government's strategy, under the direction of its Commissioner of Indian Affairs George Manypenny, and Oregon Superintendent Palmer, was the continued "extinguishing" of Indian ownership of land through purchase by treaty. In 1851 thirteen treaties had negotiated the release of six million acres for an average of three cents per acre.[46] [An extremely approximate conversion rate to year 2008 dollar value would be 77 cents per acre[47] – casting doubt on the qualification of this as an exchange of "the utmost good faith."]

Whites began taking over the land the Indians ceded, as well as some of the land that was reserved to the Indians for their use. These "pockets" of reserved Indian land, located within large tracts of land open for settlement, were an irritation to the white settlers.

Palmer did not give up the quest to get Indians on a designated reservation. If it wouldn't work to have pockets of their traditional land set aside as reservations, he would find them a new land far enough away from white settlement that they wouldn't have to worry, nor would the whites need worry about them. He told the Indians that history showed they couldn't live together with whites and there was no stopping the whites from coming, just as they could not stop the water of the Columbia from flowing, the rain from falling, or the wind from blowing. While the settlers were still few and there was still land unclaimed by them, the Indians should remove themselves to that unclaimed place and make there a new home.[48] Palmer continued to work for these goals, and for what he saw as an opportunity for the Indians to improve their circumstances and their "enlightenment."

O'Donnell writes that Luke Lea, US Commissioner of Indian Affairs, reported on the Indians in 1852:

> When civilization and barbarism are brought in such a relation that they cannot coexist together, it is right that the superiority of the former should be asserted and the latter compelled to give way. It is therefore, no matter of regret or reproach that so large a portion of our territory has been wrested from its aboriginal inhabitants and made the happy abode of an enlightened and Christian people.[49]

He continues, "And Secretary of the Interior Steward agreed: 'The only alternatives left are to civilize or exterminate them.'"[50]

As clashes between southern Oregon settlers/miners and the Indians escalated into the Rogue River Wars, Palmer tried to convince the Indians that their only hope of survival was to join together with other bands in removal to safe designated reservations. There they would be away from attack, find rest for their old and sick, safety for their women and children, and land on which to raise food and build hospitals and schools for the future.

> On 21 March 1854, Palmer wrote to the Chiefs and Head men of the Tualatin Band of Calapooia Indians: "I have been informed that some of you are still opposed to the sale of your country and to remove to another to be designated by your Great Father the President. ... Your refusing to sell your land and remove to some other place need not injure me. Why should I care about it? Nor will it injure the government. The reason why I wish you to sell is because I know it will be for your good. The whites are determined to settle on your land. We cannot prevent them and in a few years there will be no place left for you. Then what will you do? Will you live in the mountains like wolves? The deer and other game being killed off, you will have nothing to eat, your women and children crying for food, and freezing from cold; there will be no one to

care for you. I tell you this will be so. Then be wise. Take good counsel. Sell your lands. Agree to remove to such places as the Government may hereafter select for you, where they will protect you and provide for your wants. ... If you desire to do as I have proposed, come down to Dayton and sign the treaty....'" He signed the letter, "Your friend, Joel Palmer."

The Tualatins did come down to Dayton, and on 25 March the treaty was signed. In exchange for an area of 1,476 square miles, each family was promised 40 acres on the reserve – at such time as it might be established – as well as annuity goods for twenty years.[51]

An area away from settlement – the Coast Reservation – was proposed by Palmer and established by Executive Order of President Franklin Pierce in November 1855.[52] It ran east to west from the crest of the Coast Range to the ocean, and north to south nearly 125 miles long, comprising over a million acres of land. But preparations couldn't move quickly enough to have this reservation ready for all the Indians that needed to be removed from the warring areas, so Palmer also began work on a reservation approximately midway between Dayton and the Coast at Grand Ronde. He envisioned the Grand Ronde Reservation holding all the Willamette Valley Indians and, temporarily, those who would go on to the Coast Reservation from southern Oregon.

In January 1856, through cold and rains that turned roads to thick mud, the Umpqua Indians were removed to Grand Ronde. Some died along the way; one was discovered murdered; animals floundered in the mud and had to be left behind. But in early February they reached the reservation.[53] They arrived to find beds of straw, but no blankets and poor shelter.

The removal of the first group of three hundred twenty-five Indians from the Rogue River Valley to the coast began in February. It was a 263-mile journey. Eight died along the way. Eight were born. Thirty-three days later they arrived, but severe cold weather on the reservation, food shortages, and disease brought more deaths. This was all done for their own good, they were told, to protect them from harm had they remained at home.

That summer of 1856, on the Yamhill River, which is a short walk from our home, hundreds of Indians arrived for the last leg of their traumatic journey to the Grand Ronde Reservation from southwest Oregon. They had been loaded into ships in Port Orford, brought up the Pacific Coast to the Columbia River, then by boats or barges up the Willamette and Yamhill Rivers, and the rest of the way by foot to Grand Ronde.[54]

In Lafayette, just a mile from our home, people gathered to protest the location of the Grand Ronde reservation. "Not in my backyard," was the gist of their petitions to Governor Curry in Salem and Joseph Lane, Territorial Representative to Washington. Palmer was criticized severely for putting whites at such risk by allowing Indians to be located nearby. Perhaps the Coast Reservation would prove to be less controversial. However, it wasn't long before oysters were found on the coast. With markets in Portland and San Francisco ready to buy, the location proved to be lucrative. An ocean port was needed, and it was determined that money could be made selling land there to white settlers. The scope of the reservation was revised:

> In 1865 President Andrew Johnson caved to pressure and opened the central section of the reservation … to Euro-American settlement. The land hunger mounted … and attracted the interest of lumbermen, cannery owners, shipbuilders, and settlers.[55]

In 1875 Congress further opened the northern and southern sections of the reservation to settlement, on the condition that The Bureau of Indian Affairs get the consent of the Indians then living in those areas to move elsewhere. Beckham, in *Oregon Indians*, reports in the testimonials of the "Council Held With the Indians of Alsea Sub-Agency, Yachats, Oregon, 1875" that no one granted consent, but firmly and vehemently objected to being forced again from their land. "In spite of the failure to secure the assent of any of the tribes" Congress did not rescind its act, the Bureau terminated operations and withdrew, and settlers poured into the area.[56] These recorded testimonies relate, through the eyes and powerful words of a people who suffered great injustice, why they deserved at last to be heard by the Great Chief in Washington and why they refused empty promises for trinkets and money when what they needed was their home.

Treaties of the mid-1800s were soon amended to satisfy settler demands that Indians not be allowed to leave their reservations to carry out treaty-granted rights to gather berries, roots, and hunt and fish. Indians were forced to remain within the confines of the reservation, under the control of the officers of the Indian Department, or be hunted down and returned, unless they should have a written pass or permit. Infractions meant "deprivation of his or her share of the annuities, and to such other punishment as the President of the United States may direct."[57] Enforcement of this confinement was assured by the location of Army forts near the reservations. Further amendment granted right-of-way privileges to outsiders for roads, highways, and railroads through reservation lands.

Policies were adapted to change treaty terms from land reserved for the tribe or bands as a whole, to "allotments" of land given to individuals on which they were encouraged to build homes and start working farms, thus becoming "civilized." This program undermined millennia-old traditions, incurring future taxes on land held by individual owners, putting that land at risk for take-over through non-payment of taxes, and eliminating the future reserved lands of generations yet to come. Special perks – houses and additional yearly payments – were given to designated chiefs, encouraging their signing of the treaties. Payments of money were converted into goods and services that the Bureau determined were for the benefit of the Indians.

It was not explained that funds actually had to be appropriated by Congress before the promised goods – farm implements, blankets, kettles, flags, schools, hospitals, teachers or doctors – could actually be provided. When these things never came, Indians no longer having access to lands that provided their sustenance, found existence on the reservations not just a disappointment, but a challenge to life itself. Beckham reflects: "The reservations were death camps for the displaced and dispirited natives of Western Oregon."[58]

Repeatedly failed treaties and treaty terms, years of struggle and violence, forced or coerced loss of homelands, relocation and re-relocation, disease and death, and the wars brought on by all of these things were a part of the Oregon Indian story that still impacts lives here, as the Indian story has similarly impacted the lives of people in all parts of this nation.

Were there alternatives to these wars?

Of course. To get at that, let's explore another question first. Could Euro-American settlers have been stirred to do to others what they would want others to do to them?

It is hard for me to imagine my childhood and my family's life in Oregon other than what it has been. Had "the Indian Story" unfolded differently than it did, where would I have grown up? Where would my grandparents and great-grandparents have lived? What would have been the fate of my husband's family had his great-great-grandmother not made her way out on the Oregon Trail? The "what if" is almost too hard to pull off. It's easier just to accept things as they are and not question how they got this way. After all, my dad came to the family farm ninety-four years ago as a baby, the same farm that was my home after my birth. The five acres of land we found nearby when we decided to come back to Dayton with our young family has been our home for over thirty years. The fact that the deed described the land as part of the Franklin Martin Donation Land Claim seemed nothing more than a slightly interesting but irrelevant bit of history at the time. We never once considered that the claiming of that land, and the passing of it from Franklin Martin through various owners to us, had anything to do with the lives of native people, then and now. It was simply "home."

We grew up with the stories, museum displays, and the reenactments of the Oregon Trail from the pioneer perspective. My husband has been Wagon Master of the 4-H Oregon Trail Wagon Train and delights each year in hitching his mules to the covered wagon, "to help keep history alive for the kids."

Yet history is disturbing, as we have discovered, and it continues to be disturbing. In 1953 Congress implemented Termination acts that resulted in the official disbanding of tribes, to effect the assimilation of Native Americans into mainstream US society. It wasn't until thirty years later, in 1983, that the Confederated Tribes of Grand Ronde were finally restored to legal status; the Siletz, on the Coast, were restored five years earlier.

My youngest child, as a fourth-grader, was the only one of us who studied the required Oregon Trail unit from the perspective of one of the Indian tribes.

So it may be hard for descendants of white settlers to envision or even ask about alternatives, especially when we realize that in many ways we have personally taken advantage of the horrible wrongs that were done to others. But the question remains: Could basic human rights of the native population have been respected over the few centuries of settlement in North America by my ancestors and others? I believe they could have been.

First, the settlers and the US Government could have examined their reasoning about land use and ownership and the use of power over others: Do we believe in "first come first served" as a basis for land ownership or control? Is there any natural right to land use that we honor? Do we believe that tradition and occupation or prior use of land afford any rights? Do we believe that land should be occupied by those able or willing to destroy or intimidate others from using it? Do organized governing bodies have a right to determine land ownership for all? What about outside governments? Can they impose their will on others already established in a territory not under that government's control? Is military force or the use of violence a legitimate way to claim territory? Do verbal and written agreements need to be honored? What justifies their undoing? Do we expect and approve of others using the same philosophy we apply?

Once they had considered these things, they could have acted purposefully and fairly, as they would choose others to act toward them. It was a mental attitude that became prevalent that held the United States of America and its settlers to be superior to others, with the right to expand as they saw fit. It was a choice to act on that attitude and take what they wanted rather than explore the opportunity for coming as guests willing to work for a welcome and for mutual advantage.

The deaths to both native and settler populations did not need to happen. The removal of native people to increasingly lesser and ever-changing land reserves, and the taking over of lands they had used for millennia, could certainly have been avoided. The cries raised for their extermination could have been recognized as the immoral and hideous acts they were.

As the years passed, for those like Palmer who reacted to the dire conditions (imposed upon them) of the Indians, it seemed necessary, and even noble, to protect them from further loss, starvation, death. That "protection" became a dependency upon the United States Government's graces and decisions for their survival. Instead, the invaders – whom we generally prefer to call pioneers or visionaries – could have proactively evaluated the situation *before* the massive drive for territory and settlement of lands in the West was underway. Congress could have refused to condone policies or pass laws, such as the Donation Land Law of 1850, that encouraged expanded settlement, to the harm of others, and that continuously changed to support the advantage of the white settlers over the native inhabitants.

The settlers could have recognized the limits of their authority to legislate conditions for others. They could have acted with restraint and fairness, recognizing and respecting a prior claim to territory, and simply stayed out. They could have chosen to stay put until, and if, an invitation for mutually beneficial enjoyment of this new land was extended.

They could have chosen to learn from others rather than dominate them and take what they wanted from them.

Yet it must be remembered that the "indigenous people" were also once new to this land. Does arrival time, even thousands of years prior, grant eternal exclusive use? How does "use" and "ownership" of land compare? Is some give-and-take expected in the grand scheme of things? Perhaps the problem was not that outsiders, the Euro-Americans, wished to join the adventure and share the bounty, but that they felt entitled to do so regardless of the consequences to those here before them, and chose to use their power and violence to enforce their desires.

However, in our haste to disregard the "prior use" claim of ownership by indigenous people, we must not fail to ask how we would respond if the same argument were used on us today. How would we feel if outsiders came into America and told us that in the grand scheme of things it was time for us to scoot over and make room for them to take the land, that we had our turn for long enough? We know how we would feel! Yet we rarely consider the feelings of those to whom we did that exact same thing.

Perhaps there are other ways of coming to agreement on how to share resources wisely, without destroying others. The native population did not seem to mind the trading posts of the Hudson's Bay Company and those who came to run them. In fact, they found them beneficial. They didn't mind the Canadian-French who came and married into their tribes and were considered part of their own people. Terence O'Donnell quotes from Peter Burnett's *An Old California Pioneer*, to contrast the difference the Indians felt toward the pioneers:

> But when we, the American immigrants, came into what the Indians claimed as their own country, we were considerable in numbers; and we came, not to establish trade with the Indians, but to take and settle the country *exclusively* for ourselves. Consequently, we went anywhere we pleased, settled down without any treaty or consultation with the Indians, and occupied our claims without their consent and without compensation. This difference they very soon understood. [Our settlements] … rapidly encroaching more and more upon their pasture and camas grounds. They saw that we fenced in the best lands, excluding their horses from the grass and our hogs ate up their camas. They instinctively saw annihilation before them.[59]

The immigrants did not work out ways of living together here in Oregon Territory without resorting to violence and the near extermination of a people. The same story was enacted throughout the country. A successful experiment then might have paved the way for a world to look reasonably at limited resources and mutually beneficial living conditions today. Had we chosen to learn to live with less, curb the ever-reaching desire for new land, and to respect the needs and lives of others, we could have avoided the Indian Wars – and a disgraceful and sad part of our history.

Costs of the Indian wars under government direction

Estimated Dead (Whites) 14,000
Estimated Dead (Indians) 30–45,000[60]
 No Indian deaths related to disease, forced resettlement, and settler atrocities, nor settler deaths from Indian atrocities have been included here, but acknowledgment is commonly held for the near extermination of the North American native population by whites coming into North America.
Direct American War expenditures – total for all Indian Wars = not found. [The 1853 Rogue War in Oregon which lasted less than a month is reported to have cost the government $258,000[61] or, roughly estimated, $6,656,400 in year 2008 dollars[62]]. In current day figures, many billions of dollars surely were spent on the Indian Wars.
Moral impact – unknown.

2.4   The Mexican-American War (1846–1848)

An American perspective for the war

President Polk's war message is clear about the cause of this unfortunate war. He declares that Mexico has invaded US territory and spilled American blood on American soil. We are therefore forced to defend ourselves against this aggressor nation.

What other Americans said at the time

This is an act of pure aggression on the part of the United States. The most that can be said is that the incident happened on disputed territory. This Administration has failed to provide any evidence of a justified basis for war; it has purposefully deceived the American people to gain support for a war designed to accomplish its own purposes. We must reject the President's claim and acknowledge that this is a great political and moral crime of our times. Congress must have facts before it votes on war "and not merely assume that presidential claims were based on adequate evidence.... This war was begun by the President.... US troops moved into territory that Mexico considered its own and had been warned that subsequent movements would be regarded as an invasion of Mexican territory."[63]

A commonly held American belief

It is America's Manifest Destiny to carry freedom forward and to inhabit the land from sea to sea, granting all the peoples of this continent true liberty and the benefits of our way of life. Expansion into these lands can happen progressively by settlers moving into an area, rebelling against the authorities there, and requesting annexation by the United States. It can also happen by force, if needed to benefit those awaiting this destiny.

If it should come to us, America will do well to grant the people of California a welcome to our country, and at the same time make good use of the opportunities for trade that the ports on the west coast, especially San Francisco, will bring.

The perspective of the other side (Mexico)

There is no question about the southern boundary between Texas and Tamaulipas. It has always been the Nueces River, and American leaders have long accepted that. When Texas was taken from us and our President, Santa Anna, was captured, as a condition of release he was forced to agree that Mexico would grant a southern boundary change to the Rio Grande River. Our Congress immediately denied such a blatant additional claim to our territory.

When American soldiers invaded our land in 1846 by coming onto Mexican soil (that land south of the Nueces and north of the Rio Grande), we could only defend ourselves against such arrogant aggression.

Americans have claimed Texas. They will surely try to take California in the same way. Already they are sending their immigrants into our land to settle there. There will be no end to their greed. And should they overtake us, they will treat us as hated inferiors, as they do the Indians, or throw us into slavery as they've done those in their own South.

They offer us the grand "options" of being bought off or going to war to defend our homeland. How can they ask us to "sell" our nation and our honor! How can they declare war on us to take away our land!

Background

The Polk Administration and many Americans wanted California. A representative was sent to Mexico to offer to purchase both New Mexico and California for $25 million plus settlement of claims of various American citizens for damages deemed payable by the government of Mexico. The proposal was refused. Immediately after the report of refusal was given to the President, Polk ordered American troops to move into an area of disputed territory. Many believed the purpose was to provoke Mexican attack and thereby open the path to war and the potential to take the desired territory by conquest.[64] There was debate in Polk's Cabinet on whether America should go for "All Mexico" or settle for just taking New Mexico and California. In the end that question was influenced by the politics and elections of 1846, as the tone of public opinion rose against taking all of Mexico. As a result, "just" one-third of Mexican homeland was acquired as the spoils of war.

Objection to the war was strong from the beginning in some circles, and debate continued in the public and in Congress. Polk did not hesitate to use intimidation of his critics by referring to them not just as unpatriotic, but as treasonous, saying they were helping the enemy by their criticism of the war. Very few cast their votes to oppose Polk's war. There was much to be gained territorially by going to war, and those in political power recognized that the mood of the country favored having that land. Some, however, were not silenced:

> Senator John Calhoun explained why he had opposed the war from the beginning, in part because President Polk chose to put US troops into disputed territory, his initiative led to hostilities, and Polk had not properly explained the facts to Congress when he asked it to declare war: I opposed the war then, not only because I considered it unnecessary, and that it might have been easily avoided; not only because I thought the President had no authority to order a portion of the territory in dispute and in possession of the Mexicans, to be occupied by our troops; not only because I believed the allegations upon which it was sanctioned by Congress, were unfounded in truth; but from high considerations of reason and policy, because I believed it would lead to great and serious evils to the country, and greatly endanger its free institutions.[65]

Congressman Abraham Lincoln raised doubts as to the truth of Polk's assertions and asked to have the spot where American blood was shed on American soil pointed out. He further explained his concern over Polk's insistence that Mexican aggression required that we recognize we were already at war. Polk had claimed that he was fully within his rights to conduct that war. In a letter to a friend, Lincoln wrote:

> The provision of the Constitution giving the war-making power to Congress was dictated, as I understand it, by the following reasons. Kings had always been involving and impoverishing their people in wars, pretending generally, if not always, that the good of the people was the object. This, our convention understood to be the most oppressive of all Kingly oppressions; and they resolved to so frame the Constitution that no one man should hold the power of bringing this oppression upon us. But your view [that Polk had constitutional authority to act as he did] destroys the whole matter, and places our President where Kings have always stood.[66]

Lincoln pointed out a detail of tremendous importance in American history. The framers of the Constitution purposefully chose to prevent the common and "most oppressive of all Kingly oppressions" by requiring that the decision to go to war was not to be based on a President's decision or on the assumption that a certain incident defined a state of war. It was to be decided by the careful investigation and deliberation of the entire Congress of the United States. It is a bit of history that held an important vision, but one that was not always thoroughly applied, even later by Lincoln himself. President Polk chose to redefine the process and state that war already existed and he, therefore, had the right to carry on with war.

Another statesman, Rep. Isaac E. Holmes remarked:

> We know nothing more than that the two armies have come into collision within the disputed territory, and I deny that war is absolutely, necessarily, the result of it. Suppose the Mexican Congress should not recognize the conduct of their general, and condemn it, and send here a remonstrance, or rather an apology — is it war?[67]

In January 1848 Congress passed a measure by a vote of 85 to 81 to censure President Polk by stating that the war had been "unnecessarily and unconstitutionally begun by the President of the United States." But the deed was done. The war ended with the signing of the Treaty of Guadalupe Hidalgo just a month later. The United States had taken the territory it wanted.

Were there alternatives to war?

Yes. On the surface, the government could have clarified the river boundary line through negotiation. If negotiations failed, they could have designated that the question would go to arbitration. That procedure had been established in 1794 under the Jay Treaty with Britain (ratified in 1796) which dealt with unresolved conflicts remaining from the Revolutionary War. It stipulated that the northern border of the United States would be determined by arbitration. It was used again in 1814 after the war of 1812 to determine parts of the boundary between the United States and Canada. After that time arbitration became an accepted procedure in international dealings, especially for things such as boundary disputes.

The treaty which ended the Mexican-American War, signed on February 2, 1848, included the provision that future disputes between Mexico and the United States should be handled by negotiation or, that failing, by arbitration of commissioners appointed by each side or by a friendly nation. [68] The procedures were known, accepted, and already in use. They could have been applied to the conflict before the war, rather than after it!

Underneath the surface, they could have addressed their greed for land and the use of aggressive violence to gain it, and refused to go to war to take land held by another nation. Ulysses S. Grant, in his *Personal Memoir of U.S. Grant, Volume 1,* explained it this way shortly before his death in 1885:

> ... to this day [I] regard the war, which resulted, as one of the most unjust ever waged by a stronger against a weaker nation. It was an instance of a republic following the bad example of European monarchies, in not considering justice in their desire to acquire additional territory. [Ch. III] ... We were sent to provoke a fight, but it was essential that Mexico should commence it. It was very doubtful whether Congress would declare war; but if Mexico should attack our troops, the Executive could announce, 'Whereas, war exists by the acts of, etc.,' and prosecute the contest with vigor. Once initiated there were but few public men who would have the courage to oppose it. Experience proves that the man who obstructs a war in which his nation is engaged, no matter whether right or wrong, occupies no enviable place in life or history. [Ch. IV][69]

Costs of the War

DoD Estimated Dead (American) = 13,283
Estimated Wounds Not Mortal (American) = 4,152[70]
Estimated Mexican Military Dead = 8,000[71]
Direct U.S. War expenditures = $71 million
   ($1.8 billion at 2008 purchasing power)[72]
Moral impact – unknown

2.5   The Civil War (The Rebellion; The War Between the States; The War of Northern Aggression; 1861–1865)

A commonly agreed upon perspective for the war – The Confederate States of America, primarily that of property owners and those with political power

Decades of unfavorable economic treatment, growing political control, and personal arrogance of those in the northern states against us of the South have now culminated in a northern President elected on a platform which would destroy our Constitutional rights, end our livelihoods, and throw to the winds the Dred Scott Decision of the Supreme Court of the United States that acknowledges our rights to our property – our slaves.

They mock not just us, but the very Constitution of the United States of America, which, without a shadow of a doubt, reserves to the States those powers not specifically granted to the Federal Government. We are only following in the steps of those who formed this nation, when we assert that secession is one of our rights. It is our natural right as a free people desiring independence and self-rule to bring an end to oppression, as surely as our forefathers found it necessary to do in 1776. Following the lead of South Carolina, we have seceded from a Federal Union that we can no longer, in right conscience, support nor any longer be oppressed by.

As for war, there would be no war were it not for the aggression of Mr. Lincoln in sending troops into the South, an action first taken without even the consent of Congress.

Now we must defend The Constitution of the Confederate States of America and carry out its charge to "establish justice, insure domestic tranquility, and secure the blessing of liberty to ourselves and our posterity – invoking the favor and guidance of Almighty God…."[73]

No one can deny that we are already naturally divided into two nations, as our churches have led the way by breaking into Northern and Southern denominations. We in the South must stand against the ungodliness of those unfaithful to the Holy Scripture. Doesn't the very Word of God prescribe slavery! Yet the unfaithful in the North would not only disregard the Bible, but would force their vindictive heresy on us. We defend our faith and our homeland.[74]

A commonly agreed upon perspective for the war – The United States of America, primarily property owners and those with political power

The southern states have defied the very foundation and structure of our lives as a free people. They have rebelled against the United States of America and now would destroy this Union and its Destiny. We are one people, indivisible. We are one nation, indivisible. Those who defy that truth shall not be ignored in their acts of rebellion; we must uphold this nation and will do so. The rebels have fired upon American soldiers at Fort Sumpter. We will use our troops to overcome their aggression.

President Lincoln understands now that this war is upon us, we must use all powers at hand to save the Union. He has given the South 100 days to agree to surrender and return to the Union before his Proclamation goes into effect, stating that all slaves held in rebel states shall be freed on January 1, 1863.

We had no intention of forcing anything upon the south, but had this Emancipation Proclamation not been issued, Britain and France could well have given recognition to the Confederacy, greatly complicating our struggle to preserve this mighty nation. Instead, they wish to see the end of slavery as much as we do, as well as the end of the economic difficulties this war is causing their textile industry.

God is weighing our deeds and allowing this travesty into our lives in order to cleanse this nation. We seek to find His way as America is enabled to fulfill her destiny in leading the world into freedom and liberty. So, for the sake of the Union and for the God-given responsibility of ending slavery, we must fight this war through to victory.

Background

The United States of America declared independence and established a new nation based on the right and need of men to determine their own destiny. There was, however, a deeply entrenched limitation to this right of self-determination. Land ownership and thus wealth, along with gender (male) were criteria for being among the "determiners of destiny." Slavery and its denial of basic human rights to the men, women and children held as "property" of others was accepted in our political and social structure as the American way. A "live and let live" attitude prevailed, recognizing that slavery existed and there was little possibility of changing that. The only question to be worked out was: Where will it exist?

Questions were asked both in the North and in the South: Where will slavery or its prohibition support our economies? Where will slavery allow us to expand our landholdings and keep our property with us? Where can the lines be drawn so as to keep the Negroes away from us? Where can the lines be drawn so as to let us live the way we deserve? Slavery became an issue of concern primarily because it impacted economics and the political power that controlled economic benefits.

Four of America's first five presidents owned slaves, all of them during their time in office. In all, "twelve of our presidents owned slaves and eight of them owned slaves while serving as president."[75] Although there were voices for the abolition of slavery, they were generally seen as radical and unrealistic. Slavery was entrenched by the time America became a nation, and remained well entrenched thereafter.

Challenging slavery, however, was not the heart of the issue. Maintaining control over the decisions of government was. The economies of the states differed along a north/south division, with the large plantation holdings of the south being more lucrative with the use of slave labor. The north was not suited for such and slavery had not taken hold. Political control of Congress became important because of the conditions it could regulate that would show favor or disfavor to the economies of the North or the South. Thus the number of slave states and free states in the Union and their representatives in Congress were of critical importance. This was all held in balance for the first few years of our existence as a nation, but when the 1803 Louisiana Purchase added land and future states to the country, conflict arose. The question of where slavery would be allowed or prohibited became more divisive.

Then when the United States took western lands from Mexico in the Mexican-American War, the question took on explosive power. Lincoln's election in 1860 seemed proof to the South that they were soon to be controlled by the same people who would select such an outspoken proponent of limiting their rights of ownership in new territories. South Carolina seceded from the Union. Others states followed.

Lincoln tried in his inaugural address to convince the South that he had no intention of doing anything against slavery where it was already established. They had nothing to worry about by returning to or remaining in the Union. But when federal property (a military fort) was taken and held by the seceding states, Lincoln acted. The South perceived his actions as against the Constitution of the United States – calling up troops in such numbers as to raise a formidable military force without sanction of Congress, closing southern ports by executive order when such was not within his power, suspending the writ of habeas corpus by holding a private citizen without due process of law, in defiance of the request of Supreme Court Justice Taney that the case be heard.

Lincoln believed the Union must be preserved, that hard times demanded severe action, including the use of force against those working to undo the nation.

The Emancipation Proclamation enacted by President Lincoln as of January 1, 1863, was Lincoln's attempt to pressure the southern states into returning to the Union. It was not a nation-wide change in slavery laws, as it applied only to the slaves in those states that had seceded. Lincoln recognized it as a military action and claimed his right to enforce it under special war powers, saying that slaves are property which, in war, may be taken by victors (and therefore freed). Slaves in the slave states that had not seceded were not declared freed, nor were slaves held in the North.

Many expected the war to be short-lived and young men saw it as an opportunity for adventure and daring and for the glory and honor given them by those at home who said their going was patriotic, worthy, and carrying out the will of God. This was true of both sides. Instead, it lasted four years, with deplorable conditions in the camps, battles that dismembered and killed thousands upon thousands, Americans fighting Americans, even cousins and brothers fighting each other. Prison camps brought even more death, and while soldiers waited for orders to go into battle, drunkenness and rampant prostitution raged on. Venereal disease was a serious problem, and in order to lessen its heavy toll on soldiers, the Army began to license prostitutes in some locations.[76]

Timothy Levi Biel, author of *The Civil War* (*America's Wars* series) describes the impact of the war:

> [A]bout 1 out of every 50 Americans was killed in this war, or about 1 out of every 12 men and boys between the ages of fifteen and fifty. More than half of the soldiers who were not killed were either wounded or taken prisoner. In small Northern and Southern towns after the war, crippled men were seen on every street and sidewalk. Some had lost an arm; others were missing a leg or

both legs. Some towns had only a few young or middle-aged men after the war. … The bloodiest single day of the war occurred on September 17, 1862, at Antietam, where casualties for both sides totaled 22,726.[77]

Biel describes General Sherman's "March to the Sea," begun in November 1864. "The purpose, he said, was to destroy the enemy's will to fight…. He left Atlanta in flames and headed east, destroying railroad lines and burning farms and plantations all the way to Savannah, while Georgian civilians stood by with horror … a path of destruction sixty miles wide and three hundred miles long. … The charred ruins of mills, factories, and farms filled the Georgia landscape. To his critics who questioned the necessity of such destruction, Sherman replied, 'The more awful you can make war, the sooner it will be over.'"[78]

Resentment raged on in both sides after the war. Racism continued to be evidenced throughout the North as well as the South. Economic and political control over land ownership, tenant farming practices, and disparities in participation in governance resulted in former slaves continuing to live in extreme conditions of poverty. The eventual withdrawal of Union troops from the South left enforcement of newly established legal rights of freed men often in the hands of those who purposefully disregarded those rights. The nation was not to rid itself of the worst abuses for more than a hundred years.

Were there alternatives to war?

Yes. Some alternatives that could have been taken were:

- Persevere in the use of political, legal, and economic means to address the issues of tariffs and economic disparities between the industrialized North and the agrarian South.
- Address the growing polarization in both political control of Congress and the rift in religious denominations along North/South lines, before people became so entrenched in their positions, keeping dialogue open rather than giving in to splits.
- (Non-slave holding Southerners) Speak and act against secession, rather than accept the call of slave holders and those holding the wealth – the minority – to leave the Union. As Ulysses Grant observed:

There was a firm feeling that a class existed in every State with a sort of divine right to control public affairs.... The slave-owners were the minority, but governed both parties. The great bulk of the legal voters of the South were men who owned no slaves; their homes were generally in the hills and poor country; their facilities for educating their children even up to the point of reading and writing, were very limited ... they too needed emancipation. Under the old regime they were looked down upon by those who controlled all the affairs in the interest of the slave-owners, as poor white trash who were allowed the ballot so long as they cast it according to direction.[79]

- Work to end slavery by implementing plans to compensate slave owners for voluntarily dismissing their slaves, joining momentum being set by other nations (i.e. the British Parliament's abolishment of slavery in 1834), and building on cooperation with those in the South who did not favor slavery yet abhorred being "dictated to" by the North. The states could have taken the initiative as expressed in these ideas:

"Might there even have been a few visionaries beginning about 1850 to promote a centennial celebration in which the several southern states would proclaim Emancipation, voluntarily doing away with the 'peculiar institution'? It does not seem totally absurd to speculate that after a quarter-century of painstaking preparation, the southern states singly and in confederation might have brought slavery and secessionist impulses to an end, accomplishing those results on terms which they themselves had hammered out, hence found congenial." – Samuel S. Hill, Jr.[80]

"The States of Virginia and Kentucky came near abolishing slavery by their own acts, one State defeating the measure by a tie vote and the other only lacking one. But when the institution became profitable, all talk of its abolition ceased where it existed.... The cotton-gin probably had much to do with the justification of slavery." – Ulysses S. Grant [81]

- Apply some small portion of projected costs of war to devising a plan to compensate lost profitability.
- Allow secession to occur and for the nation to be divided, if necessary.

Secession? That last alternative may seem a shocking possibility to consider today, for it is nearly impossible for us to step back in time and imagine a resolution as seemingly preposterous and unnecessary as allowing secession to hold. But the fact remains that once secession had begun, the Northern States had the option of accepting it as a part of their history, just as they had accepted their own secession from Great Britain in 1776. Rather than going to war, they could have allowed the possibility that two nations could exist in the place of one, until the time came when they should choose to re-unite or accept coexistence.

Neither can we easily step back into the frame of mind that understood American territory at that time. America had taken shape through secession and declaration of independence and was still taking shape, having added land by both conquest and "purchase" in the very recent past. Some obviously believed it was fluid enough to allow for further change. Secession was not unthinkable. There had been serious talk of such in New England at the time of the War of 1812, because that war was felt by many to be entirely unnecessary. Instead, they chose not to help finance the war nor send their militia into it.[82]

Others believed secession was not an option, but neither was civil war. President James Buchanan had said that he had no power to recognize secession or to use force of arms to keep a state in the Union. He felt Congress must deal with the question, but clearly stated his opinion:

> It is manifest upon an inspection of the Constitution that this is not among the specific and enumerated powers granted to Congress. ... So far from this power having been delegated to Congress, it was expressly refused by the Convention which framed the Constitution ... it may be safely asserted that the power to make war against a State is at variance with the whole spirit and intent of the Constitution. ... Congress possesses many means of preserving it [the Union] by conciliation, but the sword was not placed in their hand to preserve it by force.[83]

Lincoln took office believing he held that power. But instead of defining his power in terms of war against his own people, what might have happened if he had defined it in terms of persuasion and mutual advantage? Others were negotiating right up through the winter of 1860–61, hoping something could be done to prevent breakdown. If Lincoln doubted the potential of further negotiations, what about non-recognition and non-cooperation with the acts of secession?

Lincoln could have acknowledged a provisional separation of states (or "Provisional Separation of States," if capital letters would cause us to pause and ponder the potential), with a set time required before reunification could be addressed – even a generation or more if needed.

For those who focus on the issue of slavery, rather than states' rights, secession, or economic and political power as a primary cause of the Civil War, the thoughts of Ron Mock, professor at George Fox University, in his book, *Loving Without Giving In,* hold great interest:

> I am convinced that violence was not the only path to the abolition of slavery. Britain itself, less democratic at the time than the United States, un-equipped with the stirring words of the Declaration of Independence, ended slavery without violence. In fact, no other country on the face of the planet had to have a war to end slavery. Are we so incompetent, so venal as a people, that for us alone it would have been impossible to end such an evil without killing each other?[84]

The cost of war was horrific. If just a percentage of the effort and cost of four years of war-making and the productivity of nearly 600,000 lives lost in that war, and more injured for life, were directed toward incentives for abolishment of slavery, fair economic policies (including the North's willingness to take on higher costs and less profits during Southern transition from slave labor to hired labor), education, and cultural exchange between North and South, the nation could have emerged from those years both healthier and more strongly united. That alternative to war would also have changed conditions of injustice and racism that continued to plague the united country over the next century and beyond.

How does one compare the value of 600,000 American lives (2% of the country at that time) with the value of an American nation united? Put in terms of today's population, that would be the equivalent of approximately six million American dead. Not including the many whose bodies were maimed for life. Six million. What exactly justifies the death of, comparably, six million Americans? Is the man who leads a nation into that kind of devastation to be unquestioningly hailed as a hero because we believe he was sincere, humble, honest, devoted, and unaware of the harm his actions could cause? Or should his decision be carefully and seriously questioned as quite possibly one of the gravest mistakes made in the history of our nation?

Costs of the War (Union and Confederate)

Estimated Dead = 524,332 [85] to 618,222[86]
Estimated Wounded = 418,206[87]
Direct American War expenditures = $4.18 billion
  ($60.4 billion at 2008 purchasing power)[88]
Moral impact – unknown.

2.6   The Spanish-American War (1898)

A commonly agreed upon American perspective for the war

The people of Cuba have been fighting for their independence from Spain's brutal control. They are subjected to terrible injustice and ill treatment. It is our duty to stop this atrocity. We have tried to negotiate on their behalf with Spain, to no avail, and now find ourselves left with no choice but to declare war.

The lives of Americans living in Cuba, as well as their property, and the investments of Americans in the sugar industry and other resources there give us reason to pacify this region and make it safe for commerce.

After months of working for peaceful change, we have now been ultimately insulted by Spanish Minister De Lome's letter concerning President McKinley that was intercepted and made public in our press. It not only greatly attacks the honor of our President, calling him weak, a crowd-pleaser, a would-be politician, but casts even more doubt upon Spain's intentions and sincerity in reaching settlement. He says outright that he wants a negotiator sent that he can toy with and use for propaganda purposes to impress our Senate. He has no intention of resolving things with the Cubans and has said as much in this "personal" letter that fortunately was made known to us all. [89]

The US battleship Maine has been sunk in the Havana harbor, with the loss of 260 American lives. We now have word from the board of inquiry investigation that it was not accidental, but was caused by an explosion of external source. What are we waiting for? Our patience can be stretched no further.

There are those who suspect our motives for war. Let them rest assured. We have passed the Teller Amendment to declare to all that we have no intentions of annexing Cuba. However, there is no reason for us to tie our hands in the future by stating now that the locals fighting for independence, and their Cuban Republic, will automatically become the legitimate government of Cuba. We need to wait and see how things unfold.

The perspective of the other side (Spain)

Cuba has been and is unquestionably, ours. The United States has neither right nor authority to intervene in our domestic affairs. We have ruled well and have worked to keep the colony running efficiently in spite of continuous rebel activity. We have just agreed to suspend hostilities in Cuba. We are willing to work with the Cubans to establish fair conditions for all, including autonomy. There is no reason to be intimidated by the United States and its demand that they and they alone shall decide what is needed in our Cuba, and when it must be done, all under the threat of war!

The perspective of the other side (Cuban nationals)

We have worked to throw off the control and cruel repression of Spain. After years of this struggle and now a three-month military involvement by the United States, the US claims the right of governance of our homeland. They have kept us out of the peace settlement with Spain. They have allowed the Spaniards who controlled our government offices the right to stay on and do what is ours to do for ourselves! They refuse to let us take over our own affairs, as if the decision is theirs to grant.

They have refused to withdraw their military presence from our country unless we agree to their Platt Amendment, giving away our newly won freedom and independence, granting them a right to coaling stations and bases in our land. What betrayal is this?! With that, they would be able to intervene in our affairs at any time they feel it necessary – for our good or theirs. What deception is this?! As the war closed, we were flooded with American businesses

nd speculators laying claim to our resources and our lands. What freedom
this?! What greed! They joined our war, and now they rob us – again – of
ur independence.

Background

Continued US economic growth at the turn of the century was tied to
markets and the potential for economic expansion into Latin America and
Asia. Many believed that a canal through Latin America was a necessary next
step for trade, along with bases to protect it, and Cuba seemed a natural part
of that picture. Americans had invested in sugar plantations and mining in
Cuba. The shipping trade also tied American business to the Cuban economy.
These Americans were vocal about needing stability in the area and expecting
the American government to see to it that their holdings were protected.

Although President Grover Cleveland had avoided war, he clearly stated
America's right to intervene in Cuba to protect American interests. McKinley
followed and restated America's right to a peaceful neighbor so near her
shores. He worked diligently to see this accomplished without resorting to
war with Spain.

Conditions in Cuba worsened under brutal "reconcentration" policies
implemented by Spain's Captain-General Weyler, in which rural areas were
completely destroyed and the people rounded up and moved into camps where
they could not lend support to national rebels. US public concern grew and
with it, the demand for war to stop this inhumanity. The war cry was led by
Congressmen eager for a way to solve the Cuba problem once and for all. It
was fed by the US press, sometimes not especially concerned about accuracy
in reporting. H. Wayne Morgan writes in *America's Road to Empire: The War
with Spain and Overseas Expansion*:

> By 1895, coincidental with the rebellion in Cuba, two powerful
> men worked on the New York newspaper scene, each determined
> to outdo the other in sensationalism. The ruthless Joseph Pulitzer
> poured his energy into the New York *World*, and William Randolph
> Hearst did the same for the *Journal*. Vivid language, striking
> sketches drawn by men who never left New York, lurid details
> composed in bars and cafes mingled with the truth about Cuba
> until the whole fabric dazzled millions into a stunned belief.[90]

Even with great public unrest, McKinley held off and worked for negotiate peace. Then when the de Lome letter was exposed and when the *Maine* wa sunk in Havana Harbor, public opinion erupted in outrage. It was not imme diately known if the sinking was caused solely from an internal explosion o board the ship or from an external cause, but Americans had made up thei minds. The cry went forth: "Remember the Maine and to hell with Spain!"⁹ McKinley called for calm as an investigation was carried out to determin the cause of the explosion. Spain asked to work together on the investigation but the United States refused and the US Navy proceeded with its investigation alone. Their results indicated that the explosion was set off from an external cause, a mine. The Navy report did not conjecture as to who was responsible. The Spanish investigation team reached a different conclusion, reporting that the explosion had an internal source. One way or the other, it didn't seem to matter much to the American public. They were convinced that there was no turning back from war.

McKinley offered final stipulations and a timeline to Spain, including his demand to arbitrate the terms of peace. Spain countered with an offer to involve the Pope in reaching settlement. Angry Congressmen demanded war, as did the press and most of the nation. McKinley had been burned in effigy and posters of him were torn off walls. Finally, with elections due the following year and support failing even within his own party, believing he had no reason to wait further, McKinley asked Congress to declare war in April of 1898.

Were there alternatives to war?

Yes. In October 1897 leadership in Spain changed. Conovas had been assas-sinated in August, and Praxedes Sagasta, whose party had criticized the harsh colonial policies of Conovas, took control. The "reconstructionist" military man Weyler was dismissed from Cuba and returned to Spain. Policies were set to change. It seemed, however, that waiting for change had become too difficult for the United States.

Though Spain's seriousness in negotiating terms of autonomy in Cuba (a suggestion to set up some kind of arrangement like that between Canada and Great Britain) had been questioned, and though many were exasperated by the seeming inability or unwillingness of Spain to act with speed on these matters, there were obvious indicators of progress. The US Ambassador in

Spain, Stewart Woodford, wired news that Spain would suspend all hostilities in Cuba and work on reform, allowing the Pope's involvement and advice. Woodford urged McKinley to hold off taking any action, believing that Spain was making an honest, timely effort and that change could come without war, as McKinley had long hoped.[92] McKinley could have made this news known and taken the advice and waited, but he did not.

H. Wayne Morgan also described what he saw as reasons war was inevitable:[93]

- power of the press to fuel the fires for war in the American public
- a public that believed war was the only alternative available
- the common opinion that insisted on American freedom of action as paramount, rather than involving European powers
- a Congress driving the President toward war
- a sense of adventure and daring to be found in war and the willingness of a growing number of Americans to go "kill a Spaniard"
- McKinley's pattern of not going public with his thinking, thus missing opportunity to inform and sway public opinion to his side
- the lack of precedence for international summits or direct Presidential involvement in such situations, thus McKinley's reluctance to exercise either
- deadlines, the perception that time had run out; the belief that America would be seen as weak to delay action further
- lack of belief in the good faith of Spain
- upcoming Congressional elections that made it more important than ever to win the favor and the vote that would be needed
- the desire of many to get Spain out of the hemisphere and enhance American economic interests
- the belief that America had a responsibility to downtrodden people and to protect the lives and prevent cruelty to our neighbors just a hundred miles off our shores.

Morgan describes things that might have been done – calling an international summit with Spain to propose and discuss settlement, asking European powers to pressure Spain, and requesting an international commission to investigate conditions in Cuba and give a final judgment on what action must be taken. But then he says, "All such suggestions seem unreal when set in their late nineteenth-century context."[94]

That does not mean, however, that no alternatives were available. It does mean that we have to go one step further and ask what could have drawn the people from "their late nineteenth-century context" and the attitudes that limited their thinking and action.

Some options come to mind. First, a vocal Presidential leadership combined with bold speaking out by people holding a vision for alternatives could have caused a shift, enough to change the perception that deadlines were more important than the process underway, and that time had run out. A strong challenge to the press and to the public perception that de Lome's letter was insulting enough to turn the country to war could have been made. The United States could have stepped back from full control of the situation, and invited other nations (including the European nations whose representatives had just come to Washington to encourage McKinley not to go to war) to play an active role in bartering the terms of peace or influencing Spain.

The leadership of the Pope, or a team of negotiators including the Pope and other religious and diplomatic or governmental leaders, could have been encouraged for Spain and Cuba, with US blessings. The United States could have recognized that the involvement of the Cubans in the process was a necessity rather than a distracting or complicating factor.

Even if the United States held that it was necessary for them to remain fully and solely involved without the assistance of others in negotiations or investigations, they could have chosen to act as a non-vested player in the negotiations between the Cubans and the Spaniards, having no demands of their own that had to be met, other than humane conditions for all. Their goals for economic development could have been separated from the decision to use war as the means to reach those goals.

As the United States was soon to show in the terms of the settlement it gained from Spain, it was not a protest against Spain's colonialization that directed their decision to go to war. Expansionism was entrenched in many minds in the United States and the idea of gaining colonies in the Pacific was seen as an assurance of expanded trade in that area and on to the Orient. If they went to war with Spain, they had a chance of gaining some of her colonial territory. (They had already positioned a fleet in the Pacific ready to go into the Philippines if war should be declared.)

Nor did America avoid in the coming war in the Philippines some of the very abuses they had protested in Spain's treatment of Cuban rebels and civilians during their struggle for liberation.[95] Their human rights violations in the American South were atrocious, with African Americans being mistreated and lynchings occurring regularly. Laws restricting their rights as free Americans perpetuated the climate of cruelty that had carried forward since days of slavery.

> Why sir, the Negro of this country is freeman and yet a slave. Talk about fighting and freeing poor Cuba and Spain's brutality of Cuba's murdered thousands, and starving *reconcentradoes*. Is America any better than Spain? Has she not subjects in her midst who are murdered daily without a trial of judge or jury? Has she not subjects in her own borders whose children are half-fed and half-clothed, because their father's skin is Black....
>
> We did not fail to inform them on the next day that the act [which required a black chaplain entering a church to sit in the extreme back seat or in the gallery, or leave] was heinous, uncivilized, unchristian, un-American. We were informed that niggers have been lynched in Alabama for saying less than that.[96]

These conditions of our own making were ignored when Americans rallied against Spanish treatment of the Cubans. Looking at our own prejudices and condescension could have created an attitude of humility and exposed a moral weakness in our drive to war.

Once the war with Spain over Cuba had ended, the peace commission traveling to Paris to finalize terms of the peace reported they had dreaded discussion with the Spaniards but instead were pleased to find their counterparts to be people of ability and dignity.[97] Had they recognized this likelihood before the war began, and met face to face, they would have had a much greater potential for reaching agreement.

Because the sinking of the Maine caused such a furious clamor for war, there was continued interest in investigating the explosion that took the ship down. A second Navy investigation was conducted in 1911 when the ship was removed from Havana harbor. It confirmed the findings of the first Navy board of inquiry report. Believing that improved scientific and research procedures might shed more light on the situation, another investigation was conducted in 1976 by Admiral Hyman Rickover, and then in 1998 by the National Geographic. Though it was agreed by all that an explosion of the ship's ammunition caused the sinking, it appears that there is no current consensus over what caused the ammunition to explode – perhaps a mine, or perhaps natural combustion in the coal storage area next to the munitions.[98] The US Department of the Navy now concludes:

> Some historians have disputed the findings in Rickover's book, maintaining that failure to detect spontaneous combustion in the coal bunker was highly unlikely. Yet evidence of a mine remains thin and such theories are based primarily on conjecture. Despite the best efforts of experts and historians in investigating this complex and technical subject, a definitive explanation for the destruction of *Maine* remains elusive.[99]

Even had the cause been certainly discovered and determined to be an external mine planted in the harbor, there was no discovery of who might have done it. Many, including newspapers, immediately blamed Spain. Others believed that Spain would have the most to lose over such an incident and had absolutely no reason to take such action. Some suspected it was the Cubans, wanting to draw the United States into war against Spain, who were more likely the offenders. At the time, however, proof of responsibility and agreement on the findings did not seem as important as acting on the "obvious" need to get on with the war.

Had the United States been committed to protecting human rights, doing all within its power to seek a just peace, and advocating for the rights of the people of Cuba to govern themselves, without economic or territorial aims in the mix, the circumstances would have been very different. Conditions of US occupancy following the war indicate human rights were not our only concern:

> General Wood and Secretary of War Elihu Root established a restrictive suffrage (limited by literacy, property, and military requirements) to disfranchise the illiterate and nationalistic masses and the working class in hopes of strengthening the political power of Cuba's conservative and largely white upper classes, many of whom favored ultimate annexation to the United States....
>
> Paralleling the extension of American political control over Cuba after 1898 was the growth of the American economic presence on the island. Large amounts of United States capital were invested in the Cuban sugar and tobacco industries and in banking facilities. By 1902 American investment in Cuba was more than double what it had been before 1898. In addition, General Wood

facilitated American investment in Cuban railroads, mining operations, and land.[100]

Without humanitarian goals being swayed by economic and political desires, it is easy to believe that the process for gaining peace could have been entirely different, and that starting this war to stop another war could have been avoided. As is always the case, the future impact of the war and the land the United States gained because of it, was not clearly seen, including its role in World War II:

> Indeed, the US acquisition of Hawaii, the Philippines, Guam, and Wake Island reads like a preview of World War II in the Pacific. It can be stated without exaggeration that the Japanese-American war in the Pacific of 1941–1945 (if there even would have been one) would have been vastly different without the prelude of the Spanish American War. It was the effects of this war that confronted the Japanese with an American intrusion into their own backyard.[101]

One thing is certain. Had this war not been fought, there is absolutely no doubt that the war which immediately followed – The Philippine-American War – could have been entirely avoided.

Costs of the War

DoD Estimated Dead (American) = 2,446
Estimated Wounds Not Mortal (American) = 1,662[102]
Spanish and Cuban deaths during the period of U.S.
    involvement, battle and disease = not found
Direct War expenditures = $283 million
    ($6.848 billion at 2008 purchasing power).[103]
Moral impact – unknown.

2.7   The Philippine-American War (1899–1902, with later continued fighting)

A commonly agreed upon US perspective for the war

Now is the time to act. Our plan has been in place so that if war is declared against Spain in Cuba, Commodore Dewey is ready to move the Navy and take Spain's Philippine colonies in the Pacific. Our troops will move into Manila. Having accomplished this, with Spain capitulating, the Philippines will be ours.

If we don't take control, other countries could move in. If we do, we have access not only to potential markets there, but we also have a foothold nearer the great Orient. We can bring the Filipinos political savvy, culture, and Christian salvation. We will bring education, health, and economic growth to "our little brown brothers."[104] It is our duty and our destiny.

The perspective of one other side (Spain)

You must know that we also have a public that demands fairness in the terms of peace. You sunk our ships in Manila harbor. Manila is not the Philippine Islands. You did not conquer the Islands and you cannot claim that land as yours through conquest. How can you expect us to capitulate to your demands over our colonies and face the loss of support of our own people? Only your offer of payment will make agreement possible. Yes, in exchange for $20 million, we will give you the Philippines, Guam, and Puerto Rico.

The perspective of the other side (Philippines)

Why should we throw off domination and control by one nation and now lie down to be run over and controlled by another nation, one who supposedly believes in freedom for the oppressed and now becomes the oppressor? These Americans appeared to join us in our cause for independence and self-rule, and then declared their own control over us. How condescending and cruel such a betrayal is! No! We will fight for our freedom.

Background

Many Americans had not heard of the Philippines. They had no idea where the islands were, yet they were impatient for the war against Spain to get underway once it had been declared. They expected it would be in Cuba, but when that was delayed, they were elated to receive word that Spain had been hit hard, its fleet in Manila Bay sunk.

> Millions of hearts thrilled to the sounds of martial music, the sight of fireworks, and the thought of victory's meaning.... That victory came in another hemisphere and in a place of which most Americans had never heard did not matter.[105]

One senator spoke what others felt: "The fear I have about this war [the Spanish American War] is that peace will be declared before we can get full occupation of the Philippines and Porto Rico [sic]."[106]

A riddle in a newspaper asked, "Why is Uncle Sam like a lady throwing a stone?" The answer came back: "Because he aimed at Cuba and hit the Philippines."[107]

However, not everyone was happy about such a radical change of US policy and action. Many saw this as an unjustifiable and criminal act of aggression, an experience of absolute imperialism against the very spirit and form of our nation and our Constitution. The idea of taking the Philippines was abhorrent to them.

But in the end, the voices for US control of all the Philippines carried the day.

President McKinley said:

> I walked the floor of the White House night after night until midnight; and I am not ashamed to tell you, gentlemen, that I went down on my knees and prayed Almighty God for light and guidance more than one night. And one night late it came to me this way – I don't know how it was, but it came: (1) That we could not give them back to Spain – that would be cowardly and dishonorable; (2) that we could not turn them over to France or Germany – our commercial rivals in the Orient – that would be bad business and discreditable; (3) that we could not leave them to themselves – they were unfit for self-government – and they would soon have anarchy and misrule over there worse than Spain's was; and (4) that there

was nothing left for us to do but to take them all, and to educate the Filipinos, and uplift and civilize and Christianize them, and by God's grace do the very best we could by them, as our fellow-men for whom Christ also died. And then I went to bed, and went to sleep, and slept soundly ...[108]

As the war carried on for forty-one months, brutality was intense on both sides, and the United States ended up using some of the same policies against Filipino civilians that had been used by Spain in Cuba and were held up as a basis for our declaring war on Spain.[109, 110]

Historian Howard Zinn, quoting a November 1901 Manila war correspondent's report in the Philadelphia *Public Ledger,* gives us a feeling for the conditions of the war we waged against the Filipinos:

> [O]ur men have been relentless, have killed to exterminate men, women, children, prisoners and captives, active insurgents and suspected people from lads of ten up, the idea prevailing that the Filipino as such was little better than a dog. ... Our soldiers have pumped salt water into men to make them talk, and have taken prisoners people who held up their hands and peacefully surrendered, and an hour later, without an atom of evidence to show that they were even *insurrectos,* stood them on a bridge and shot them down one by one, to drop into the water below and float down, as examples to those who found their bullet-loaded corpses.[111]

Sean McEnroe, writing in the *Oregon Historical Quarterly,* describes the "justification" given for such measures:

> The testimony of General Robert P. Hughes, who commanded American troops around Manila in 1898, included this exchange with Senator Joseph Rawlins (D-Utah) on the practice of burning Filipino villages:
>
> Rawlins: The punishment in this case would fall, not upon the men, who could go elsewhere, but mainly upon the women and little children.
>
> Hughes: The women and children are part of the family, and where you wish to inflict a punishment you can punish the man probably worse in that way than in any other.

Rawlins: But is that within the ordinary rules of civilized warfare?...
Hughes: These people are not civilized. [112]

McEnroe further describes the conditions of the war:

In a letter to his wife, [George] Telfer described his daily routine without apology: "We perform no duty during the day – but put out pickets at night. Scouting parties are made up from volunteers – every now and then. It is great fun for the men to go on 'nigger hunts.' The air would be delightful were it not for the odor from dead niggers which have been left unburied...."

The American soldiers treated the civilians as enemies, heedless of protestations to the contrary, and either executed them or used them for forced labor. [Albert] Southwick's men made a general attack on all people and property within the area of their military operations. The following passages are typical: "the 'nigs' were so well hidden and using smokeless powder, it was almost impossible to find any of them, but we filled the trees and bushes full of lead.... and sent a shot into every clump of bushes and houses thick leaved trees, or anything that looked like a place for a 'nigger' to hide." Among his [Southwick's] favorite activities were what he called "nigger hunting," "foraging," and hunting for "curios" and "relics" – that is, tracking down and killing Filipino enemies and looting the area for food, drink, and valuables. In war, Southwick considered his enemies black, savage, and undeserving of the protections of civilization. ...

The personal papers of members of the Oregon Volunteers indicate that they burned villages, killed prisoners and civilians, impressed labor gangs, and looted the countryside. Read a century later, the soldiers' candid accounts may shock us, but they also raise many questions. [113]

Were there alternatives to war?

Absolutely. In 1904, two years after the war ended by treaty, Grover Cleveland spoke about what had happened:

No sincerely thoughtful American can recall what followed without amazement, nor without sadly realizing how the apathy of our people's trustfulness and their unreflecting acceptance of alluring representations can be played upon.

No greater national fall from grace was ever known than that of the Government of the United States ... while still professing to exemplify before the world a great Republic's love for self-government ... it embraced an opportunity ... to possess itself of territory thousands of miles from our coast, and to conquer and govern, without pretense of their consent, millions of resisting people ... it slaughtered thousands of the abject possessors of the soil it coveted, and sent messages of death and disease to thousands of American homes. [114]

The US Government was under no compulsion of any kind to wage a war against the Filipino people in their own land. They did not have to take over control of the Philippines, Guam, or Puerto Rico as prizes of conquest in the war with Spain over conditions in Cuba.

Hawaii was also taken by the United States during this same time period. The Hawaiian monarchy had been overthrown in 1893 by American businessmen, the sons of missionaries who had subsequently established themselves as large land holders and who no longer wanted to be restricted economically by the policies of the Hawaiians. Their revolt was supported by the landing of US Marines. They asked the United States to recognize Hawaii as a US territory. After sending an investigator to study the situation, President Cleveland declared the takeover illegal and ordered that power be returned to Queen Lili'uokalani. The Americans refused and assembled weapons to fight off any US forces that might come to carry out the President's instructions.

Rather than fire upon Americans, Cleveland back-tracked and referred the question to Congress. McKinley replaced Cleveland as President in March 1897. Time passed. The desire for economic gain on the islands was added to by others hoping to gain economically throughout the Pacific and in the Orient, and hesitancy shifted. (Among the many accounts of this happening, the reader may find those sources footnoted here to hold helpful highlights of the period of US dealings with Hawaii as just described.[115] [116] [117] [118])

Morgan summarized the impetus for taking Hawaii as follows:

In July [1898], using the war and its resulting need for naval
bases in the Pacific, pointing out that Hawaii would be the major
stepping stone to American penetration in the Orient, the administration pushed through a joint resolution annexing the islands,
and the President signed it on July 7. ... The expansionists easily
saw Hawaii's importance; it was a beginning, not an end. If it could
be acquired, what would stop the acquisition of the Philippines?[119]

The US Government could have chosen not to take over the lands and
homes of other people – Hawaiians by force and by vote (that of Congress,
not the Hawaiian people), Guam and Puerto Ricans by purchase from a third
party, and Filipinos by war.

They could have chosen to support the Filipino people in ways that they
might ask, helping their pursuit of independence, working cooperatively for
mutual economic gain and friendship. This war was unnecessary. It was a
decision by the United States to take and control another people's homeland
through aggression and violence.

Costs of the War

Estimated Dead (American) = 4,234
Estimated Wounded (American) = nearly 3,000
   "Thousands more died later of diseases they had
   contracted in the Philippines."[120]
Estimated Dead (Filipino) = 16,000–20,000
Estimated Filipino civilian deaths = 200,000–
   225,000[121]
Direct War Expenditures = (Estimates vary: $200
   million[122] / $400 million[123] / $600 million[124]
   ($4.8 – 14.5 billion at 2008 purchasing power)[125]
Moral impact – unknown.

2.8   The Tampico/Veracruz, México, Military Action (1914)

The Tampico/Veracruz military action of 1914 is probably unknown to most Americans. Sadly, our gallop through America's wars includes the nearly unbelievable.

A commonly agreed upon perspective for America (through President Wilson's concern carried to Congress)

A grave travesty has occurred against the United States of America. US sailors in Tampico have been taken at gunpoint and held, only later to be released. Our Admiral in Mexico considers the arrest of these men so serious a happening that he is not satisfied with an apology. Admiral Mayo demands that Mexico fly the American flag and give a 21-gun salute in a special ceremony. They have refused. This is not a trivial incident. General Huerta and his people continually disregard our dignity, and treat us differently than they do other countries, as far as I can learn.[126] If we let things like this go unchallenged we may be faced one day with something so bad that our only option would be to respond with armed force. This is the time to let the people know we are serious. We must insist that our demands be met.

We hope this will not force the United States into war with the people of Mexico. We do not want that. If it should happen because of General Huerta's attitude, we will only be fighting him and those who support him, in order to grant the people of Mexico the opportunity to return to their own laws and government. (The words of President Wilson to members of Congress):

> There can in what we do be no thought of aggression or of selfish aggrandizement. We seek to maintain the dignity and authority of the United States only because we wish always to keep our great influence unimpaired for the uses of liberty, both in the United States and wherever else it may be employed for the benefit of mankind.[127]

The perspective of the other side (Mexico's General Huerta)

A mistake was made. A superior officer immediately challenged the actions of the arresting officer, and shortly thereafter released those taken, with apology. I myself have apologized. The United States is dangerously meddling – again.

Background

In April 1914 Mexico was embroiled in revolution. American warships were stationed near Tampico, a port city on the Gulf of Mexico, to protect the many US citizens who had settled in the area because of the lucrative oil industry, and the investment of US oil companies there. When the group of sailors went ashore to get supplies, they were arrested by Mexican federal soldiers. Neither group could speak the other's language, adding to the confusion. They were held for an hour and a half, and then released with apologies from the military personnel responsible. They later received a personal word of apology from General Huerta, who had claimed leadership over Mexico. Admiral Mayo was not satisfied and asked President Wilson's intervention. In his address to Congress asking for approval to use armed force in this situation, Wilson said:

> I, therefore, felt it my duty to sustain Admiral Mayo in the whole of his demand and to insist that the flag of the United States should be saluted in such a way as to indicate a new spirit and attitude on the part of the Huertistas. Such a salute General Huerta has refused, and I have come to ask your approval and support in the course I now purpose to pursue. … No doubt I could do what is necessary in the circumstances to enforce respect for our government without recourse to the Congress and yet not exceed my constitutional powers as President; but I do not wish to act in a matter possibly of so grave consequence except in close conference and cooperation with both the Senate and House. I, therefore, come to ask your approval that I should use the armed forces of the United States in such ways and to such an extent as may be necessary to obtain from General Huerta and his adherents the fullest recognition of the rights and dignity of the United States, even amidst the distressing conditions now unhappily obtaining in Mexico.[128]

This is the same President Wilson who was soon to work with extreme persistence and diligence over many months to try to keep America out of World War I; the same President who was to encourage the development of an international forum for dialogue and peacemaking. Yet in this situation in Tampico he was willing to go along with the demand for a certain form of flag salute to *enforce respect*, or to ask Congress for the go-ahead to use armed forces to get it. From the viewpoint of time and distant observation, Wilson's actions seem inexcusable, certainly not an example of judicious restraint and leadership one would hope to find in a US President.

But before Wilson's plan to force appropriate honor of the United States could be carried out, he got word of an impending shipment of arms from Germany to arrive the next day in another port city, Veracruz. He hastily ordered that Veracruz be taken in order to prevent the shipment from being delivered. He suspected the arms could get into the hands of Huerta, whom the United States was hoping would be deposed, and he wanted to prevent that.

Forty-one US ships began bombarding Veracruz on April 21, 1914. Marines landed, and by April 24 the fighting had stopped. The United States took control of the port and its administration and remained in Veracruz for seven months, bringing the United States and Mexico to the brink of war, necessitating outside negotiation, and worsening relations between the countries for years.

Were there alternatives to this warring act?

Yes. Acknowledge, officially, that demanding the American flag be raised on Mexican soil to a 21-gun salute might not be the only, or even the best, way to gain respect for the dignity of our nation. Accept an apology. Encourage language study.

The US Government could have re-examined their involvement in Mexico through arms embargos and the lifting of them. Were the embargos put in place in order not to fuel war, but then lifted for the economic gain of US arms manufacturers, or for impacting the outcome of the Mexican revolution? There could also have been an examination of US citizens' ownership of the resources and land of other countries and the resulting need to protect those individuals and their holdings with violence.

Costs of the War

Estimated Dead (American) = 17
Estimated Wounded (American) = 61
Estimated Dead (Mexican) = 152–172
Estimated Wounded (Mexican) 195–250[129]
Direct War expenditures = not found
Moral impact – unknown.

2.9   World War I ("The Great War", 1914–1918)

A commonly agreed upon American early-on perspective for the war

What a pity that the nations of Europe have brought upon themselves this great calamity. It is not our duty to join the battle, for there is not just one side, but both sides are with fault, and both have at times tried our patience to the breaking point. Rather, we must act as the mediators of peace and do all we can to bring this conflict to a hasty and permanent resolution.

Background (on the surface)

Gavrilo Princip of the Austro-Hungarian province of Serbia killed Franz Ferdinand, heir to the Austro-Hungarian throne, and his wife Sophie, when they were visiting Serbia in June 1914. Austria-Hungary determined this to be an assassination plot by those working for the independence of Serbia. They issued an ultimatum to Serbia, which many believed was purposefully done to provoke a refusal and serve as an excuse to declare war on them and wipe out their independence movement. Partial terms were refused; war was declared.

Russia, allied to Serbia, joined war on Serbia's side, as did Montenegro. Germany, allied to Austria-Hungary, joined war against Russia. France, allied to Russia, joined war against Germany and Austria-Hungary. Germany headed through Belgium to get to Paris. Britain, holding agreements with both France and Russia and an old agreement with Belgium, joined war against Germany and Austria-Hungary. Colonies of Britain – Australia, Canada, India, New Zealand, Rhodesia, and the Union of South Africa – joined war on Britain's side. Japan held agreements with Britain, and joined war against Germany. Austria-Hungary declared war on Japan. Turkey attacked Russian ports in the Black Sea. Italy and the United States declared their neutrality during the early months of the war, but joined the war in 1915 and 1917, respectively. Bulgaria joined in 1915. Romania stayed neutral at first, but joined the war in 1916 hoping to gain territory from Austria-Hungary. Portugal seized German ships in Portuguese harbors so Germany declared war on them in 1916. Greece joined on the Allies' side in 1917. Soon the world was at war. [130]

Background (under the surface)

In the century before World War I began, Europe and many other areas of the world were in upheaval. Control of territory and wars to gain more, grabbing up colonies, changing national and kingdom borders and forms of governance, and ethnic groups' struggles for independence – these were the reality. Perceived economic advantage raised animosity among those in power and between those controlling wealth and those without control.

Political and economic power was concentrated in the hands of an increasingly interwoven family of aristocracy. Buildup of armed forces and weaponry escalated. Alliances were formed in hopes of maintaining one's own power or limiting others'. So once the war began, countries fell like dominoes into the conflict along the lines of their alliances.

At first, the US public and government watched, and President Woodrow Wilson took a position he felt to be that of a majority of the American people and of his own ethics and wisdom – that of neutrality.

> It was clear to Wilson that all the belligerents sincerely believed that they were fighting for their existence, but that all of them desired a smashing victory in order to enhance their power, win new territory, and impose crushing indemnities upon their enemies. … [H]e suspected that the financiers and industrialists favored preparedness and a strong foreign policy in order to increase profits and provoke a war that would end the reform [labor] movement at home.[131]

The US Decision to Join the War

In 1914 as the war began, Wilson and the State Department, holding fast to the stance of neutrality, implemented a ban on all credit to all of the fighting nations. By 1915, however, it was evident that this impacted the US economy negatively by hampering US trade, and the policy was changed. The economy had slowed dramatically and only began turning around as the United States was able to supply war materials as well as other goods to those in conflict in Europe.

Britain, with its advanced naval force, was largely in control of the seas and the shipping routes to Europe and, through blockades and other policies, gradually became able to prevent almost all US trade with the Central Powers (Austria-Hungary, Germany, the Ottoman Empire, and Bulgaria) and monopolize the US trade for its own benefit, both economically and for its war effort. Thus shipping and trade with Britain became the primary factor of US economic health.

But all was not well between America and Great Britain. Britain had blacklisted American firms who managed to trade with the Central Powers. British forces carried out "search and seizure" of American ships, reminiscent in Wilson's opinion of the very reasons the United States had gone to war with Britain in 1812. They captured US ships and took them into British ports. And they spurned all efforts Wilson had taken to mediate a peace. It seemed to Wilson that the war was largely based on Britain's having taken control of much of the world and Germany wanting the same thing for itself. "Wilson asserted that 'the objects which the statesmen of the belligerent on both sides have in mind in this war are virtually the same, as stated in general terms to their own people and to the world.'"[132] Wilson was determined to keep the United States out of others' dispute.

However, since trade largely excluded the Central Powers, and US financiers had made large interest-bearing loans to Britain, US economic success became tied to the continued dealings with and success of the Entente (Allied) Powers in the war.

Another factor troubling to the United States was German attacks with a new weapon – the submarine – that did not fit into the "rules of the game" and international law. German submarines were seen as something different than the irritating British search and seizure of US ships. This new weapon was simply cruel. In May of 1915 a German submarine sank the Lusitania, a

British passenger liner, and 1200 people died, including 128 Americans. Little did it matter that the Lusitania was found to have been carrying arms for the war effort and that Germany had warned Americans of such potential and advised them not to travel in war zone waters. Such facts could not override the sense of outrage that stirred the country toward retaliation, entering the war to protect American lives, and stopping Germany's use of such a despicable weapon as the submarine.

Still Wilson urged caution and did not give up his desire for neutrality. He threw himself into the task of getting an agreement from Germany regarding use of its subs against unarmed vessels. This effort became complicated since the Allies had previously encouraged commercial ships to "arm themselves against submarines and ram them whenever possible."[133] When negotiations bogged down with Germany, Wilson turned his hopes to becoming the mediator of a peace initiated with Britain.

But Britain turned cold to the idea, as did France, choosing to push on for full victory in the war instead. The Allies wanted to win and take what they could, and be assured that Germany would be broken, unable to keep the territory it was currently holding. There would be no peace without victory.

After the proposal for mediation broke down, Britain implemented more economic policies against the United States. Wilson got approval from Congress to close our ports to any nation discriminating against US trade [i.e., Britain] and to use military force if necessary to enforce the closure. American bankers were warned that money loaned to the Allies could be lost if the Allies lost the war and were unable to repay the loans.

But again things shifted. Germany was successful in implementing a submarine blockade of the British Isles. Germany believed they would now earn the victory they wanted, on their own, without Wilson's attempts to mediate peace. Their unrestricted submarine warfare continued. Then it was learned that the German Foreign Secretary Arthur Zimmerman, through his Minister to Mexico, proposed an alliance with Mexico & Japan against the United States to result in Mexico joining the war and taking back Texas, New Mexico, and Arizona. Prior to this Wilson had agonized over the possibility of America joining the war:

> He spoke of war as a cancer or infection. "Once lead this people into war," said Wilson, "and they'll forget there was such a thing as tolerance. To fight you must be brutal and ruthless, and the spirit of ruthless brutality will enter the very fibre [sic] of our national

life, infecting Congress, the courts, the policeman on the beat, the man in the street."[134]

But such an insulting and aggressive act now brought a shift in public opinion, and Wilson acknowledged he had done what he could, and that his initiatives for reaching peace were not working. Wilson asked for and received from Congress a declaration of war in April 1917. It was to be:

> ... [a war] for democracy, for the right of those who submit to authority to have a voice in their own governments, for the rights and liberties of small nations, for a universal dominion of right by such a concert of free peoples as shall bring peace and safety to all nations and make the world itself at last free.[135]

Yet others used these words to express the reasons for going to war:

> While Wilson said the United States was going to war to make the world safe for democracy, he in fact entered for the less lofty principle of making it safe for American citizens to sail on the armed ships of belligerents.[136]

The machinery and equipment of war enabled slaughter, lifelong debilitating injury, and destruction that the world had never before seen. Use of machine guns, "advanced" artillery, gas warfare, mining of international waters, tangled masses of barbed wire or wire constructions that funneled troops into killing zones, and submarine attacks, all contributed to the mass killings of those in battle in trenches, on ships, or in civilian life in the way of war. Gas warfare, banned by treaty, was used and further developed by those who had decried its use (including the US Government), as necessary because it had been unleashed on them. Millions died and millions more were injured, both military and civilians, in World War I.

Were there alternatives to war?

The surface issue that sparked the war – the murder of Franz Ferdinand and his wife – could have been treated as a crime to be dealt with by law. Nineteen year-old Gavrilo Princip was apprehended, tried, and sentenced to twenty years in prison, though he died less than four years later of tuberculosis, still imprisoned.

The war did not solve the underlying issues: nationalism and the quest for independence and self-determination, disputed territorial holdings and colonialism, military and economic dominance, centuries old racial and class prejudices, escalation of militarism, economic inequality of nations and of individuals, and political control and leadership. Nor did the armistice or the terms of the peace resolve these issues. Many of these things were remnants of previous wars that resurfaced and that remained to plague the world after the war ended. Simply put, one cannot say that the war was necessary to resolve issues that it did not resolve.

In the end Germany was required to take all responsibility and guilt for the war, and was to repay all damage done by the war, though the amount was not set at the time. The League of Nations was created. Arms limitations, though supposed to apply to all nations, in reality only applied to "the solely guilty" Germany.

> Wilson argued that the victorious powers should disarm just as they were insisting that Germany be disarmed. Thus, the American president proposed the abolishment of conscription, the prohibition of the manufacturing of implements of war by private parties, and the maintenance of armies large enough to preserve order and fulfill international obligations but no larger.[137]

Though disarmament became the topic of negotiations for a decade and a half, Britain managed never to have the right timing with the right support or willingness to give up its superiority in offensive weapons. The plan of then US President, Herbert Hoover, was presented at the World Disarmament Conference in June 1932, proposing a ban on all offensive weaponry:

> Hoover proposed the elimination of all bombing aircraft, all tanks, all chemical warfare, all large mobile guns, and the reduction by one third of battleships and submarines.... Hoover's proposals were met with a veritable 'explosion' of applause from the delegates, from the press, and – quite improperly – from the well informed public gallery.[138]

But debate bogged down when open public sessions were replaced by closed sessions at which only select countries were allowed, to the exclusion of the USSR, Germany, and all "lesser powers." The reluctance of Britain, unwilling to give up its air forces and other offensive weaponry, caused a major undermining of the Hoover Proposal and other plans for disarmament. The opportunity for world arms limitations was lost in a continued and accelerated rise in militarism, including Germany's unwillingness to be limited by an agreement that others were not keeping, paving the way for German re-armament, the rise of Hitler, the Nazis, and World War II.

In the end, the Alsace-Lorraine land was returned to France, as it had been before the Franco-Prussian War. According to terms of the League of Nations, self-determination of all people was to be the basis for formation of nations. However, as it worked out, this too applied only to "the losers" while "the winners" kept their lands and colonies. Some people in Central Europe did gain independence, but Germany's overseas territories and commercial "rights" were divided up as spoils of war, Britain getting some and France and other Allied countries others. Some of Germany itself was split off.

Turkey's Ottoman Empire met a similar fate, with France getting Syria and Lebanon and Britain getting Palestine/Transjordan and Mesopotamia (Iraq) as "Mandates" under the League of Nations, breaking British promises to the Arabs who were told their independence would be granted if they helped fight the war. The geo-political chopping up of the Middle East during this time continues to impact world conflict to the present.

Did the United States have to enter the war in 1917? The government refused in 1914 to become involved, believing the reasons for war were territorially and economically motivated and that both sides, all sides, were at fault. It was expected that our economic boycotts would eventually contribute to a decision to cease hostilities. However, the government chose not to continue those policies. For one thing, it was too hard for some to resist the desire for profits that bank loans and sales of military goods and other materials would bring, and the stimulation it gave to the economy. As time went on, these economic decisions appeared to give support to the Allies and withhold support from the Central Powers, and most certainly led us toward involvement in the war.

David Dellinger in his story, "Why I Refused to Register in the October 1940 Draft and a Little of What It Led To," says:

> Even Woodrow Wilson, the president who had demanded US participation in "A War to Make the World Safe for Democracy" reached a point of utter disillusionment when he said, "Is there any man, woman or child in America – let me repeat, is there any child – who does not know that this was an industrial and commercial

war?" I knew those words by heart long before the United States came close to entering what is known as the Second World War.[139]

The war would have ended eventually. The US Government could have chosen to sit it out, and America could have kept out of European waters if need be for their safety, focusing instead on living with less growth and developing mutually beneficial options for trade with Latin America and in the Pacific.

Those Americans who stood to reap huge profits from banking loans and arms sales and used their leverage to influence the country toward war could have been boldly challenged for their greed and its moral consequences.

The government could have avoided the experience and cost of a massive self-propaganda campaign to sell the war to America, and even more importantly, avoided the undemocratic and freedom-destroying legislation and practices that punished those who believed differently from the official government stance for war and chose to speak accordingly and were imprisoned for doing so.

The US Government could have chosen to continue encouraging a halt to the bloodbath, instead of joining it.

Costs of the War

DoD Estimated Dead (American) = 116,516
Estimated Wounds Not Mortal (American) =
    204,002[140]
Estimated Dead (Total, Military) = 8.5 million
Estimated Dead (Civilian Total) = 6.6–9 million[141]
Estimated Wounded (Total Military) = 19,536,000[142]
    Direct U.S. War Expenditures (American) = $20
    billion ($253 billion at 2008 purchasing power)[143]
Moral impact – unknown.

2.10   World War II (1939–1945)

A commonly agreed upon American perspective for the war

We have been attacked. American lives have been lost at the hands of the deceptive and villainous Japanese aggressors in the bombing of Pearl Harbor. The world saw the atrocities they committed against the people of China. The Nanking Massacre will never be forgotten. We will defend our nation against such barbarity. Japan's unprovoked attacks on America have proven to us and to the world that their aggression will not end unless we stop it. We will fight for the right of all people to live free of such evil.

President Franklin Roosevelt has addressed Congress and the nation (December 8, 1941) saying:

> The attack yesterday on the Hawaiian Islands has caused severe damage to American naval and military forces. I regret to tell you that very many American lives have been lost. ... The facts of yesterday and today speak for themselves. The people of the United States have already formed their opinions and well understand the implications to the very life and safety of our nation.
>
> I believe that I interpret the will of the Congress and of the people when I assert that we will not only defend ourselves to the uttermost but will make it very certain that this form of treachery shall never again endanger us.
>
> ... I ask that the Congress declare that since the unprovoked and dastardly attack by Japan on Sunday, December 7th, 1941, a state of war has existed between the United States and the Japanese Empire.[144]

Now, on December 11, 1941, Germany has declared war on us. Many of us have known for years that we cannot isolate ourselves from the world and watch as harsh dictatorship overruns Europe. We were pulling the wool over our own eyes, in pretence that we were safe simply because an ocean separated us from them. We should have been fighting in this war long ago.

Even those who have said we must stay out of Europe's never ending mess, that we learned our lessons from the Great War, now concede that we no longer have that choice. When America is attacked, we stand ready to defend our nation.

The perspective of the other side (Japan)

For the past two hundred years East Asia has been the victim of Anglo-American prosperity and imperial exploitation. You intend to carry that on even now, even after you cried it would no longer be so. We have proposed that all nations be free to enjoy their own liberty. We can no longer bow down to your imperialistic control. We must protect and save Asia for Asians.

You cripple our nation and our people's very existence by cutting off our oil and iron ore supplies. You seek control of the rich resources of the region, and of the markets, for yourselves, and will use any means to accomplish that. In your aggression, you have determined to strangle our nation and the well-being of our people, and we cannot allow this to happen. Your Pacific fleet is located to be able to carry out these evil acts. You leave us no choice.

For so long you have armed Britain and taken your navy to sea yet cry, "We are neutral!" and insist that we must ignore our prior pact with Germany and Italy. That is neutrality?

You propose that international conflict not be handled by military pressure, yet you use economic pressure that is often more inhumane than military action.

In order to survive, we will act. In the end, we seek only a fair peace for ourselves and for East Asia.[145]

The perspective of the other side (Germany)

We know what it means to live in desperation and poverty. Starvation has been no stranger to us. We know what it is to be trampled underfoot and forced to live as others dictate, crippling us in any way they can. We know what it is to have our homeland split apart at others' whims. And all of this has been done in the name of peace!

Did not this Treaty of Versailles prescribe that all nations begin demilitarization? And yet you all continue to build up arms as we are forced into subservience. We are Germany! We can no longer stand by. We have a right to live. We have a right to re-arm to protect ourselves.

History has taught us that to be wise and well, one must act when opportunity allows. That time is now. We need a place to grow and be, and we will find that place and in the process bring new hope to the people of this continent who are looking for a better way. The National Socialist German Workers Party knows we are strong, we are proud, and we will change our world for the better.

Background and Reflections

A misconception held by many Americans to this day is that the United States was the innocent victim of an entirely unprovoked attack on Pearl Harbor. In as much as that belief continues to be used as a major justification for our involvement in World War II, it is good to review the circumstances.

Whether one believes that Japan's conquest in China in the 1930s and later in French Indochina (including present day Vietnam) in 1940 was purely cruel imperialistic aggression for economic gain and political control, or a strategy to promote national self-interest by opening trade and access to natural resources, or "keeping Asia for the Asians" and holding Western imperialism at bay, will most likely depend upon who's writing the history and from whose perspective. It is commonly agreed, however, that Japan was following fairly closely in the footsteps trod by Western colonialism in reaching for and taking additional territory.

In September 1940 Japan took control of French Indochina from Vichy France, at least in part to block imports into China, including US weaponry being used against Japan. In response, the United States froze Japanese assets in America and implemented an embargo on US oil exports to Japan.[146] With eighty percent of Japan's oil supply coming from the United States, Japan saw its economy and its ability to support its military in danger of being fully destroyed, and determined the only road open to them was to move ahead with plans to take the oil rich Dutch East Indies. They would need to do this without US intervention. And the oil would have to be transported back to Japan by ship, without being blocked by the US Naval fleet, which they expected the United States would attempt to do.

Diplomatic negotiations between Japan and the United States were pursued through late fall of 1941. Japan insisted that they had special interests and rights in China. The United States had long-and-loud declared its stance regarding China: the Open Door Policy that allowed unrestricted trade by all nations and excluded any one country, Japan included, from taking any control in China. That piece, we were not willing to put on the negotiation table. Though there were occasions of movement in negotiations, in the end, the US response to Japan's proposals of November 1941 confirmed what both sides suspected – there would be no agreement. Japan moved forward with plans to attack the US Pacific fleet and do so before we became aware of their intentions.

The United States had broken the Japanese military code and knew all of this. They knew attack was coming, imminently, and they knew why. Some believe they did not know where; others believe it was evident that it was Pearl Harbor, the heart of the US fleet that had been relocated to the Pacific. Much controversy has been raised about Roosevelt's purposes and actions and brought numerous investigations into the attack on Pearl Harbor and Roosevelt's leadership of US entry into World War II. It continues to be examined up to the present time. A *TIME Magazine* article of April 1946, described the investigation that brought to light Secretary of War Henry Stimson's diaries of November and December 1941, which seemed to highlight the viewpoint that Roosevelt felt that war was inevitable, he needed the country to get behind it, and recognized that an attack by Japan would bring America together for war:

> In its fifth month of prospecting, the Pearl Harbor Committee at last unearthed a rich find—a broad, deep vein of comment and discussion of the 1941 tragedy by ex-War Secretary Henry L. Stimson, studded with pure history in the form of notes from his diary. Significant excerpts:
>
> "Nov. 25. The President brought up the event that we were likely to be attacked, perhaps (as soon as) next Monday, for the Japanese are notorious for making an attack without warning, and the question was what we should do. The question was how we should maneuver them into the position of firing the first shot without allowing too much danger to ourselves.... "
>
> "Nov. 28. G-2 had sent me a summary of the information in regard to the movements of the Japanese in the Far East and it amounted to such a formidable statement of dangerous possibilities that I decided to take it to the President before he got up."
>
> "Dec. 2. The President is still deliberating the possibility of a message to the Emperor, although all the rest of us are rather against it, but in addition to that he is quite settled, I think, that

he will make a message to the Congress and will perhaps back that up with a speech to the country. He said that he was going to take the matters right up when he left us."

"Dec. 7. Just about 2 o'clock, while I was sitting at lunch, the President called me up on the telephone and in a rather excited voice asked me, 'Have you heard the news? ... They have attacked Hawaii. They are now bombing Hawaii....'"

"My first feeling was of relief that the indecision was over and that a crisis had come in a way which would unite all our people.... Our General Staff officers were working under a terrific pressure in the face of global war which they felt was probably imminent. Yet they were surrounded, outside their offices and almost throughout the country, by a spirit of isolationism and disbelief in danger which now seems incredible."[147]

Franklin Roosevelt and Winston Churchill, along with their military staffs had met earlier in 1941. Roosevelt had believed for many months that the United States needed to be prepared for war, and he led the country into those preparations. The United States had long claimed neutrality in the war in Europe and thus immunity from attack, all the while actively financing the war for Britain and manufacturing and delivering the weapons and war equipment Britain and the Allies were using, through Lend Lease provisions (and the earlier "Cash and Carry" policy). The United States had sold munitions to France and Britain, traded destroyers to Britain in exchange for bases, escorted Allied ships at sea, attacked German U-boats, and replaced British troops guarding Iceland with 40,000 American soldiers. These were all hostile actions yet all technically initiated under the claim of neutrality. The first peacetime military draft was instituted in America in 1940, and a massive build up of US troops followed. [148] [149]

The American Naval Fleet had been moved from San Diego to Pearl Harbor, seemingly to act as a restraint on Japan. However, the Japanese saw it as a move indicating hostility and preparation for a war to be waged against them. Their response followed an observably predictable course. It was the American people, reluctant to relive another World War, who chose to hold back, even amidst all the preparations for war – until the hour came when America was attacked.

The attack on Pearl Harbor came as a surprise to the American public and to the military in Hawaii, but it was not unprovoked, unless one uses a very narrow definition of provocation. It was in direct response to the American embargo of resources Japan felt to be critical to the survival of its people and their economy, and to the policy of a nation they perceived as an imperialistic intruder into their affairs in East Asia.

In Europe, the situation unfolded differently. Some say that World War II began during World War I, and certainly at that war's end, in seeds planted by the Treaty of Versailles and the conditions of war. Sheldon Richman, in "The Roots of World War II," describes the situation in this way:

> Not all the hardship resulted from the treaty. During the war the Allies imposed a starvation blockade on Germany. Due to French insistence, that blockade remained in place until the treaty was signed in June 1919. The German people were made to watch their children starve for six months after the guns fell silent. The blockade killed an estimated 800,000 people.
>
> In the 1920s, many people – Germans and others – would call for revision of the unjust treaty. But no one in a position to do anything about it heeded the call. Can one imagine ground more fertile for the growth of the poisonous vine called Nazism? [150]

The political and cultural conditions described earlier in this chapter – aspects of Europe and the world at the beginning of World War I – were still very real, although anti-colonialism and the struggle for self-rule had continued to rise. The terms of peace after "The Great War" were felt by the victors to be justified restitution and reasonable restriction (though President Wilson worked diligently to obtain other less punishment-driven terms and was overridden). The losers felt them to be unbearably controlling, harsh, and unjust.

The world was in the midst of the Great Depression. Germany, feeling its effects and believing them to be tied to vindictive terms of peace, moved to correct those wrongs and determined to do it through power and force, if needed. The return of militarism followed. Not wanting to lose lucrative economic gain from sale of arms, victor countries renegotiated their earlier restrictions to Germany's rearmament.

The "unification" of Austria with Germany, or its "forced annexation" in March 1938 began Germany's move to build the Empire it wanted. The demo-cratic governmental and legal processes that had been in place for elections, appointments, and party politics were followed in Germany until the power was there to override them and usurp control. With control came the violent push to take more territory and carry out the policies and aims of the Nazi party and leadership, in disregard for human rights and human decency. By 1940 Germany held most of Western Europe.

People remain, more than sixty years after World War II, unable to understand how the German people could have allowed themselves to be swept up into the Nazi furor that was Adolph Hitler. A variety of explanations are given: he told us there was an answer when we desperately needed an answer; he understood our hurt and our desperation and proposed to do something about it, but we didn't know it would end this way; he held power over us and we could do nothing to resist; we resisted in every way we could; we tried to stop him and we would have kept trying until we succeeded. From others, there comes only acknowledgment, apology, or silence.

A German exchange student to our community explained the reaction of many German youth of today: "When we first hear of this as children, we wonder if it is only a wild tale. We ask our parents, and they say it is true. We talk about it. Then when we are old enough, we study it in school. My class made a trip to one of the concentration camps. We know it happened. And we know how bad it was. Sometimes we think that enough is enough. Even though it's very important not to forget, we can't keep thinking only about this. It wasn't our generation. We don't have to repeat the ignorance of that time. And we won't. It happened in Germany. That is bad. But it won't happen again."[151]

Like them we want to know with certainty that it will never happen again, anywhere, and knowing why it happened might help bring that assurance. A massive cruelty of thought coupled with power to carry it out resulted in millions of deaths once the Nazis had taken control of an area. Deaths occurring in the process of gaining territory or meeting military objectives had long been seen as necessary to the immediate goal of war. But containment of large populations in concentration camps for the purposes of forced labor and the "disposal" through murder of those no longer fit for labor or seen as "excess" was something horridly new.

More than any response I have heard to the proposal that war be questioned is this: "But what about Hitler? How else could a madman be stopped from killing six million Jews?"

It's a fair question to ask. We must look at what war did and did not do and what people intended and did not intend to do by going to war.

First, the war did not stop the Nazis from killing six million Jews. That happened. So something else was needed to prevent that: a common habit of religious and ethnic tolerance; a healthy society in which people of all walks of life live and work together cooperatively, recognizing the human rights of all; education that supports respect; the active participation in governance by the people; practical means of resolving conflict and injustice within communities; effective processes for early detection of abuse of power and a populace motivated, informed, and practiced in ways to pressure leaders into compliance; laws that protect against abuse and allow for the enforcement of its prevention; and a common base of economic justice, decency, and empathy felt and experienced by all people. This is a tall order for any society, but it is also the work that brings about safety, the protection of human rights, and the prevention of mass abuse. Any effort in these areas contributes to a culture in which abuse such as occurred in World War II is less able to take hold.

The reality was, most of the world did not much care about what was happening to the Jews, or did not care enough, or didn't know how to impact the situation. Although America would like to believe it now, and many do believe so, America did not enter the war to stop Hitler from killing Jews. America would not even offer Jews begging for asylum in this country a place to come. A depression had hit the world. People were concerned about their own unemployment problems and didn't want to risk others taking their jobs. A shipload of over 900 Jews coming to the United States from Germany got as far as Cuba and waited there for visa processing. The entire ship was refused entry into the United States and was sent back to Germany.[152]

Saul Friedman in his book, *No Haven for the Oppressed*, says, "While thousands of Jews were gassed daily in Europe, only 4,705 Jews entered the United States that year [1943]."[153] More than 200,000 German and Italian POWs were brought to the United States in 1943; military camps in 45 states eventually held over 426,000 POWs by the end of May 1945.[154] Yet there was no room for Jewish refugees.

Those in office didn't want to risk an unpopular stance with their voters. Friedman relates that Roosevelt "may have been motivated more by the distressing public opinion soundings taken during this period which indicated that Jews were the most unpopular racial or religious group in this country, fully four times as unpopular as Germans or Japanese."[155] Transport ships returning to the United States empty of the supplies and troops delivered to Europe weren't used to bring refugees away from harm. Railway lines that could have been bombed to stop transport of the Jews to the concentration camps were not targeted.[156] Even after the war ended, the Jews were left in horrid conditions: "Months after VE-Day, Jewish displaced persons were still living under guard behind barbed wire in some of the most notorious concentration camps of Germany, Austria, and Poland. Within two months of liberation 18,000 Jews died of starvation and disease in Bergen-Belsen. Throughout 1945 the death rate at Dachau was sixty to a hundred a day."[157]

American journalist Marvin Kalb notes that the information about what was happening to European Jews was available, but it was "published as four inches of copy on page 12."[158] Saving the Jews was not America's goal; winning the war was. Roosevelt knew what was happening, Kalb points out, but could not be distracted. Anti-Semitism was strong throughout the country. These things surely could not be true of the German people. This was not the kind of war news the papers wanted to run as headlines, not even occasionally, so they didn't.

So to say that we went to war to stop Hitler from killing the Jews is simply not true. What did stop Hitler from killing Jews? It was those people who refused to cooperate with his orders or who defied what was being done and risked their lives personally or collectively to protect the Jews and prevent their deportation.

Bulgaria, though aligned with Germany, was ordered by Hitler to send the Jews by rail to the death camps. As in other places, it would happen swiftly, and be finished. Word of the order was leaked, and the vice-president of the parliament immediately called for and received written protest against the German mandate from its members. Students joined with political leaders and others in all walks of life, and protested and marched in the streets. The first group of nearly 9,000 Jews was assembled at the rail station, cordoned off in barbed wire areas, awaiting the final orders for loading into the trains. Church people under the leadership of their bishop approached and threatened to lie down on the railroad tracks to prevent any train from taking them away. Their actions were powerful. In the end, the Jews were told to take their bags and go back home.

But things weren't over yet. The Germans filed a report on the difficulty of carrying out orders in this area. The pressure to have the Jews deported continued. However, local officials, under the constant vigilance of the people, reported that the Jews were needed for work within the country, and they refused to allow them to be deported. Though conditions were not good and treatment was often not honorable, and although confusion existed, none of the 50,000 Jews living there lost their lives to Hitler's policies. (The reader may find the resources footnoted here to hold helpful highlights of the story of Bulgaria's Jews during the time period just related.[159] [160] [161] [162] [163])

The people of Denmark also saved the lives of Jews:

> In the fall of that same year [1943], the Danes were able to foil Hitler's secret plans to round up Danish Jews. Almost the entire nation worked together to smuggle 7,500 Jews to Sweden before the Gestapo could ship them off to the crematoria.[164]

This is the kind of actions that stopped Hitler from killing Jews. Others throughout Europe, acting as individuals or in networks, hiding or helping in the escape of the Jews, prevented other deaths.

But at least the war saved more of the Jews held in concentration camps from being killed, we counter. Because once the war ended and the camps were liberated, the killing stopped. It is true that the end of the war brought the end of the concentration camp killings, and this important fact must be included in our questioning as we consider the possibility of alternatives to war.

Were there alternatives to war?

> *"One day President Roosevelt told me that he was asking publicly for suggestions about what the war should be called. I said at once 'the unnecessary war.' There never was a war more easy to stop than that which has just wrecked what was left of the world from the previous struggle."* – Winston S. Churchill[165]

It was not only Churchill who believed World War II did not have to happen. Today many propose that the conditions dictated by the "victors" of World War I directly contributed to the rise of Nazism, nationalism, totalitarianism, and Hitler's power. Many propose that Japan was simply watching the West as it moved into its own role of imperialism. The Japanese were carrying on the status quo: taking what one wants and needs, by force if necessary, as the way to assure progress and sufficiency for one's people.

The United States entered the war in the Pacific to stop Japanese aggression, defend its Pacific holdings from Japanese takeover, and assure its continued access to the rich natural resources and growing markets in the Pacific and

East Asian areas. America entered war in Europe a few days later when war
against us was declared by Germany, in order to stop German aggression,
assure the safety of nations under attack, and help restore the balance of power
needed for a healthy world and a prosperous America.

But could America have avoided war? In the Pacific, preventive actions
could have been taken decades earlier. The US Government could have worked
for the independence and self-determination of the Pacific and East Asian
peoples, including those controlled by the United States, by never under-
taking empire building in the first place, with its accompanying alienation
and pattern-setting.

Our government could have been a voice for freedom, specifically negotiating on behalf of the people of French Indochina, rather than treating them
as a pawn in our international dealings. The United States could have added
to the practical ability of the League of Nations to be a place of effective international conflict resolution by finding the conditions under which we could
support that organization, and through it promote problem-solving rather
than power-over (both militarily and economically) by our own example.
We could have avoided actions that escalate rather than diminish the risk of
war – sale of armaments to others, appearances of aggression through location of our defenses.

The US Government even missed "late in the game" alternatives to war in
the Pacific. As late as July 1941 the Emperor of Japan had urged his ministers to work for peace; Japanese Prime Minister Konoye proposed a summit
conference with Roosevelt, but the offer was rejected, and with it the opportunity.[166] Melvin Small, Professor and Chair in the Wayne State University
History Department stated in *Was War Necessary? National Security and
U.S. Entry into War*:

> [US Secretary of State Cordell] Hull argued long and hard and
> eventually successfully against the meeting suspecting that it would
> not have been beyond his chief [President Roosevelt] to make some
> unprincipled deal that would have slighted our interests in China.
> Had Roosevelt met Konoye, the Japanese might have offered a
> face-saving, peace-keeping compromise we could have matched.
> What was to be lost by meeting him? At worst, we might have
> gained a few more months before a Japanese attack; at best, a firm
> commitment from them to retire from Indochina and portions of
> China proper. [167]

That could quite possibly have shifted the momentum away from war, improved relations, and returned the United States to a period of more cooperative and mutually beneficial policies with Japan. America could have recognized the economic potential of trade with Japan, for the "fabled China Market had never materialized. The Japanese-American trade link was our most important Asian economic connection" at that time.[168]

What about in Europe, Africa, Asia, and the Middle East? It started somewhat "quietly," with Germany reclaiming territory taken from it in the settlement of the First World War. But it was soon boiling over. Could it have been stopped at that point? Perhaps, but there was much anger, breakdown of international relations, disrespect, and desire for retaliation and conquest. War as a means of control was well entrenched, and control was wanted. So America stopping the war then would have been very difficult.

Could the United States have stayed out of it? Yes. Without US Government violation of neutrality, America likely would not have become a direct target of the Axis powers: "We were paying for and shipping material to the Allies, convoying their vessels across the Atlantic, shooting at submarines that dared challenge us, and planning war and peace with England.... Each month brought new provocative policies."[169]

What would have happened to those nations already involved? There is no way of knowing. Hitler might have expanded the rule of the Nazi Party even further, and held power over Europe in a forced European union under dire and repressive conditions. He may have carried on the plan of forced labor and extermination of "undesirables" so that more died.

On the other hand, people may have wearied of years of oppression, and other leaders from within the people could have emerged to loosen the grip of Nazi control. The power of nonviolent resistance, trained or untrained, spontaneous or planned, could have caught fire and caused a turning away from the status quo. In Barbara Ash's report titled "The Day Hitler Blinked," regarding the research conducted by Dr. Nathan Stoltzfus, we learn: "By January 1943, German women in general were particularly influential in any collective effort to oppose the Nazi regime... Not only had they lost husbands, sons, brothers, but they also were expected to cut back on food and material consumption..." Hundreds of unarmed German "Aryan" women, along with relatives and others sympathetic to their cause, stood in defiance of even machine gun threats, and demanded that their Jewish husbands held on Rosenstrasse in Berlin be released to them rather than being sent away. She continues:

> In 1941 outcries by the Roman Catholic Church and victims' families curtailed the regime's centralized program of euthanasia, of which mentally and physically 'defective' Germans were victims. And millions of German homemakers defied [the] 1943 call for 'total war' by refusing to be conscripted into the workforce. ... Even toward the end of the war, during years marked by increased violence and terror, resistance was possible. The regime backed down when even its most basic ideology of racial purity was challenged. ... [I]t contradicts the notion that Germans had to chose [sic] between resistance and martyrdom.[170]

The impact of public resistance held great power and, had it become widespread enough, could have stopped Nazi control.

Those within and outside of Germany who knew the conditions of the Jews and others being put to death, could have found ways to spread the shocking word so that resistance grew and with resistance, the end of "looking the other way" and of cooperation.

These are conjectures, but had the United States not taken part in the war, things would have gone differently. Those differences would have impacted America and others' lives, and they are worth considering.

- The United States would not have killed hundreds of thousands of civilians in the cities and villages of Japan and Germany nor destroyed their land and homes, injuring thousands more.
- Hundreds of thousands of American lives would have been saved and many thousands more able to live in health without being maimed physically or damaged mentally and emotionally.
- The United States would have saved or been able to use in other ways the trillions of dollars of costs paid for the war.
- America would have avoided one of its great shames – the rounding up of Japanese Americans and transporting them to concentration camps, causing the loss of their homes and belongings, forcing them into confinement, covering up for years the immorality and devastation of what had been done.
- America would not have so entrenched within its people and national mentality a pattern of racism geared to develop hate for the "other." Although ill will toward the Japanese and Germans eventually faded, America lived

out the practice of defining, fearing, and hating "the enemy" and find it a path we can easily take again. A friend of mine recalls as a child asking his classmates why a Japanese family in their town should lose their home and be taken away. The response from the children was, "You dirty yellow Jap lover!"[171] Are we even aware of the lingering effects of such intensely and deeply practiced racism that flourished, and was officially promoted, during World War II?

- The United States could have experienced the defiance of technology-deter-mining-the-boundaries-of-humanity, and instead experienced humanity-setting-boundaries-on-the-use-of-technology. We all could know that science can do much, but that we do not have to let it dictate to us and accept as inevitable and normal what we had earlier found so abhorrent. The US military would not have killed, as they did, more than a hundred thousand civilians in the firestorm that Dresden bombs created nor 80,000 in one night in Tokyo's blaze, nor directed the vaporizing and scorching deaths of the victims of the atomic bombing of Hiroshima and Nagasaki. The story of nuclear weaponry begun in World War II is not over. There is no way of knowing now what cost the world will pay in the future for the choice to develop and use nuclear weapons on others in that war.

- Americans would not have to learn and hold the dreadful incriminating knowledge within them that many believe that Japan was clearly devastated as a nation and ready to surrender before the first atomic bomb was ever dropped on Hiroshima. They would not have to wonder why the second bomb – on Nagasaki – was dropped, so soon. [The first had been uranium; this was plutonium. Was this some sickly horrid experiment?]

- The forced relocation of soldiers and civilians after the war caused millions of deaths. The role America played in those deaths could have been avoided.

- Reports of rape by US soldiers are sadly and cruelly a part of the story of war. Beyond that cruelty is the question of US military association and cooperation with the Allies in World War II and any responsibility we share for what our Allies did:

> Natalya Gesse, a close friend of the scientist Andrei Sakharov, had observed the Red Army in action in 1945 as a Soviet war correspondent. "The Russian soldiers were raping every German female from eight to eighty," she recounted later. "It was an army of rapists." … Nuns, young girls, old women, pregnant women and mothers who had just given birth were all raped without pity. …

Altogether at least two million German women are thought to have been raped, and a substantial minority, if not a majority, appear to have suffered multiple rape.[172]

In war, what responsibility does a nation carry for the crimes committed by their allies, the other soldiers and nations with whom they collaborate on the planning and implementation of the war, even if they act insanely? Or is that also war? America would not have been an associate to such horrific acts.

- The US Espionage Act of WWI was added to by the Smith Act, cracking down on those who spoke out against the war.

  Personal liberties were dismissed as unimportant. Fear remained and grew, even after the war, causing a backlash of government surveillance and control that threatened the very liberty (and lives, of some) of America. America could instead have thrived in the kind of liberty we longed for the world to experience.

- America would not have ended up jointly controlling a divided Korea with Russia (another war could thus have been avoided). What would the impact on the Cold War have been, and on the billions of dollars spent on tools of destruction, many of which remain to threaten the world today?

- The reliance on war as *the* means of settling crisis would be less entrenched. America would have an additional experience of a non-warring solution from which to learn.

- The United States would have a more realistic sense of its place as one nation in a world community, rather than perceiving itself as dominating victor, ever ready to use war again.

Though "rewind" does not happen in real life, there are enough questions raised by these "what ifs?" that we must at least wonder, and refuse to claim that World War II was an unquestionably necessary war. Nor can we accept its happening as sure evidence that when such conditions exist, war, and only war, will be required for their resolution.

We must also stop laying the ground for the fire, piling up kindling and logs all around us, then dousing it down with gasoline, and finally, when the match is airborne and headed toward the heart of the explosive pile we have built in our midst, cry that there is no option but one: We must call the fire engines and the firefighters with the hoses so they can put the fire out and save us. If we don't, everything will be lost. There is no choice, we say. Yet we are blind to the role of kindling, logs, gasoline, matches, and our own hands, when we say there is no other way to be saved.

~

When someone says, "But what about Hitler?" we can answer, "Yes. What about Hitler must we always remember? What might have been done both before and during Hitler's rise to power that would have changed the course of history? (We need to remember that he was elected and appointed into office.) What could have been done to stop that horrid abuse of power? What could have been done so that violent and cruel actions would not have been condoned? What things do we participate in or allow that hold similarities to the conditions that contributed to the rise of Hitler's power, militarism, and Nazism?

I learned of a US Department of Defense program called Starbase which targets elementary school children (5th grade, especially those from low income areas) to be taken onto military bases and given training in math, science, engineering, technology, and careers, with a goal of building a "workforce that can meet the advanced technological requirements of the Department of Defense."[173]

One must ask if the decision to divert this educational responsibility for 10 and 11 year olds from our public schools and allow it to be handled directly by the military (and to fund the program with Department of Defense money when schools struggle for funding to keep their teachers) should cause us concern. Are there any ways in which it could bear resemblance to the indoctrination of youth and the rise of militarism in Nazi Germany in the late 1930s?

Costs of the War

DoD Estimated Dead (American) = 405,399
Estimated Wounds Not Mortal (American) = 670,846[174]
Estimated Total World War II Death Toll = 50 million,
   including an estimated 27,930,500 civilians[175]
Total Estimated Wounded = unknown, but estimated at
   well over the number of deaths
Direct U.S. War expenditures = $296 billion
   ($4.114 trillion at 2008 purchasing power)[176]
Moral impact – partially unknown; partially known: *The
   war changed America's perception and acceptance of
   inhumane atrocity.** (Read on …)

*More About Changing Morals During World War II

Something big happened to established military procedures in World War I and the time leading up to and during World War II. New technology brought capability for massive aerial bombing, never before possible in the history of the world. And it was extended to the deliberate bombing of civilian populations. When this happened in 1937 during the Spanish Civil War at the hands of Germans assisting General Franco, and in Nanking, China, at the hands of the Japanese, the reaction was one of horror:

> The United States government strongly protested the latter. "Any general bombing of an extensive area wherein there resides a large populace engaged in peaceful pursuits is unwarranted and contrary to the principles of law and humanity."[177]
>
> At the outbreak of war in Europe, Roosevelt urgently appealed to the parties involved to affirm that they would not engage in air bombardment of civilian populations or unfortified cities. A year later he declared that the bombing of helpless and unprotected civilians was a tragedy that aroused the horror of mankind: "I recall with pride that the United States has consistently taken the lead in urging that this inhuman practice be prohibited." [178]

The bombing of Nanjing and Canton, which began on the 22nd and 23rd of September 1937, called forth widespread protests culminating in a resolution by the Far Eastern Advisory Committee of the League of Nations. Lord Cranborne, the British Under-Secretary of State for Foreign Affairs, expressed his indignation: "Words cannot express the feelings of profound horror with which the news of these raids had been received by the whole civilized world. They are often directed against places far from the actual area of hostilities. The military objective, where it exists, seems to take a completely second place. The main object seems to be to inspire terror by the indiscriminate slaughter of civilians..."[179]

However, just as with the development and use of gas warfare in World War I, the US Government found such bombing hard to resist when they wanted to win the war and felt they were at a disadvantage by not doing what the enemy did, regardless of how bad they thought it was. The US policy changed from one of stated condemnation of the acts as inhuman slaughter, to standard protocol. The US military used bombs to destroy the morale of the people, doing as much damage as possible. They began fire bombing the cities of Germany, leaving tens of thousands of civilians dead and more homeless. The numbers went up as they bombed Japanese cities, creating a mass inferno and burning to death an estimated 280,000 Japanese,[180] destroying their homes and cities. In the end, it was just one bomb needed to burn and maim a hundred thousand at a time. And then three days later, one more.

It wasn't just the US military or the government that had changed its perception. A 1945 survey of Americans, published in Fortune magazine in December of that year, showed that while just over 4% of those questioned felt the United States should not have used an atomic bomb at all and nearly 14 % believed one should have been dropped on an unpopulated area first to give Japan a chance to surrender, 53% believed the United States should have done just as they did. And nearly a fourth of those surveyed felt the US military should have quickly dropped many more atomic bombs before Japan had a chance to surrender.[181]

Soldiers of World War II still speak about the use of atomic bombs on Japan. Their words echo what President Truman told the American public – that it was a hard thing to do, but it had to be done to save lives and bring an end to the war. Winston Churchill wrote later:

At any rate, there never was a moment's discussion as to whether the atomic bomb should be used or not. To avert a vast, indefinite butchery, to bring the war to an end, to give peace to the world, to lay healing hands upon its tortured peoples by a manifestation of overwhelming power at the cost of a few explosions, seemed, after all our toils and perils, a miracle of deliverance.[182]

As the evidence of what actually happened was learned, it was undoubtedly a reassuring thought – that in order to avoid enormous losses of human life and to end the war in the shortest time possible, the US military did what they had to do. Many believed that such weapons and happenings would make war a thing of the past and would assure the peace forever.

But even at the time there was not full agreement on what exactly the course of action of the war would be. The Army's view was that a ground invasion of Japan would be needed in order to get surrender; the Navy disagreed. Admiral William Leahy, Chief of Naval Operations before the war and personal advisor to both President Roosevelt and President Truman on military matters, wrote in his memoirs: "It is my opinion that the use of this barbarous weapon at Hiroshima and Nagasaki was of no material assistance in our war against Japan. The Japanese were already defeated and ready to surrender because of the effective sea blockade and the successful bombing with conventional weapons."[183]

Further echoing this view was the United States Strategic Bombing Survey which was "established by Presidential order toward the end of the war to investigate the effects of our aerial attacks on Germany and Japan."[184] They reported:

Based on a detailed investigation of all the facts and supported by the testimony of the surviving Japanese leaders involved, it is the Survey's opinion that certainly prior to 31 December 1945, and in all probability prior to 1 November 1945, Japan would have surrendered even if the atomic bombs had not been dropped, even if Russia had not entered the war, and even if no invasion had been planned or contemplated."[185]

It had been assumed earlier that Germany was developing a similar bomb, and a race for the weapon that cost the United States two billion dollars was run in great secrecy. When it was learned that Germany was not even close to making an atomic bomb, scientists involved began to question its use. By August of 1945 Germany was no longer a threat.

Some suggested that the bomb be tested away from civilian populations in a barren location where representatives from all nations could see its power. The United States could hold back using this weapon and agree to establishment of international control. In protest to its possible use in Japan, some of those working on the project described the potential backlash of horror that might well be felt by the world. They went on to say:

> Nuclear bombs cannot possibly remain a "secret weapon" at the exclusive disposal of this country for more than a few years. The scientific facts on which their construction is based are well known to scientists of other countries. … Within ten years other countries may have nuclear bombs, each of which weighing less than a ton, could destroy an urban area of more than ten square miles.[186]

Edward Teller, physicist on site where the bomb was being developed, later said that he took his concern to Robert Oppenheimer, the authority at the Los Alamos center:

> Oppenheimer told me, in a polite and convincing way, that he thought it improper for a scientist to use his prestige as a platform for political pronouncements. He conveyed to me in glowing terms the deep concern, thoroughness, and wisdom with which these questions were being handled in Washington. Our fate was in the hands of the best, the most conscientious men of our nation. And they had information which we did not possess. Oppenheimer's words lifted a great weight from my heart. I was happy to accept his word and his authority. I did not circulate Szilard's petition. Today I regret that I did not. … We could have exploded the bomb at a very high altitude over Tokyo in the evening. Triggered at a high altitude, the bomb would have created a sudden, frightening daylight over the city. But it would have killed no one. … [W]e could have told the Japanese what it was and what would happen if another atomic bomb were detonated at low altitude.[187]

The reality of what happened was described in Charles Pellegrino's book, *The Last Train From Hiroshima: The Survivors Look Back*, as reported in a *New York Times'* book review:

He describes the so-called "ant-walking alligators" that the survivors saw everywhere, men and women who "were now eyeless and faceless – with their heads transformed into blackened alligator hides displaying red holes, indicating mouths."

The author continues:

"The alligator people did not scream. Their mouths could not form the sounds. The noise they made was worse than screaming. They uttered a continuous murmur – like locusts on a midsummer night. One man, staggering on charred stumps of legs, was carrying a dead baby upside down."[188]

Challenging a myth can be difficult if it causes us to give up a belief that holds great comfort. Questioning the official word of our leaders and the official "story" of our nation, takes courage, especially when that story is told us by people we respect and care about. We may tend to say, "Let sleeping dogs lie. It's a thing of the past and can't be undone anyway." Yet the weaponry of World War II has only "progressed" in its development to even more deadly and destructive power. It is important that we not turn away from the hard questions, even if what we find is ugly and painful, for the answers they bring affect us today. Is the common explanation given for our use of the atomic bomb a myth that has only served to lull America, with its rapidly changing morals about what is "acceptable" in war, back into a trusting sleep?

Should we instead have been thrown into the nightmarish acknowledgment that something went terribly wrong in our world, and it was the work of the United States Government? Does the story continue to contribute to acceptance of and complacency about nuclear weaponry's "acceptability" today?

Similarly, German submarine warfare had been highly criticized during World War I and was used as an argument justifying our entrance into the war. Its use again in World War II was criticized and German Admiral Karl Dönitz was tried at Nuremberg for war crimes including ordering unrestricted submarine warfare. But the British and US Navies had issued the same unrestricted submarine warfare orders that we had at first considered immoral.

The German U-boats of the 1914–1918 conflict gave American officers and designers reason for pause … they provided the paradigm for American interwar development. ...[T]he community of submarine officers struggled with a problem.... How should the Navy use submarines? What was their proper strategic role? ... [I]ncidents like the sinking of the passenger liner RMS *Lusitania* painted this style of warfare with a dark brush, suggesting immorality when submersibles operated without restriction. ... American submarine strategy could not include unrestricted submarine warfare, which might turn neutral commercial vessels and innocent civilians into victims.[189]

But with time, thoughts changed.

American officers realized that war in all of its brutality, not peacetime politics or worthy ethical concerns, would determine the future challenges faced by the submarine force. In spite of official policy, the boats under construction in the 1930s reflected assertive, offensive strategic thinking.... By 1940, the submarine force had answered its fundamental strategic questions and had the vessels to carry out the consequent roles and missions. Thus, when Admiral Thomas Hart proclaimed unrestricted submarine warfare against Japan on 8 December 1941, it came as no surprise. The submarine force knew what to do.[190]

They used the submarines for "unrestricted" warfare – exactly what was earlier found so abhorrent in our enemy. This was done in spite of "worthy ethical concerns."

~

As the war in Europe drew to a close, millions of German prisoners of war were taken under the Allies' control, including direct US military control. Makeshift prison camps were set up in open fields, inside barbed wire fences, many times with no shelter, and on rations that contributed to the deaths of thousands. According to the International Committee of the Red Cross:

The surrender of Germany on 8 May 1945 led to the capture of millions of German soldiers who could no longer count on the assistance of their government or on that of their families, themselves in a situation of dire poverty. On the victorious side, public opinion held that the Germans were only getting what they deserved, and the ICRC found itself virtually alone in interceding on their behalf.

The ICRC made approaches to the authorities of the four occupation zones and, in the autumn of 1945, it received authorization to send both relief and delegates into the French and British zones. On 4 February 1946, the ICRC was allowed to send relief into the American zone, and on 13 April 1946 it obtained permission to extend this activity to the Soviet zone.

The quantities received by the ICRC for these captives remained very small, however. During their visits, the delegates observed that German prisoners of war were often detained in appalling conditions.[191]

For nearly a year, the United States had refused entry to the Red Cross, and only granted them access when most of the camps had been closed down. General Dwight Eisenhower requested that the United States designate the POWs as "Disarmed Enemy Forces" (DEFs), in order that we not be held to the 1929 Geneva Conventions on the treatment of POWs. The US military just didn't know how it could feed or house that many POWs under the conditions required by the Geneva Conventions. With DEF status, it would not be required to do so. The prisoners could be given rations that were more "realistic" to a Europe destroyed by war and crippled by loss of agriculture and infrastructure to get food to the people. That these rations were near starvation level for many and that the camps offered poor, if any, shelter in harsh conditions, is a difficult thing for Americans to learn.

That thousands died under the care of their American military victors is disturbing. It was more pleasant to hold the images of the joyous celebrations of crowds filling the streets in America over news of the war's end than to picture the emaciated and dead bodies of DEFs in US barbed wire camps after victory. So the parades became the pictures that anchored the end of World War II in Americans' memories, not the deaths in the holding camps that the United States was in charge of.

To think that the American military could simply create a new name for POWs with a new acronym and thereby avoid the commitment to keep international war conventions that had been considered a just, moral responsibility – because they saw no way they could abide by them – shows how difficult it can be to predict the consequences of waging war. Stephen Ambrose, Eisenhower biographer conceded, "We as Americans can't duck the fact that terrible things happened. And they happened at the end of a war we fought for decency and freedom, and they are not excusable."[192]

~

The secret agreement made with Stalin at the Yalta Conference in February 1945 for the transfer of Soviet POWs back to Russia, also caused unimaginable consequences, as described in *Wars of America: Christian Views*:

> Some were aware that Stalin regarded as traitors all Russians who had surrendered to the Germans without fighting to the death, and they did not want to see British and American war prisoners treated the same by the Soviets. After V-E Day the British and Americans held to their word and began transferring to Soviet control the two million Russian prisoners and displaced persons who were in Western Germany and Austria.
>
> What followed were incredibly shocking scenes, as Russians who expected to receive political asylum resisted the efforts of their Western captors to send them back. The riots, mass suicides, and repeated incidents where doomed men were clubbed and forced into railroad cars at gunpoint constituted a melancholy final chapter in the Allied war effort, one that was faintly reminiscent of the Holocaust. The full extent of the operation was covered up, the victims were lied to and deceived regarding their fate, and the military personnel involved in the operation excused themselves by pleading that they were just "following orders."[193]

That was another sad example of the difficulty in predicting the consequences of war.

~

Though information gathering, learning, understanding, and examination and evaluating of circumstances are all important in decision-making, it is also true that war can tend to blur the decision-making process and turn it into a rally for support (in more generous terms) and for obedience or subservience (in less generous terms) of the people to their political and military leaders. War propaganda reached new intensity on all sides during World War II, partially because of the advancement in the film industry and in marketing and communication. The German propaganda effort likened

Jews to disease-carrying rats, and portrayed such in films geared to further enrage racism. By repeating the message that Germans were a superior race destined for greatness and deserving to be free from limitations caused by undesirables, thinking was replaced by hearing. And the way was opened for mass genocide.

The Japanese carried the message of decadent and corrupt America, whereas Japan was a divine land, and the Japanese superior to other races. And what America criticized in the enemy, the US Government also did. Materials housed in the US National Archives illustrate the propaganda effort:

> Guns, tanks, and bombs were the principal weapons of World War II, but there were other, more subtle forms of warfare as well. Words, posters, and films waged a constant battle for the hearts and minds of the American citizenry just as surely as military weapons engaged the enemy. Persuading the American public became a wartime industry, almost as important as the manufacturing of bullets and planes. The Government launched an aggressive propaganda campaign with clearly articulated goals and strategies to galvanize public support, and it recruited some of the nation's foremost intellectuals, artists, and filmmakers to wage the war on that front.[194]

> Public relations specialists advised the U.S. Government that the most effective war posters were the ones that appealed to the emotions.... [The posters] played on the public's fear of the enemy.... A study of commercial posters undertaken by the U.S. Government found that images of women and children in danger were effective emotional devices.[195]

The government tapped into Hollywood to make film shorts and cartoons that carried the message they had for the American public. As propaganda is designed to do, complicated issues became simple, the enemy became the embodiment of evil, and America's cause became fully innocent, just, and holy. This was perhaps not so much a shift in morals, as it was an acceptance, even though unknowingly or unwillingly received, of what others wanted America to know – a distortion of inquiry and informed decision making. It reinforced a tendency to accept what was told rather than to seek out and evaluate the complexities of an issue. It allowed America to believe the government without having to question.

~

It wasn't just the war planners and military leaders on both sides who committed acts previously felt to be atrocities. US soldiers too were instigators. Stories, letters, and photographs sent home showed the gold teeth knocked out and the ears cut off Japanese enemy dead to take as souvenirs of the war. Though practices condemned by military leaders, they happened, along with the taking of Japanese skulls as war trophies. There is evidence of torture and massacres carried out by American soldiers after taking the enemy.

Deep American moral outrage against what had been seen as atrocious, despicable, grossly offensive acts of brutality and inhumanity in others turned into simple acceptance of how one runs a war. When speaking of the atomic bomb on August 9, 1945, the day Nagasaki was bombed and three days after Hiroshima was destroyed, President Harry Truman told the American public: "We thank God that it has come to us instead of to our enemies; and we pray that He may guide us to use it in His ways and for His purposes."[196]

America had moved from the stance of decrying aerial bombing as against the principles of law and humanity, a tragedy arousing the horror of mankind, an inhuman practice, to asking God's guidance in using it for His purposes. And the "it" was so much more destructive than ever imagined when spoken of earlier. Instead of feeling deeply the horror and shame of unspeakably cruel violence, America let it go, kicked up her heels, and paraded in the streets with joy that the war was over!

Once lost, how does one regain the eyes to see anew what at one time was putrid and horribly, deeply wrong? What is the cost to a nation and to individuals of such a shift in morals?

2.11 The Korean War (1950 to the present; Armistice 1953)

A commonly agreed upon American perspective
for the "police action"

North Korean troops have crossed the 38th parallel and moved into the South, aggressively, violently, and illegally, attempting to spread their communistic government and take control of the people of the South. We have been requested by the United Nations to come to the aid of the people of South Korea, to repel the attack, and to restore the peace. We will do so, with all the speed, wisdom, and force within our power. We will stop the aggression of communism in East Asia, an aggression that has clearly taken the form of violence against the free people of the Republic of Korea.

The perspective of the other side
(the Democratic People's Republic of Korea)

The people of the South are waiting to be liberated. For centuries we have been a free and united people. Two generations passed with our people under Japanese cruelty and control. When the war ended, we became pawns in the hands of others, lines on a map. We were promised our independence under the Cairo Declaration. That should have been enacted when the Japanese surrendered. We are one nation, one people, and we will be that again. We will throw off the rule and domination of others, including those of the South who do the bidding of the United States of America against the will of the Korean people.

Background

Japan's surrender in World War II meant that their long-time control over Korea would end. Koreans believed they were set for independence, with differing factions in the country bidding to take the leadership. Reform nationalists intended that the end of Japanese occupation would also be the end of control by those Koreans who had held political, economic, and social advantage in the country before and during Japanese occupation. On the other hand, there were those who were ready to regain and strengthen their favored status through political control under an economic system that worked well for them. The potential for civil conflict was high as the question of leadership for the independent nation was being disputed.

But independence did not come. The Allies determined that the Koreans were not ready to take over leadership of their country, even though they had already moved toward establishing their government. Instead Korea was to be held under trusteeship of the Allies for five years. As victors of the war, they proceeded to carry out these plans.

With Britain fully occupied with the task of rebuilding at the close of the war, it was the United States and the USSR. that moved into the country militarily to accept the surrender of the Japanese and then to control the direction the trusteeship would take in Korea. It was soon agreed that each country would administer one half of Korea, dividing it geographically along the 38th parallel. To the disbelief and anger of South Koreans, the United States restored some of the Japanese to administrative positions, also re-igniting Soviet concern over the potential for Japanese aggression from a location so near their border.[197]

Korean factions within both halves of the country began to rally support for their claim as the legitimate power over a unified nation. Kim Il-sung, a Korean whose family had fled from Japanese occupation to Manchuria, and who later fought against the Japanese and for Korean independence, took leadership in the North. Syngman Rhee, a Korean who had long worked for Korean independence, and who had lived and studied in the United States to avoid persecution under Japanese occupation, returned to Korea with US support and took leadership in the South. Rhee was known to the United States, but his leadership was not without problems and was described as having "tendencies toward dictatorship."[198]

> "Unfortunately, Syngman Rhee was an authoritarian leader who had many old scores to settle. He often used his military forces more harshly against internal opposition than he did against the armies of North Korea."[199]

Military buildup occurred for both sides, with military advisors and equipment from the United States staying on in the South and from the USSR remaining in the North. Skirmishes across the 38th parallel became frequent. In June 1950 the North moved in a major military action over the line into the South.

The United States, fearful of communist takeover throughout the world, saw this as one violent attempt which could and must be stopped. An emergency session of the UN Security Council was called at US prompting on June 25, 1950, the day after news of the invasion reached the United States. The UN Security Council (without the USSR who was boycotting all UN meetings) called for support of the South and immediate withdrawal by the North.

> On June 26, as the battle reports became grimmer, we realized that the American-trained South Korean troops were unreliable. [President Harry] Truman was thus compelled to order American naval and air forces into combat. He issued this directive to the Pacific Command without consulting Congress and *before* the United Nations authorized its members to offer all possible assistance to the victims of aggression. In a technical sense, we had gone to war without authorization from the United Nations. Only the next day, June 27, did we receive legitimation from the world body. At the same time, the President summoned congressional leaders to the White House to explain what he had done. … Few in Washington objected either to the methods or substance of Truman's policies. The challenge the military incursion posed to our national security could not await the pleasure of Congressmen in the manner prescribed by our Founding Fathers during an earlier epoch.[200]

General Douglas MacArthur was chosen to lead the UN troops, predominantly American and South Korean forces but with contingencies from several other countries, and reported directly to Truman.

On the US-South Korean side of the war, after heavy losses and confinement of troops to a small area of the south, MacArthur pushed north back to the 38th parallel, and drove on through the North to the border with The People's Republic of China. China, finding its industrially rich Manchurian area threatened, and the "buffer zone" that kept US troops from its borders now eliminated, entered the battle and attacked U.N./US troops.

The United States undertook a massive bombing effort, making rubble of much of North Korea, destroying cities and villages along with their inhabitants as attacks with even more lethal weaponry were carried out. The deadly creation of napalm – used near the end of World War II – was let loose fully on the Koreans. Those who survived the asphyxiation and immediate death of the bombs, suffered damage that left their bodies horrendously burned, deformed, and in need of intense medical care that was simply not available. They were left to the ravages of shock, infection, and painful, slow recovery or death.

Use of atomic bombs to greatly increase the speed and extent of the devastation, and thus the military victory, was considered. MacArthur, hailed by the American public as a hero, eventually chaffed under the limitations placed upon his military plans by President Truman and was later dismissed for insubordination. It was found that fighting a "limited war" was challenging. However, the nuclear weapons were not used, fearing they could set off a nuclear war with the Soviet Union.

The Korean War came to a halt three years after it began. The last two years included continuous efforts from both sides to negotiate an armistice. The cease-fire armistice was signed in July 1953, leaving things pretty much as they had been before the war started, with a DMZ (demilitarized zone) being added at the division line at the 38th parallel, but with Korea in shambles and millions dead or injured.

For a war that many Americans don't know much about and that was referred to as a "police action," further softening the historical image of what transpired, we must acknowledge that the Korean War took American military personnel through dire, freezing battle conditions resulting in tens of thousands of casualties. Both sides committed atrocities now admitted.

Besides the total military and civilian deaths, wounded, and missing during months of horror at the hands of their fellow Koreans, Chinese, Soviets, Americans, and others, "half of Korea's industry was destroyed and a third of all homes. The disruption of civilian life was almost complete."[201]

Were there alternatives to war?

Had the USSR and the United States *not* divided Korea in half, there would have been no opportunity or need for a US Korean War, unless the U.S. simply decided to move in its military to enforce our control over the form of government to be implemented or to join the possible civil war of another nation.[202] The strongly divergent political positions held within the country in 1945 intensified because of this US-USSR division, and over the next few years erupted into incidents of violence. The direction that this conflict might have gone, without outside intervention and division of the country, is unknowable, though it is likely that a reformist government would have been established through rising socialist leadership. The US Government was not interested in encouraging peaceful national unification if it meant that the type of government we wished to see in place might not happen. The US policy was to enact division and trusteeship in order to control communist expansion in East Asia. Half a country would at least give us a place to say to the communists, "No farther."

The geo-political division which the United States and the USSR created, certainly contributed to the struggle the Koreans faced, solidifying their differences and allowing them to form into fully opposing quasi-national administrations in two separated "nations." The people's intentions for a unified, independent Korea were overrun.

The United States and others could have recognized and encouraged the benefits to the Korean people of remaining united as they began working toward the goal of establishing their independence and setting up their governmental system. We could have worked to overcome our disagreements with the USSR over how to conduct the nation-wide election which was to have taken place in 1948, rather than resort to a South-only election that locked in the militarily supported division of the nation. We could have let the Koreans decide the fate of their own nation.

Countries and leaders with little power (not the United States or the USSR), but practical experience in governance, could have offered their services as advisors, if the Korean people felt the Japanese occupation had left them with a gap in their abilities to administer their own government.

When the US Government decided that it would settle for keeping one-half of the nation under US direction in order to assure the kind of government wanted, it failed to consider what a forced, long-term division of their homeland would mean to the people of Korea. This division and this "police action" war have deeply impacted the lives and thoughts of the Korean people, North and South. Putting ourselves in the shoes of the people of North Korea – with memory of a nation divided against the will of the people, a homeland bombed into ruin, a people living under fear of nuclear destruction as had so recently been unleashed on Japan – might help us understand their hesitancy to believe in the goodwill of those who carried out such actions. The impact of that war remains today.[203]

Costs of the War

DoD Estimated Dead (American) = 36,574
Estimated Wounds Not Mortal (American) = 103,284[204]
Estimated Dead
    Other United Nations Military = 3,155
    South Korean Military & Civilians = 660,248
    North Korean Military & Civilians = 1,316,579
    Chinese = 460,000[205]
Direct U.S. War Expenditures = $30 billion
    ($320 billion at 2008 purchasing power)[206]
Moral impact – unknown, but memory of the war
    remains in those still living today, a war that officially
    continues, though under ceasefire.

2.12   The Vietnam War (1965–1973 segment)

A commonly agreed upon American perspective for the war

There was no commonly agreed upon perspective.

The Vietnam War was very divisive and seen from a variety of viewpoints. The US Government proposed, and many Americans believed, especially in the early years, that war was necessary to protect the rights of the people of South Vietnam who were seeking freedom and democracy and forced to do so through war against those in the north who would usurp that right from them. Without intervention, they would become the victims of cruel, Godless, communistic rule. The war would show our commitment as a nation to the rights of all people to liberty. It was seen as preventing the fall of Vietnam, and thereafter of Southeast Asia, and indeed perhaps of the entire world, to the tyranny of communism.

Soldiers volunteered or were drafted to carry out this mission of bringing help, hope, and freedom to the people of Vietnam. President Johnson reported to the Congress and the American people that the United States had been attacked – twice – in the Gulf of Tonkin and that he needed authorization to respond. It was granted.

To other Americans the war was a blatant example of forceful and destructive US intervention in the lives and rights of others, the people of Vietnam who sought independence and self-rule. It was seen as a transfer of support from the colonialism of France to control by the United States, control that benefited the corruption and violent and dogmatic internal repression of US-backed leadership in South Vietnam. As the war progressed, it became evident to many Americans that they had not heard the truth about the war, its probability of success, and the history of our involvement. The 1968 Tet Offensive gave America a new picture of the determination and strength of the North and the repeated underestimations of the number of troops needed to win. The My Lai massacre shocked the world with the atrocities committed by US troops on Vietnamese civilians. Many Americans believed that we had no business being in Vietnam and protested to end the war.

The perspective of the other side (North Vietnam)

We have lived under the yoke of French colonial repression for generations. The suffering continued under the Japanese occupation of our land during the war. When the war ended, we knew our time for independence was finally here. Our Congress convened and Ho Chi Minh was elected leader of the provisional government. What pride there was on September 2, 1945, when Ho Chi Minh read our Declaration of Independence:[207] "All men are created equal. They are endowed by their Creator with certain inalienable rights; among these are Life, Liberty, and the pursuit of Happiness…."[208] Little did we know that the imperialist powers of the United States and Europe had already decided our fate at their Potsdam Conference. They bargained away our nation and our lives: They agreed that France should return as colonial lords over us. This we could not let happen, and we went to war to prevent such wretchedness. We were victorious over the French and those who aided them. The peace terms that followed in the Geneva Accords called for the temporary division of our country, our one nation, into two, until elections could be held.

Knowing full well that Ho Chi Minh would be chosen in a nation-wide election, the puppets in the South, doing the bidding of the United States, prevented the election and the reunification of our country. The United States took over the oppressor's role. We had no choice but to fight for our homeland and our people. This is a war for liberation and independence of our country. They may do what they will, kill ten of us for every one we kill, but we will never stop nor be defeated until Vietnam once again belongs to the people.

Background

During European colonial takeover of other lands in the 1800s, France claimed resource-rich Indochina (Laos, Cambodia, Vietnam) as a French colony. Still claiming the area as its own when France was overrun by Germany in 1940 during World War II, the new Vichy France government, who collaborated with Germany, took over. Japan sensed the opportunity at hand and moved in to take control of the area. Those who had been working for national independence against the French – the Viet Minh – turned their struggle against Japan. The Viet Minh recognized that this time of shifting power gave them an opportunity to advance their drive for independence, and they determined not to let Japan destroy their dream.

Once the United States was at war with Japan, the O.S.S. (Office of Strategic Security, forerunner of the CIA) supported Ho Chi Minh and the Viet Minh against Japan, instructing the Viet Minh in guerilla warfare and providing weaponry against the mutual enemy – Japan. The United States was willing to acknowledge a satisfactory goal – national independence for Vietnam – in exchange for help defeating the Japanese.

However, as the war came to a close both in Europe and in the Pacific, US priorities changed. America needed the support of France for NATO and in allowing Germany to become economically strong as a deterrent against the spread of communism in Europe.[209] The United States would let France retake control in French Indo-China in exchange for their cooperation in Europe. The Viet Minh declared independence for their nation in September. However, the country after which they modeled their declaration began working against their cause; the United States supported the French return to power. Seven years of war followed as the Viet Mihn fought a renewed struggle with the French for their independence, with the United States financing much of the war for France.

In 1954 the French finally surrendered. The terms of peace secured by the 1954 Geneva Accord called for a temporarily divided Vietnam along the 17th Parallel, to be unified under leadership determined by elections to be held in 1956. The US Government didn't sign the agreement but stated that it would not block its terms. Over time, however, the United States took on the role of the French, supporting division of the country and building up South Vietnam with millions of dollars of economic and military aid. The United States supported a divided country, with the South under the leadership of Diem, chosen by the United States but not by the people of Vietnam, a leader mired in corruption and whom the United States also eventually turned against.

The US Government determined that the 1956 elections should not take place. It was generally believed that the popularity of Ho Chi Minh would bring him the victory and therefore leadership of a united Vietnam under communism. The United States also found unacceptable France's call for moderation which suggested that it might be time to end the days of aggression and work toward coexistence. Coexistence would only assure the spread of communism, and America could not accept that.

The United States defined Vietnam's quest for independence as a communist drive to take over the country and part of a much grander plot of the USSR to spread communism throughout Southeast Asia and the world.

Ho Chi Minh had long held active and strong ties with communism. Later, when the People's Republic of China attained victory over Nationalist China in their civil war, they began supplying arms to the Viet Minh. This again was clear evidence to the United States that communism was the end goal, not the independence of the Vietnamese people. In a memo from the Joint Chiefs of Staff to the Department of Defense, the threat of Communism was made clear:

> Southeast Asia is a vital segment in the line of containment of Communism stretching from Japan southward and around to the Indian Peninsula... The security of the three major non-Communist base areas in this quarter of the world – Japan, India, and Australia – depends in a large measure on the denial of Southeast Asia to the Communists. ... The fall of Indochina would undoubtedly lead to the fall of the other mainland states of Southeast Asia.[210]

Oregon's Governor, and later Senator, Mark Hatfield, saw it differently. He had visited the area in 1945 while in the Navy. He wrote to his parents at that time:

> It was sickening to see the absolute poverty and the rags these people are in. We thought the Philippines were in a bad way, but

they are wealthy compared to these exploited people. ... [P]eople here have never known anything but squalor since the French heel has been on them. ... I tell you, it is a crime the way we occidentals have enslaved these people in our mad desire for money.... I certainly see why these people don't want us to return and continue to spit upon them.[211]

Hatfield continued to be a firm and vocal opponent of the Vietnam War. He believed it was nationalism, not communism, behind the drive for a united Vietnam under leadership of Ho Chi Minh, a people longing to throw off the shackles of foreign domination. He described in his book, *Not So Simple*, the many false precepts being marketed by the United States to justify the war, including the declaration that we must support the free and democratic South Vietnam against communist aggression.

Hatfield demonstrated that the South Vietnamese did not have freedom of the press, freedom of speech, freedom of assembly, or the freedom to petition the government for redress of grievances. He accused the Saigon government of using Gestapo tactics and conducting dishonest elections. The senator also condemned the bombing of Vietnam as useless and brutal. He proceeded to defend the rights of those Americans who opposed the war.[212]

In a 1967 interview with HIS magazine, Hatfield said,

I just cannot accept the idea that ultimate victory will be achieved by killing more people, killing more people, and killing more people. I think we should take peace, prosperity, and food and love to these people ... and we ought to use our genius and our ingenuity to find an honorable way to solve this problem.[213]

The build-up to the war happened over time. In May 1961 the United States sent 500 military advisors, followed by 15,000 more in 1963. Then in August 1964 President Johnson reported that a US ship had been attacked by North Vietnam in international waters. He issued a warning to North Vietnam that any such unprovoked actions in the future would have grave consequences, and he let the American public know that his Administration would not let such aggression go unnoticed.

Two days later Johnson announced that a second deliberate and unprovoked attack on two American ships had occurred; he asked for Congressional approval for the use of force to defend American forces and our right to navigate peacefully in international waters. He received passage of the

Gulf of Tonkin Resolution with only two dissenting votes in the Senate. The following day the United States bombed North Vietnamese naval facilities in retaliation.

What was not explained to the American public was that the United States was planning and training for hit-and-run raids on North Vietnamese coastal installations and facilities which were being carried out by the South Vietnamese, and that the USS Maddox had regularly moved to within eight miles of the North Vietnamese coastline and within four miles of its islands to accomplish its intelligence gathering. The August 2nd attack was in retaliation for those raids. Nor did we learn that the Maddox had fired first to warn off the boats that were approaching it; Johnson insisted that the Vietnamese boats fired first. In spite of increased tension between the North Vietnamese and the United States, the coastal raids were not called off. On the night of August 3rd/4th a North Vietnamese radar station and security post were shelled by the South. Yet the United States righteously stated that it would not only drive away, but would destroy, any force that carried out an unprovoked attack.

The story of the second unprovoked "attack" on the night of August 4th/5th that propelled Congressional passage of the Tonkin Gulf Resolution and gave Johnson the go-ahead to use military force against the North Vietnamese, pulling America fully into war in Vietnam, is told in the review and evaluation of secret documents finally released forty years after the fact – 2005, 2006, and 2008.[214] In *Spartans in Darkness: American SIGINT and the Indochina War, 1945–1975*, Robert Hanyok of the Center for Cryptologic History in a report for the National Security Agency marked "Top Secret" – until unclassified and approved for release by them in November of 2005 – describes what the evidence clearly showed: There was no second attack, and the happenings unfolded differently than what the American public was told.[215]

The first news of attack that originally reached Washington, D.C. was incomplete but eagerly received. It was a report from the ship, later determined to be based on false radar readings that showed the Maddox was being surrounded by a large number of enemy boats. The planes directly overhead giving them air protection saw no evidence of any North Vietnamese boat in the area. They fired out into the darkness at the "boats" attacking them, boats that intercepted intelligence codes identified as being miles away in another area of the sea, being towed back to port by tug boats salvaging them from the battle two days earlier.

Although the captain of the Maddox followed up with an immediate correcting report of "many doubts" about the action and noted that they had "never positively identified a boat as such,"[216] and even though other conflicting reports came in from intelligence services, Secretary of Defense Robert McNamara reported that the evidence of attack was "unimpeachable." Johnson had the evidence that he needed. According to Hanyok, the National Security Agency bolstered the case for proof of attack by selective inclusion and exclusion of intelligence, as well as creative translation, rearranging of texts, and pulling things out of context. He doesn't say that it was purposeful deception, but simply that because they "knew" what happened, they found the information that seemed to back up their understanding. "As much as anything else, it was an awareness that President Johnson would brook no uncertainty that could undermine his position."[217]

When the alleged attack was questioned, both by some in government and the public, a request went back to the intelligence personnel to "supply urgently all intercept that provided proof of DRV attack on 4 August on U.S. Naval vessels."

No proof was available. No proof was sent.

Two months earlier, William Bundy, Assistant Secretary of State for Far Eastern Affairs had prepared a proposal for Congress to allow the President to defend any nation that was under threat by "communist aggression or subversion." The President would have the power to decide how the defense was to be carried out. However, fearing this would blemish his stance of moderation in his bid for re-election against Barry Goldwater, Johnson let the proposal go. But in August 1964 the time was right. America had been attacked, and Congress speedily passed the Tonkin Gulf Resolution. Johnson had his power to act. (The released reports and commentary on them describing events differently from what was related to the American public forty years earlier, can be read in the references listed here.[218 219 220 221])

A commentary on Hanyok's research summarizes the claim of attack which propelled passage of the Tonkin Gulf Resolution and launched the United States into full scale war in Vietnam as follows:

> The most sensational part of the history [US National Security Administration's release of the 500 page "Spartans in Darkness" history of the Vietnam War] … is the recounting of the 1964 Gulf of Tonkin Incident, in which a *second* reported North Vietnamese attack on U.S. forces, *following another attack two days before*, trig-

gered a major escalation of the war. The author demonstrates that not only is it not true, as Secretary of Defense Robert McNamara told Congress, that the evidence of a *second* attack was "unimpeachable," but that to the contrary, a review of the classified signals intelligence proves that "no attack happened that night."[222]

The Gulf of Tonkin Resolution opened the way for America's Vietnam War, with troop increases, massive bombing campaigns, with such names as "Rolling Thunder," and promises of victory that didn't come. Vietnam War spending replaced Johnson's "War on Poverty" at home.

In Vietnam, the country and its inhabitants, as well as American soldiers, were being exposed to a new tool of war – Agent Orange – as was described in a Veterans Health Initiative report:

> Agent Orange is the name given to a specific blend of herbicides used for military purposes in Vietnam from 1965 to 1971. It was developed by the US military for the purpose of eliminating plants and leaves from foliage in Vietnam that could have provided cover to the enemy. (p. 8)
>
> Before the military spraying program ended, estimates are that at least 17 to 19 million gallons (more than 100 million pounds) of herbicide were sprayed over approximately six million acres in Vietnam. In fact, all regions in Vietnam were sprayed at least once, and some on multiple occasions. The most heavily sprayed areas included inland forests near the boundary between North and South Vietnam, inland forests at the junction of the borders of Cambodia, Laos, and South Vietnam, inland forests north and northwest of Saigon, mangrove forests of the southernmost peninsula of Vietnam and mangrove forests along major shipping channels southeast of Saigon. (p. 9)
>
> Based upon findings contained in the initial 1994 NAS [the National Academy of Sciences Institute of Medicine] report, VA [the Veteran's Administration] decided to recognize a range of illnesses as presumptively service connected for Vietnam War veterans diagnosed with soft tissue sarcoma, non-Hodgkin's lymphoma, Hodgkin's disease, chloracne, porphyria cutanea tarda, multiple myeloma and respiratory cancers (including laryngeal cancer, and cancer of the lung, bronchus and trachea). In fact, VA and Congress

had previously recognized chloracne, non-Hodgkin's lymphoma and soft tissue sarcoma as related to herbicide or dioxin exposure for Vietnam veterans – the NAS review process confirmed the validity of these earlier decisions and added additional diseases to the list. (p. 14)[223]

Concerning the fate of their children, the report concludes:

> In summary, among men veterans, Vietnam service has not been associated with adverse reproductive outcomes, except for spina bifida. Among women veterans, Vietnam service has been associated with the risk of having children with a wide range of birth defects.[224]

One must wonder about the harm to Vietnam and its people who suffered and still suffer the effects of this defoliation tool developed by the US military, including those born after the war ended. They are left to live on with the consequences of the US use of chemicals in warfare.

Protests against the war increased as more draftees were called to military duty, intensifying awareness of the war and the deaths it brought throughout all sectors of the population. A broad range of Americans were impacted intensely and personally. Draftees who believed it to be an immoral war were still ordered to join the military and go. Some sought deferments. Many fled to Canada and Sweden to avoid taking part; others, having no way of knowing that a general amnesty would later be declared, and being unwilling to give up their American homeland, their families, and all that life in America meant to them, believing they had no viable option, reluctantly left for Vietnam.

Because of division within the Democratic Party and increasing criticism of the war which undermined his support, Johnson announced he would not run for re-election in 1968. Richard Nixon was elected President on a peace platform. However, four more years of war followed, including bombing in Laos and Cambodia (which had started much earlier, secretly and with official US denial). Public opinion against the war grew as newsreel images poured back into America, and protests and demonstrations continued. College campuses continued to be a center of outspoken determination to bring an end to the war.

In 1970 immediately after Nixon went on TV and radio to announce that he had ordered bombing in Cambodia, demonstrations against the war increased. Confrontations with police in Kent, Ohio, and burning of the

ROTC building on Kent State's campus brought the National Guard in to disburse demonstrators at Kent State; four students were killed and nine others wounded. A massive student strike followed, temporarily closing hundreds of colleges and universities.[225]

In 1971 parts of the secret "Pentagon Papers" ["United States–Vietnam Relations, 1945–1967: A Study Prepared by the Department of Defense," commissioned by Robert McNamara in 1967, completed in 1968] were leaked to the *New York Times,* and further publication was blocked by the Government. This action was challenged by those believing these materials needed to be seen by the American public, and the US Supreme Court ruled in favor of release of the information. Providing wider public access to the contents, Beacon Press stepped forward and published the multi-volume study which contained documents that illuminated a history unknown to the American people as it incriminated the US Presidency and the government's actions in the 50s and 60s and further galvanized public opinion against the war.

Nixon eventually responded to public pressure by advocating Vietnamization of the war, whereby South Vietnam itself would conduct the war without US troops but with US aid. Troop withdrawals began. Then in January 1973 the United States and North Vietnamese signed the Paris Peace Accords ending US participation in the war (except for aid that continued to support the South).

The United States went home, having sixty days to evacuate their remaining soldiers.

In 1974 Congress cut off all military funding for the war. South Vietnam, overcome militarily by the North and left on its own by the United States, surrendered in April 1975. That same month the US Congress passed the War Powers Resolution, requiring the President to obtain the approval of Congress for any troops committed to action for a period exceeding sixty days.

North and South became a united Vietnam on July 2, 1976.

Were there alternatives to war?

Yes. The United States could have acted consistently with what it had recognized to be the rights of all people to self-determination, rather than aiding the re-establishment of French colonialism. The United States could have supported Vietnamese independence immediately after World War II, and denied funding France in a renewed war, which would likely have prevented

France from retaking the country as a colony. Even after supporting the French in their war, the United States could have agreed to and honored the Geneva Accords which required elections in 1956, thus avoiding the Vietnam War.

US Government's plans to become politically and militarily involved, even after the Geneva Accords, could have been challenged, recognizing that paranoia can blind one to see only what is already perceived as truth. In this case, the United States "saw" a nationalistic quest for independence, driven and supported by communists, as a part of a worldwide communist take-over, and our fear of the USSR reinforced that "truth." The *Pentagon Papers* of 1968 included a critique of US policy and a memo posed to the National Security Council in the spring of 1954, asking:

- Just how important is Southeast Asia to the security interests of the United States? … Is the area important enough to fight for?
- How important is Indochina in the defense of Southeast Asia? Is the "domino theory" valid? Is Indochina important enough to fight for? If not, what are the strategic consequences of the loss of all or part of Indochina?
- If the United States intervenes in Indochina, can we count on the support of the natives? Can we fight as allies of the French and avoid the stigma of colonialism?
- Is there a strategic concept for the conduct of a war in Indochina which offers promise of early success…?[226]

When the American public learned what had happened and was happening, they answered those questions very differently than the US policymakers had earlier. One must wonder what criteria were used in arriving at the answers to those questions in 1954. More careful questioning could have very likely – again, even after other opportunities had been missed – avoided the Vietnam War entirely.

US political leadership could have slowed down and searched for truth, rather than pulling together "facts" to substantiate their "right" to do what they wanted to do regardless of what had actually happened.

Costs of the War

DoD Estimated Dead (American) – 58,220
Estimated Wounds Requiring Hospitalization
(American) – 153,303
Wounds without hospitalization
(American) – 150,341[227]
Estimated Dead
S. Korea, Philippines, Thailand, Australia – 6,855
South Vietnamese military – 224,000
South Vietnamese Civilians – 300,000
North Vietnamese Military/Viet Cong – 666,000
North Vietnamese Civilian– 300,000[228]
Direct War expenditures – $111 billion
($686 billion at 2008 purchasing power)[229]
Moral impact – unknown

2.13   The Gulf War (1991)

A commonly held American perspective for the war

President George H.W. Bush, in an address to the US Congress on September 11, 1990, has said:

> In the early morning hours of August 2nd, following negotiations and promises by Iraq's dictator Saddam Hussein not to use force, a powerful Iraqi army invaded its trusting and much weaker neighbor, Kuwait. Within 3 days, 120,000 Iraqi troops with 850 tanks had poured into Kuwait and moved south to threaten Saudi Arabia. It was then that I decided to act to check that aggression.
>
> … Our objectives in the Persian Gulf are clear, our goals defined and familiar: Iraq must withdraw from Kuwait completely, immediately, and without condition. Kuwait's legitimate government must be restored. The security and stability of the Persian Gulf must be

assured. And American citizens abroad must be protected. These goals are not ours alone. They've been endorsed by the United Nations Security Council five times in as many weeks.... This is not, as Saddam Hussein would have it, the United States against Iraq. It is Iraq against the world.

We stand today at a unique and extraordinary moment. The crisis in the Persian Gulf, as grave as it is, also offers a rare opportunity to move toward an historic period of cooperation. ... [A] new world order – can emerge: a new era – freer from the threat of terror, stronger in the pursuit of justice, and more secure in the quest for peace. ... A world where the rule of law supplants the rule of the jungle. A world in which nations recognize the shared responsibility for freedom and justice. A world where the strong respect the rights of the weak.

... Vital issues of principle are at stake. Saddam Hussein is literally trying to wipe a country off the face of the Earth. We do not exaggerate. ... Vital economic interests are at risk as well. Iraq itself controls some 10 percent of the world's proven oil reserves. Iraq plus Kuwait controls twice that. An Iraq permitted to swallow Kuwait would have the economic and military power, as well as the arrogance, to intimidate and coerce its neighbors – neighbors who control the lion's share of the world's remaining oil reserves. We cannot permit a resource so vital to be dominated by one so ruthless. And we won't.

... Iraq will not be permitted to annex Kuwait. That's not a threat, that's not a boast, that's just the way it's going to be.[230]

Iraq remains determined in its lawless, violent aggression, in spite of UN sanctions and deadlines for withdrawal. The nation of Kuwait and its people must now be liberated from this tyrant.

The perspective of the other side (Iraq)[231]

Our people struggled through eight years of war with Iran. So many lives were lost and so much was destroyed. We ended the war with $40 billion in debts, not including the aid given us by the Arab states. It was with great determination that we turned to the task of rebuilding our land and our lives. Then another war struck our people, a war against our right to live and to heal, a war against our children's rights to milk, our war widows' and orphans' right to receive help to survive. Some wars kill by taking blood; this war kills by taking away our future and condemning us to a desperate struggle for existence.

This is the war Kuwait waged against us – an economic war carried out by manipulation of oil production, against agreement, so that prices plummeted so low that our only real source of income for rebuilding is cut by billions of dollars. It would have strangled us, but we won't be held hostage to such economic warfare. Such action is also a direct attack on our defense, robbing us of the funds to maintain our military strength. Without that, we cannot defend our homeland. If Iran decided to war again, or Israel determined to attack us as they did in 1981, we would be ill-prepared. We cannot allow this to happen.

We did everything we could. At the meeting of the oil ministers in Amman in May, we made clear what Kuwait was doing. Our Foreign Minister Tariq Aziz contacted the Arab League, describing the Kuwaiti violations of OPEC agreements. We were encouraged to meet face to face in Jeddah, which we did. The conclusion was not an agreement we could live with. We cannot withstand the loss of billions of dollars of revenue caused by Kuwait's belligerent actions, when our people are so in need. Their direct thievery of our oil, by slant drilling into our oil fields, has continued defiantly.

We asked that the aid given by our Arab Brothers be forgiven of repayment. These funds were as surely used to protect them from the control of the Islamist revolutionaries of Iran as it was for our protection. Instead, they declare this is a war debt that will not be forgiven and insist on collection, making our recovery impossible.

The Americans, who gave us support during the war in many ways, and re-established relations with us, have now turned away and are supporting this warfare of Kuwait's. They have started a media campaign in the United States to turn the American people against us. They apologize for some of these attacks, but then start them up again. They say they don't understand all that we do. That is to be expected. They have not had dealings with us over the centuries, nor do they know our long history. But sometimes we also don't understand what the Americans do. We could learn by working with each other.

They said they wanted better relationships with Iraq. We too want this, but see how America always talks about democracy but doesn't take time to look at any other viewpoint. America tries to stir the world against us and lead the UN to turn nations to war with us. You have a right to choose your friends, America, but you should not do this by rewarding Kuwait for their aggression against our people.

We told the Arab Kings and Presidents that some brothers were making war against us. We promised not to do anything until we could meet together. If we found there was hope, then nothing would happen, but if there was no solution, they had to understand that Iraq will not accept death. They made the choice. Our patience ran out and we had to act. So we moved into Kuwait to protect our rights to survive, as is necessary for any government responsible to its people. The United States and their supporters would do no differently if they were us.

We have only sought to bring our own territory back to us. The Europeans wreaked havoc with the Arab people after the First World War. They took it upon themselves to divide us into states according to their wishes and for their own economic and political power and benefits. That is exactly what the British did with Kuwait, a part of our Basra district. We only moved to restore, never to usurp what was not ours.

Knowing full well what we would have to do in Kuwait, the US Ambassador told us that they had no intentions of becoming involved in our Arab affairs or with our border concerns, yet now, after we were finally compelled to act, they determined to bring us down. They stir the anger of the world against us, drive the UN Security Council against us, never seeking to understand the truth.

Even with all this, we have offered many times to bring this situation to negotiation so it may be resolved, along with other issues that must no longer be ignored. America refuses to negotiate.

Background

Let's begin in the middle, and then move back in time, then forward.

Iraq moved troops into Kuwait and forced the Kuwaiti government to flee for safety in August of 1990. "Minutes after national security advisor Brent Scowcroft told him [US President George H.W. Bush] of the invasion, Bush phoned U.N. Ambassador Thomas Pickering, instructing him to call for a session of the Security Council to condemn Saddam's action."[232] The Security Council responded. A series of resolutions followed in the coming weeks – demand for immediate withdrawal, implementation of trade embargo and financial sanctions against Iraq, and, in late November 1990, their final resolution authorized all means necessary to uphold the other resolutions unless complied with by January 15, 1991. Use of military force was to be a last option, if and after all else had failed.

> To win, build, and maintain his coalition, Bush ... kept up a barrage of personal phone calls and visits to world leaders. ... America would join with the Soviet Union and other nations to oppose 'naked aggression' and replace the old superpower spheres of influence with respect for international law. But he was practical enough to know that a little logrolling makes idealism easier to swallow. So the U.S. forgave $7.1 billion in military loans to Egypt, granted textile trade concessions to Turkey, and lifted political sanctions imposed on China after the Tiananmen Square massacre, among other moves. The President and his men worked overtime to quash freelance peacemakers in the Arab world, France, and the Soviet Union who threatened to give Saddam a face-saving way out of the box Bush was building. Over and over, Bush repeated the mantra: no negotiations, no deals, no face-saving, no rewards, and specifically, no linkage to a Palestinian peace conference.[233]

Though the UN Security Council had acted, the US Congress had not. There was disagreement in America over what seemed to be the drive toward inevitable war as the only or best means of resolving the situation with Iraq and Kuwait. Some said economic sanctions against Iraq would motivate them to withdraw from Kuwait, but there hadn't been time for them to work. Others said the Arab nations held the most potential for pressuring Iraq and should have that opportunity without the threat of military intervention by the United States. President Bush recorded in his diary in October 1990, "The news is saying some members of Congress feel I might use a minor incident to go to war, and they may be right. We must get this over with."[234]

President Bush raised the image of Saddam Hussein as the new Hitler,[235] a dictator who must be stopped. Americans held in the embassy in Kuwait or hiding in the city from Iraqi troops were described as hostages. Lloyd Gardner noted in his book, *The Long Road to Baghdad,* that this hostage image could provide the provocation needed for military action if nothing else turned up, yet he mentions that other embassies had shut down and their nationals had left the country:

> Asked why the United States did not do the same, an adminis-
> tration official replied, "Because we don't want to acquiesce to the
> annexation of Kuwait." ... Saddam backed off, offering passage out
> of Kuwait to all the Americans in early December, coupled with
> various invitations to what Baghdad insisted would be serious nego-
> tiations – always, of course, to involve the Arab-Israeli question.[236]

Saddam Hussein invited negotiations beginning as early as August 11, 1990, asking for deliberations on oil policies and access to the Gulf in exchange for withdrawal.[237] His offers of withdrawal continued to come, but always referenced issues besides withdrawal, saying other current instances of occupation in the region – the long time Israeli occupation of the West Bank and Gaza Strip and Syrian occupation of Lebanon – needed to be on the table as well. The US Government refused to negotiate under such conditions. It was not going to be side-tracked from the issue at hand – Iraq's invasion of Kuwait – and refused any consideration of negotiation on a broader scope.

A clear opportunity for peaceful settlement came on September 9, 1990 during a meeting of President Bush and Soviet President Gorbachev:

> Gorbachev brought out a proposal to end the crisis peacefully.
> Iraq offered to release the hostages, withdraw from Kuwait, and
> restore the Kuwaiti government. In return, the United States would
> promise (just a promise) that it would not strike Iraq and would
> reduce its forces in the area, which would be replaced by an Arab
> peace-keeping force. An agreement for an international conference
> on the Middle East would follow.[238]

Because the wording of this proposal, again, linked settlement of the crisis to Israel via a conference on the broader Middle East situation, it was rejected.[239]

The final exchange was a meeting between Secretary of State Baker and Iraqi Foreign Minister Aziz at which Baker delivered US ultimatums in a letter which Aziz refused to accept "saying it was nothing but 'threats.'"[240]

Bush continued working for Congressional approval of military action against Iraq at the same time he was ordering massive troop build-up in Saudi Arabia:

In the early months of the trade [sanctions] blockade, Bush and his aides worried that the 230,000 U.S. troops they had initially deployed were vulnerable to Iraqi attack.... By October, [Collin] Powell was pushing for a major increase in the U.S. military presence. Even before the midterm elections on November 6, Bush decided to nearly double America's troop strength. But to avoid making it a campaign issue ... delayed his announcement until November 8. Critics who warned that Bush had set the clock ticking on Saddam's withdrawal from Kuwait were correctly stating what the President had in mind.[241]

President Bush began using Iraq's potential for nuclear weaponry as justification for force. Gardner notes that the argument was working with the public and that a *New York Times/CBS* poll gave 54 percent of respondents agreeing that military action was justified to prevent Iraq from getting nuclear weapons. But voices still spoke of alternatives:

The leading American historian of the Manhattan Project and its consequences down through the years, Richard Rhodes, took sharp issue with the administration's case for war. ... Nuclear proliferation was not good, obviously, and having another power with such weapons was destabilizing, whether it was Iraq or any other nation. But an embargo on potential weapons material was a first step, not war, followed by serious attention to an overall Middle East settlement, and finally general nuclear disarmament.[242]

Perhaps most impacting of all arguments on the American public was the deeply emotional and horrific statement of a young hospital volunteer from Kuwait City, testifying before the non-governmental Congressional Human Rights Caucus, relating that she had personally witnessed the brutal actions of Iraqi soldiers rushing into the hospital, seizing babies from incubators, leaving them on the floor to die, and packing off the incubators. The story was later discovered to be a fake, the work of a US public relations firm hired by Citizens for a Free Kuwait to assure US support for the war, yet the story was repeated over and over, including by President Bush, before it was exposed as a yarn. Gardner explains that the "hospital volunteer" turned out to be the daughter of the Kuwaiti ambassador to the United States and a member of the ruling royal family – as well as a participant in a major PR deception.

However, the uncovering of the deception took place after the US bombing had begun.[243]

Details of the extensive Kuwaiti-funded PR campaign to sell the war to the American public are described in "How PR Sold the War in the Persian Gulf," an excerpt from *Toxic Sludge is Good for You: Lies, Damn Lies, and the Public Relations Industry:*

> The American Public was notoriously reluctant to send its young into foreign battles on behalf of any cause. Selling war in the Middle East to the American people would not be easy. Bush would need to convince Americans that former ally Saddam Hussein now embodied evil, and that the oil fiefdom of Kuwait was a struggling young democracy. How could the Bush Administration build US support for "liberating" a country so fundamentally opposed to democratic values? How could the war appear noble and necessary rather than a crass grab to save cheap oil?
>
> "If and when a shooting war starts, reporters will begin to wonder why American soldiers are dying for oil-rich sheiks," warned Hal Steward, a retired army PR official. "The US military had better get cracking to come up with a public relations plan that will supply the answers the public can accept."
>
> Steward needn't have worried. A pubic relation plan was already in place, paid for almost entirely by the "oil-rich sheiks" themselves.[244]

The authors describe several other pieces of the public relations campaign – giving away tens of thousands of "Free Kuwait" t-shirts on college campuses, TV and newspaper ads, speakers available for rallies, news briefings, calls and mailings, press conferences, bumper stickers, media information kits, video news releases, opinion polls, and direct contact of politicians. It was a multi-million dollar PR project to sell the war.[245]

The question of official US diplomatic efforts and their impact on the situation were raised when *The New York Times International* printed "Excerpts From Iraqi Document on Meeting with U.S. Envoy" on September 23, 1990, concerning the July 25, 1990, meeting of Saddam Hussein and US Ambassador to Baghdad, April Glaspie. The document was an Iraqi Government transcript, translated into English from Arabic, of the meeting that took place before the Iraqi invasion of Kuwait. The comments attributed to Glaspie acknowledged that the United States wanted "to seek better relations with Iraq." When Hussein described their concern over oil prices being forced down by Kuwait and U.A.E. and thereby impacting the Iraqi budget by $6 or $7 billion dollars – a disaster for their nation – Glaspie noted that many Americans from oil-producing states would like to see oil prices go above $25 a barrel, the figure Hussein mentioned as a reasonable price. Then she said:

> I think I understand this. I have lived here for years. I admire your extraordinary efforts to rebuild your country. I know you need funds. We understand that and our opinion is that you should have the opportunity to rebuild your country. But we have no opinion on the Arab-Arab conflicts, like your border disagreement with Kuwait.
>
> I was in the American Embassy in Kuwait during the late 60's. The instruction we had during this period was that we should express no opinion on this issue and that the issue is not associated with America. James Baker has directed our official spokesmen to emphasize this instruction.[246]

Glaspie said she clearly understood what President Hussein was describing, and that our American history "taught us to say freedom or death." She went on to say that she hoped the problem would be resolved quickly using "any suitable methods via Klibi [Secretary General of the Arab League] or via President Mubarak [of Egypt]." She expressed concern that the "the massive troops" deployed in the south, coupled with the Iraqi point of view that recent actions of Kuwait and U.A.E. were equal to military aggression, required that she ask about the intentions of Iraq toward them. Hussein acknowledged the legitimacy of being concerned when peace is at stake, but put forth the challenge to the United States to show concern in a way that the aggressor [Kuwait] would not feel supported for its aggression. He mentioned upcoming talks and said the Kuwaitis could be assured that "When we meet and when we see that there is hope, then nothing will happen. But if we are unable to find a solution, then it will be natural that Iraq will not accept death."[247]

The release of this information raised concern that US diplomatic efforts were at least partially responsible for causing Iraq to interpret US reaction to a possible Iraqi military action in Kuwait as "no opinion," and therefore the United States had even more responsibility to work to resolve the issue diplomatically rather than militarily.

There were other questions raised by those calling for restraint. The photos that were used to convince Saudi Arabia that they needed to invite US troops and weaponry into their country, to deter the Iraqis from invading Saudi, "became the subject of intense controversy" as other photos discovered by an investigative reporter showed no evidence of a build-up near Saudi Arabia as had been described to King Fahd.[248] Furthermore, Iraq accused Kuwait of "slant drilling" into Iraqi oil wells. The long-unresolved border issues between Iraq and Kuwait remained, with Iraqi claims that Kuwait was part of its territory. These issues were not the ones to gain multi-million dollar PR attention.

The administration's certitude that war was necessary and justified continued to be projected:

> Bush claimed that he did not need a congressional declaration of war to use military force against Iraq. However, to bolster political support for the commencement of hostilities with Iraq, and to obtain legislative legitimacy for the participation of US troops in a multinational coalition, the president requested a congressional resolution supporting the implementation of the UN Security Council resolution authorizing member states to use 'all necessary means' to restore peace to the region.[249]

Senator Sam Nunn of Georgia, Chairman of the Senate Armed Forces Committee, held a series of televised hearings on US policy and the threatening war. Testimony was strong for giving sanctions time to work, which no one expected could happen in just five and a half months, and recognizing that peaceful efforts to resolve the conflict could yet be pursued. Double standards were cited in that the United States failed to challenge years-long Israeli occupation of Palestinian lands, nor was the United States pushing for enforcement of existing UN resolutions against that occupation, in comparison to the immediacy of the position taken regarding Iraqi occupation of Kuwait:

> On November 28, 1990, the Committee listened to General David Jones and Admiral William Crowe. ... General Jones stated that coalition members had preference, from the beginning, for diplomatic and economic measures over offensive military action with particular sensitivity about attacking Iraq itself. ... Admiral Crowe argued that force should be used only if sanctions fail to achieve their objectives. He explained that using force would not solve the problems of the Middle East. Actually it would exacer-

bate them, particularly the Palestinian-Israeli conflict, stability of Arab regimes, boundary disputes, the US links to Israel, and the dominant position of American oil companies in foreign policy. He mentioned that many Arabs would deeply resent a campaign, which would kill large numbers of Arabs and Muslims. ... James Webb, former Secretary of the Navy, ... mentioned that "had the President dispatched a modestly-structured air-ground presence to Saudi Arabia, and then begun negotiating a mutual withdrawal of American and Iraqi forces from their respective positions, the crisis may have been over by now."[250]

Congressional consideration continued. Though the vote was close, on January 12, 1991, the US Senate approved Senate Joint Resolution 2, 52 to 47,[251] and House Joint Resolution 77 was approved the same day by a vote of 250 to 183.[252] Public Law 102–1, the "Authorization for the Use of Military Force Against Iraq Resolution" was signed by the President on January 14, 1991.

The US-led bombing began on January 17, 1991. The air campaign hit Iraq's military, industrial, and transportation infrastructure including power stations, bridges, and oil facilities. It was followed by a ground war begun February 24 and ending February 28, 1991, with Iraq out of Kuwait, the Kuwaiti government restored, and in the end, what was later to be called a slaughter on the "Highway of Death" as retreating Iraqi soldiers were pursued by forces from the United States, United Kingdom, and France.

The victory over Iraq was celebrated as having accomplished its goal of liberating Kuwait. It was said to have incidentally "kicked the Vietnam Syndrome" once and for all, proving that the American military would not be bogged down in a never-ending war with thousands of American casualties. This one was done with decisive, effective, powerful action in a matter of days, with minimal American deaths. Some criticized President Bush for not going further, straight to Baghdad and destroying Saddam Hussein and his potential nuclear weapons. Dick Cheney was to explain that decision eighteen months later at a talk given in Seattle, Washington:

> I would guess if we had gone in there, I would still have forces in Baghdad today. We'd be running the country. We would not have been able to get everybody out and bring everybody home. And the final point that I think needs to be made is the question of casualties. I don't think you could have done all of that without

significant additional US casualties. And while everybody was tremendously impressed with the low cost of the (1991) conflict, for the 146 Americans who were killed in action and for their families, it wasn't a cheap war. And the question in my mind is how many additional American casualties is Saddam (Hussein) worth? And the answer is not that damned many. So, I think we got it right, both when we decided to expel him from Kuwait, but also when the president made the decision that we'd achieved our objectives and we were not going to go get bogged down in the problems of trying to take over and govern Iraq.[253]

Though the choice to take Baghdad was not made, the bombing managed to destroy much of Iraq's infrastructure. According to the New York based Center for Economic and Social Rights' fact sheet "Costs and Consequences of War in Iraq":

In the 1991 Gulf War, US-led forces dropped 84,200 tons of munitions on Iraq and Kuwait during 43 days of bombing. ... They caused major damage to Iraq's civilian infrastructure, including electricity generation and water and sanitation facilities. A total of 110,000 Iraqi civilians, including 70,000 children under the age of five and 7,000 elderly, died as a result of "war-induced adverse health effects" caused by the destruction of infrastructure.[254]

Sanctions remained in place and, as a response to the Iraqi government's counterattack against civilian uprisings (uprisings urged by the United States to overthrow Saddam Hussein), in both the south and north of Iraq at the conclusion of the war, "No Fly Zones" were established. US and UK air strikes continued sporadically in these "No Fly Zones" over the next decade. Many thousands of deaths of the Iraqi people have been attributed to the sanctions and these bombing raids.

~

Dr. Hassan A. El-Najjar, Associate Professor of Sociology & Anthropology at Dalton State College, Georgia, describes in his book *The Gulf War: Overreaction & Excessiveness,* his strong belief that the actions taken by Iraq in 1990 must be examined through a knowledge of history that was not brought to the attention of the American people nor debated or understood during the months that preceded the January and February 1991 Gulf War.

He relates that Britain had shown great interest in Kuwait in the 18th century. They established a trade center there and maintained Indian soldiers as guards. But their real opportunity to develop a strong presence came in 1896 when they protected and supported Shaikh Mubarak, a man who murdered his two half-brothers in order to exclusively claim the family's rule over Kuwait. The British signed an agreement of protection with Mubarak, recognizing him and his heirs as the legitimate rulers of Kuwait. He, in turn, agreed to obtain British approval before dealing with any other foreign nations.

El-Najjar describes Kuwait as having been a part of the governorate of Basra (Iraq) within the Ottoman Empire, but Mubarak became uncooperative, except with the British. Ottoman troops determined to bring Kuwait back into line. They withdrew their intentions, however, after being challenged by the British Navy. They agreed to the status quo, recognizing that there still remained unresolved border disputes. When the Ottoman Empire was defeated in World War I, its lands were divided into areas of control by the victorious European powers, instead of the Arabs being granted their independence as had been promised. Britain took jurisdiction over both Kuwait and Iraq, and decided the long-standing border disputes needed to be resolved. The borders they chose were not accepted as legitimate by Iraq.

Oil was first produced in Kuwait in 1934 by British and American oil companies. The population of Kuwait was about 75,000 at the time, and it grew quickly as foreign workers were brought in. In the following years a move for independence was stirring in colonies and protectorates around the world. Kuwait was among those affected.

On June 19, 1961, Kuwait's 1899 protection agreement with Britain was replaced with a friendship agreement, and Kuwait became independent. Six days later:

> Iraq declared its intention to annex Kuwait claiming that it was an Iraqi territory before the protection agreement. The former Iraqi President, Abudl-Karim Qassem, moved his troops to the borders in order to restore Kuwait following the British withdrawal. To prevent that, Britain sent 5,000 troops to the borders between Iraq and Kuwait…. This time, the British interests in Kuwait were much more important than at the turn of the century. … [T]he British government owned one-fourth of the Kuwait Oil Company (KOC), and Britain imported about 40 percent of its oil needs from Kuwait. The crisis ended by accepting Kuwait as a member of

the Arab League, on July 20, 1961, then as member of the United Nations Organization on May 17, 1963.[255]

In October 1963 the Iraqi Prime Minister recognized Kuwait's sovereignty and independence, but the Iraqi Parliament never ratified his decision to do so and instead kept their claims that Kuwait was a part of Iraqi territory.[256]

The current grievance raised by the Iraqi government was that these long-held border disputes were integral to the conflict, yet they were not given consideration or even recognition as impacting the conflict. Neither was any attention given to Iraq's concerns over Kuwaiti disregard of oil production quotas or Iraq's subsequent oil revenue loss, conflict over ownership of borderland oil fields, nor inconsistency in dealing with territorial integrity as in the case of Israeli occupation of Palestinian lands.

Were there alternatives to war?

To exercise honesty and humility could have opened doors to alternatives to war. President George H.W. Bush rallied support for war by demonizing Saddam Hussein and describing his chemical and biological weapons program as an evidence of the kind of atrocities the man and the Iraqi government were capable of if not stopped. He did not bring to the attention of the American people and to members of Congress the American complicity and collaboration in that work, nor did he highlight America's role in providing other military assistance to Iraq during the preceding Iran-Iraq war.

It was Senator Riegle of Michigan who learned much and reported to Congress in 1994 what his office had discovered during its attempts to help Gulf War veterans and their families. The veterans had come to him because they were suffering from serious illnesses, some life-threatening, which came to be called "Gulf War Syndrome." Senator Riegle's report became a matter of Congressional Record on February 9, 1994, about three years after the Gulf War ended. He described the chemical weapons in Iraq that our soldiers were exposed to, saying:

> Some researchers feel that the symptoms may not only be a result of exposure to chemical warfare agents, but also as a result of exposure to biological warfare agents. Now we are pursuing that line of inquiry. Before laying out the evidence that we have found, I want to emphasize that this is an extremely serious issue with

very powerful consequences. These kinds of exposure may begin to explain the alarming and growing evidence that the illnesses some of our gulf war veterans are experiencing appear to be moving through their families, causing health problems in the wives and in their children.[257]

He went on to describe the great injustice done to veterans because of lack of interest in their condition on behalf of the Defense Department that was "looking ahead to other things. They are not looking back at the large number of sick veterans who are out there." Riegle's outrage seemed heightened by what he had learned in the search to discover what the soldiers might have been exposed to:

> I asked my staff to contact the Department of Commerce to request information on any biological materials that might have been exported from the United States to Iraq in the years prior to the gulf war. After we finally got the information from the Commerce Department, we then contacted a principal supplier of these materials to determine exactly what materials were exported to Iraq which could have contributed to their biological weapons capability. ... We found that pathogenic, which means disease-producing items, and toxigenic, meaning poisonous items, and other hazardous materials were exported from the United States to Iraq following a licensing and application procedure actually set forth by our own United States Department of Commerce. That means our own Government had to approve the shipment of these materials and obviously did so – approving the shipment of these items to Iraq before the war started. ... Between the years of 1985 and 1989, the United States Government approved the sales of quantities of potentially lethal biological agents that could have been cultured and grown in very large quantities in an Iraqi biological warfare program.[258]

Riegle spelled out for the record exactly what the United States sent, in page after page of listings, including the name of the material, shipping dates, and the Iraqi governmental agency receiving it. (Among the many listed, incidentally, is "bacillus anthracis" or anthrax.) He continues:

We should have gotten this information from the Department of Defense. We did not. We had to generate it ourselves. ... So let's get cracking on this. We know we sent the stuff. We know our own Government approved it. Why, I will never know – to send it on over to Saddam Hussein. Maybe because at the time the policymakers in the administration thought he would use these weapons on the Iranians. Well it looks as if they may have gotten used on our people.[259]

Riegle's report came too late to stir America to consider complexities and look at alternatives to the war in January 1991, but it does show that America kept aside or used information in the way it chose, which was to support its drive for military action. Had the US Government admitted its own complicity in providing Iraq with materials it later held up as signs of atrocious, cruel behavior (and similarly its role in down-playing Iranian complaints of use of chemical weapons by Iraq), there might have been enough humility to at least be willing to listen to the voices that urged restraint and time to seek resolution.

The use of arbitration to settle boundary disputes has been mentioned in the review of earlier wars. It was an accepted and established mechanism for peaceful resolution of international conflict that was not attempted in this situation, either before the Iraqi invasion into Kuwait or after it. It could have provided a base upon which alternatives to war could have been explored. It is startling to learn more of the background of the November 29, 1990 UN Security Council Resolution 678, which authorized the use of force to accomplish Iraqi withdrawal from Kuwait. According to El-Najjar, Secretary of State Baker:

... admitted in his memoirs that if the member states in the Security Council resisted his pressures, he was ready for two major concessions. First the U.S. was willing to withdraw a fixed percentage of American troops from Saudi Arabia, if Iraq withdrew. Second, the U.S. was ready to call for the creation of an Iraq-Kuwait claims tribunal at The Hague to deal with their border dispute.[260]

But this never happened. The buying of votes to okay going to war overrode this concession, never offered, that could have made the war unnecessary. Yemen and Cuba refused to go along with the resolution. El-Najjar goes on to explain how other UN Security Council votes were rounded up:

[Zaire] demanded that the U.S. foreign aid be restored ... for a yes vote. ... [Ivory Coast] asked that the G-7 countries forgive his country's debt in return for a yes vote. ... [The Romanian vote] was bought for just $80 million in humanitarian aid. ... He [Baker] threatened [Malaysian Foreign Minister] that a negative vote would 'affect relations between the two countries.' At that moment, the Foreign Minister 'became dead silent,' and gave a yes vote.[261]

None of these examples reflect a decision based on the merits of the situation. It is a sad commentary on the manipulation of the purpose for which the United Nations was formed.

Although Ambassador Glaspie in July 1990 described understanding and empathizing with Iraq's desperate economic situation and the right to rebuild its homeland after the Iraq-Iran War, it does not appear that the US Government was motivated to act on that understanding and empathy. One must wonder what would have happened if the effort and expense used to convince Saudi Arabia's King Fahd to allow a huge US troop buildup in Saudi Arabia had – before the Iraqi invasion began – instead been used to convince Kuwait and Saudi Arabia that war debt forgiveness or reduction could be to their mutual advantage with a healthy economy returning to the region.

Debt forgiveness was not an impossibility, as was seen later when the United States worked extensively on such a plan for Iraq during the war that America initiated in 2003. Once Saddam Hussein had been ousted, the United States recognized that, even though there would be oil revenue that could be used to fund Iraq's debt, the amount of the debt was unsustainable in that it wouldn't allow for current and future needs of the nation as well. The United States forgave 4.1 billion of its own debt and lobbied for billions of dollars of debt forgiveness by others, which was agreed to.[262]

After the Iran-Iraq war ended in August 1988, Hussein had worked for debt forgiveness. None was granted. In July 1990 he expressed desperation over the crippling debt. Could US support for debt forgiveness at that time have caused a shift that worked to positively influence others and at the same time strengthen relations – relations not based on military build-up and arms sales or on control of oil resources, but on mutually beneficial cooperative trade and understanding between people?

During the weeks after occupation, alternatives arose. Although France had agreed to a military response to bring about Iraqi withdrawal from Kuwait, should all peaceful efforts fail, they continued to work for those peaceful methods right up to the deadline given by the U.N. Security Council. They proposed the rapid withdrawal from Kuwait be accompanied by a commitment of the U.N. Security Council to convene an international conference on the Arab-Israeli conflict, opening the possibility of dialogue and action on an issue that the United States refused to tie to the Iraqi-Kuwait situation in any way.

Was the adamant US stand against linking issues, done from a worthy determination not to encourage or promote aggression by granting negotiations on unrelated issues? Or was it a hard-headed stubbornness that prevented America from recognizing what others around the world saw as an issue long overdue for examination (the Israeli occupation of Palestinian lands), and one that could support the search for truth and justice throughout this region of the world? Could America not see any inconsistency in punishing Iraq for invading Kuwait while ignoring Israeli invasion of others' territory? Others working with the United States didn't seem to feel it was unreasonable to broaden negotiations, as noted by the French proposal and that of Soviet President Gorbachev.

Had negotiations been allowed to take place, in good faith and in search for solutions for both situations, this Gulf War of 1990 might well never have happened, and the conditions that followed it and contributed to the drive for war again in 2003, and the many deaths caused in the interim both by direct military action and by sanctions might have been avoided.

The United States also had available the untapped wisdom of the United Nations in implementing alternatives to war, one of the reasons for its existence. Had we replaced our telling the Security Council what needed to happen, how, and by when, with asking representatives of all nations of the General Assembly what could be done to restore justice, it is quite possible that an alternative to war could have been discovered, with lasting results.

Had we made certain that the history of the Arabian Peninsula and the Middle East in general were intimately known, and that the voice and wisdom of Arabs was sought, we may have been able to look more objectively at a situation that many believe was biased heavily toward an Israeli perspective. If men and women of Arab heritage were active in roles of political leadership in the United States, or were invited to share background and viewpoints with such leadership, a more balanced picture may have emerged that could have supported a peaceful resolution.

Had we looked at Iraq's militarization and potential for developing nuclear weapons in the light of Israel's militarization and possession of nuclear weapons (and the US's), and the way in which force was used by both nations, we could have chosen to work for disarmament in the entire region, rather than pushing arms sales to Iraq and maintaining millions of dollars of military aid for Israel over many years. Working for disarmament instead of military build-up, acting on a commitment to a just peace in the Middle East, implementing a willingness to buy oil on just economic terms rather than control oil access through military force, and supporting democracy through education and example, could have laid the foundation for a tradition of working to peacefully resolve conflict that could have avoided the Gulf War.

The possibility that the September 11, 2001, attacks in the United States were in retaliation for US troops retained in Saudi Arabia after the1991 Gulf War, increases the possible casualties tied to this war by the total number of those deaths, and by the number of deaths caused by the US retaliation for that retaliation. Those figures are not reflected in the box below.

Costs of the War

DoD Estimated Dead (American In-Theater Deaths) – 383
  (147 battle deaths)
  Estimated American Wounded – not mortal – 467[263]
Estimated Dead
  Iraqi Military – 10,000 – 56,000[264]
  Iraqi Civilians – 1,000 – 3500[265]
  Iraqi Civilians by Infrastructure Destruction – 110,000[266]
Direct War expenditures – $61 Billion [$54 Billion of which was
  reported to have been offset by in-kind contributions or cash of
  allied governments] ($102 Billion in FY2011 dollars)[267]
Estimated American Military Deaths from "Gulf War Syndrome" –
  unknown
Estimated Veteran and Family of Veteran incidence of illness from
  "Gulf War Syndrome" – unknown
Estimated Iraqi Civilian Illness/Deaths Attributed to U.S. use of
  depleted uranium in weaponry – unknown
UNICEF Estimated Increase in Iraqi Children Deaths from 1991–
  1998 – 500,000[268]
Moral impact – unknown.

More About the Costs of War

The boxed "Costs of the War" tabulations given throughout this chapter ignore other extremely significant costs. One is the cost of ongoing mental, emotional, spiritual, and physical pain and damage caused to those who, even though not counted among the dead or wounded listed above, continue to experience the impact of war. They may or may not have received treatment or help for these conditions, and the cost to them and their families and others has not been measured nor reflected in the tallies given above.

The cost of refugee resettlement within the countries at war or other countries to which they have fled and the ongoing difficulties encountered thereby are not generally included, nor is the value of man-made property and infrastructure destroyed in the war, or the reconstruction of such damage by those suffering it.

A third area of war cost not listed is damage to the earth and the non-human environment. Even while recognizing that research and study of the environmental impacts of war are still in early stages, clear patterns have emerged and are considered in the essays included in *Natural Enemy, Natural Ally: Toward an Environmental History of War*.[269] The range of topics is broad – wildlife, from massive consumption of songbirds to counter food shortages, to whales mistaken for enemy submarines and blown up; forests, from the total destruction of old growth stands to development of forest management policies; from land mines to nuclear fallout. The sampling of examples which follow will at least cause us to ponder the need to more broadly define "cost of war":

The demand for lumber skyrocketed in war time. The logs often desired for ships and port facilities came from the tallest ancient trees and contributed to the destruction of old growth primary forests throughout the world. Reconstruction of bombed cities, the building of military camps, warehouses, and shipyards, along with the demand for wood as fuel and for railway construction brought further intensive logging. The old ecologically diverse multi-species forests, if replaced at all, were generally replaced by reforestation programs of single-species trees.

This perspective perceived forests as timber, not as entire webs of life ... they were tree farms, not full-spectrum forests. In this important sense even the forest conservation programs did serious ecological damage, reducing the species diversity of natural forests to the few species required for strategic priorities.[270]

Clear-cutting practices during the world wars led to soil erosion, flooding, and extensive damage to downstream water sources, as well as establishing a "model for the clear-cutting of the tropical world's rain forests later in the century."[271]

Disease had always played a large part in the death toll from war, yet progress in combating those losses had unexpected consequences during and after World War II. "Malaria itself caused nearly ten times as many casualties as battles for the American forces until 1943. But DDT almost totally controlled the disease among the troops before the war's end. No one at the time foresaw the massive environmental damage which DDT would produce in the following peacetime."[272]

Chemical weapons developed through the United States Chemical Warfare Service for use in World War I contributed to the development and extensive use of insecticides and the dove-tailing of research efforts by the Chemical Warfare Service and the Bureau of Entomology of the Department of Agriculture. The long term impact of war's role in proliferation of chemicals in agriculture and the subsequent effects on the environment is not yet known.

The practice of precaution in spreading animal diseases was also affected by war. One example of this is disease in cattle. Because of the unique geography of the area, quarantine and shipping procedures had been able to keep targeted animal diseases that were endemic elsewhere, from spreading into areas of the Pacific Islands. During World War II, these precautions took a back seat to the decision to use haste in supplying horses to the US military stationed in New Caledonia. Horses carrying ticks from infected areas in Australia were brought in, and the ticks soon spread to the cattle in New Caledonia, causing millions of dollars of continuing loss to the cattle industry.[273]

Land mines have caused more destruction than their human toll, and they remain to do even more damage: "Some one hundred million unexploded anti-personnel mines remain around the planet now ... grievously retarding the restoration of postwar farms, pastures, forests, and water regimes."[274]

Nuclear weaponry, described as "the most ominous environmental threat in history," holds unequaled destructive power.[275] That potential destruction is precariously contained. The testing of nuclear weaponry alone made areas in the southern Pacific Ocean unfit for life. The thousands of nuclear weapons held by the United States and Russia and the hundreds by other nations are unimaginably dangerous to human existence and to all life on our planet. But because their destructive power is not easily comprehended – except to acknowledge that it is nothing like what the United States did in Japan in 1945 – some set the worry aside with explanations that "surely no one would be that stupid." Yet the danger is real and the ever present possibility of use through accident or by individuals set on control or retaliation is real, all a part of the story of war that must be challenged.

Military activities have sometimes lessened adverse impacts on the environment at such times, for example, when scarcity of fuel, transportation, or other pollutants made them simply unavailable for use, or when a military base has been isolated from development and retains the characteristics that allow for wildlife and plant diversity that would otherwise be lost to urbanization. Tucker and Russell conclude in *Natural Enemy, Natural Ally:* "Overall, the evidence in this book leaves little doubt that modern warfare has accelerated long-term damage to the biosphere, as a direct consequence of the intensifying destructive capacity of military technology."[276] War also delayed the growing concern and vision for care of the environment:

> World War II had a fatal and long-lasting impact on environmental discussion, policies, and protection. [It] put an end to all environmental activism in the public and private sectors for two or three decades. The war caused a long break in environmental policy-making that recovered in most countries only gradually in the postwar decades, causing the false impression that environmental protection was a new postwar phenomenon that was born in the 1960s or even later. This essay argues that the world wars, and above all World War II, were socio-ecological interventions that delayed the long-term development of environmental politics and protection perhaps more than any other single factor over the twentieth century. From the point of view of environmental policy making, war was probably the worst possible alternative to peace.[277]

And finally, the costs of war shown do not include the costs of maintaining a standing military force of the magnitude that the United States has, or the benefits granted soldiers once out of war. The *Statistical Summary of America's Major Wars* lists each war's costs in billions of dollars, breaks the cost of war down into "per capita" figures, and clarifies further: "Note that the figures are for direct costs only, omitting pension costs, which tended to triple the ultimate outlays. The table also omits the cost of damage to the national infrastructure during those wars waged on American soil."[278] (It goes unspoken that it also omits the cost of damage to the infrastructure of those nations on whose soil the United States waged war, as well as the harm caused to the people of those nations.) It is important to recognize the very real limitations of any attempt to quantify "Costs of War."

2.14   Acts of Military Violence Outside of War

The United States has gone to war in situations where there has been issued a formal "Declaration of War." It has also gone to war in other situations with Congressional authorization or approval. There have been undeclared wars and "incidents," including officially ordered bombings, at various times in various locations, without a full-scale military invasion or declaration. An example of the latter is that of April 1986 when President Reagan ordered the bombing of several sites in Libya in retaliation for the bombing of a Berlin disco often visited by US troops, and in order to convey a message to Libya that support of terrorism will not be ignored.[279]

Tensions between Libya and the United States had been high for years, including Libyan claims that US Navy ships were routinely patrolling in its territorial waters and the United States claiming that it had a right to be where it was, within international water boundaries. Libyans had been killed at the hands of the United States in March 1986 when both countries fired on each other's military in the Gulf of Sidra waters, when the United States crossed into waters claimed by Libya exclusively. The April disco bombing was alleged to have been in retaliation for those lost lives.

In the Berlin bombing three died and nearly 200 were injured. In the April Libya bombing, which included the home of Libyan leader Muammar Gadhafi [Khadafi], an estimated 60 died. In retaliation for that retaliation, 270 died in a Pan-Am jet bombing in 1988. A cycle of violence, death, and retaliation spiraled.

International opinion on the April 1986 US bombing of Libya was strong and varied. The United Nations General Assembly overwhelmingly condemned it as a violation of the Charter of the United Nations and of international law.

In looking back on this type of limited, but deadly, military action, as well as at declared or undeclared wars, one must examine the circumstances and ask what perspective was held by each side, what other alternatives were available, how vigorously they were pursued, and what the short-term and long-term impacts of the action taken have been. Historian Howard Zinn was one in the United States who commented on the moral impact of the Libyan incident when he observed:

> Too bad Khadafi's infant daughter died, one columnist wrote. Too bad, he said, but that's the game of war. Well, if that's the game, then let's get the hell out of it, because it is poisoning us morally, and not solving any problem. It is only continuing and escalating the endless cycle of retaliation which will one day, if we don't kick our habits, kill us all.[280]

The Navy Department Library website lists thirty pages of single-spaced summaries of "Instances of Use of United States Armed Forces Abroad, 1798–2004"[281]. The list is introduced with:

> The instances differ greatly in number of forces, purpose, extent of hostilities, and legal authorization. ... Some of the instances were extended military engagements that might be considered undeclared wars. ... The majority of the instances listed prior to World War II were brief Marine or Navy actions to protect US citizens or promote US interests. A number were actions against pirates or bandits. Covert actions, disaster relief, and routine alliance stationing and training exercises are not included here, nor are the Civil and Revolutionary Wars and the continual use of US military units in the exploration, settlement, and pacification of the Western part of the United States.[282]

There are 320 listed "instances," including the 1983 invasion of Grenada (Operation Urgent Fury) and the 1989 invasion of Panama (Operation Just Cause), both condemned by the General Assembly of the United Nations as flagrant violations of international law.[283]

This report is a part of the story of America's past and present, showing that there is much to learn: what constitutes "US interests" and whose interests are they, exactly? How has it been decided that the use of military force is the most reasonable way to accomplish those ends – at what financial cost and cost of life, to whom? What impact have these actions had? What alternatives were available and not used? Who is in control?

2.15   Recent US Wars

The Afghanistan War of 2001 to date (Operation Enduring Freedom, renamed Operation Resolute Support) and the Iraq War begun in March 2003 (Operation Iraqi Freedom) are within the experience and lifetime of most readers of this book. I suggest that you follow a similar pattern as has been laid out here and reflect on one or both of these wars. Read, research, and talk with people who were there and who weren't there.

Copy the blank "Evaluation of War" template that follows, and use it for your reflections. Write out a common US perspective on the war (or the perspective of your homeland), the perspective from "the other side," some background information, and the casualties and cost of the war so far. Learning about civilian casualties will take some digging for recent US wars, as the US Government has chosen not to keep track.

In referring to the civilian death toll from the Iraq War initiated by the United States in March 2003, *USA Today* reported on June 11, 2003: "Lt. Col. Jim Cassella, a Pentagon spokesman, said Tuesday that the US military did not count civilian casualties. 'Our efforts focus on destroying the enemy's capabilities, so we never target civilians and have no reason to try to count such unintended deaths,' he said."[284] Many disagree vehemently with his statement, believing there is extremely compelling reason to count and consider the number of civilian casualties.

Please include in your study of the Iraq War the report of Human Rights Watch, titled "Off Target: The Conduct of the War and Civilian Casualties in Iraq" concerning their mission to Iraq in April, May, and June 2003 to study civilian casualties that might have been avoided. The following excerpt from their report may spark your interest:

> The widespread use of cluster munitions, especially by the U.S. and U.K. ground forces, caused at least hundreds of civilian casualties. Cluster munitions, which are large weapons containing dozens or hundreds of submunitions, endanger civilians because of their broad dispersal, or "footprint," and the high number of submunitions that do not explode on impact. U.S. Central Command (CENTCOM) reported that it used 10,782 cluster munitions, which could contain at least 1.8 million submunitions. ... Although cluster munition strikes are particularly dangerous in populated areas, U.S. and U.K. ground forces repeatedly used these weapons

in attacks on Iraqi positions in residential neighborhoods. ... Many of the civilian casualties from the air war occurred during U.S. attacks targeting senior Iraqi leaders. The United States used an unsound targeting methodology.... All of the fifty acknowledged attacks targeting Iraqi leadership failed. While they did not kill a single targeted individual, the strikes killed and injured dozens of civilians.[285]

The report goes on to make recommendations, including the type of munitions which should be used, especially in populated areas, in order to reduce the number of civilian casualties. (With an organization holding the name and respect of Human Rights Watch, one must wonder about the power that would come from declaring war itself the violation of human rights. In the 1980s, when Physicians for Social Responsibility refused to develop a medical plan and protocol for survival of nuclear war, their message came across loud and clear – there is no cure for nuclear war, only prevention.)

Once you have studied the perspectives of each side and the background, take the time to consider and write down what alternatives to war might have been available.

Another question to add to the research is: Who benefited or who is benefiting from the war as time goes on? Nearly seven years after the most recent US war in Iraq began, the Portland, Oregon, *Oregonian* ran an article that sheds light on that question for one war:

> *U.S. Companies race to cash in on Iraqi oil projects: Baghdad* – U.S. companies have been arriving in Iraq in waves in recent months to pursue what is expected to be a multibillion-dollar bonanza of projects to revive the country's stagnant petroleum industry as Iraq seeks to establish itself as a rival to Saudi Arabia as the world's top oil producer.
>
> Since the 2003 U.S.-led invasion, nearly all of the biggest reconstruction projects in Iraq have been controlled by the United States. But many rebuilding contracts are expected to be awarded as soon as this month for drilling hundreds of wells, repairing thousands of miles of pipeline and building several giant floating oil terminals in the Persian Gulf, and possibly a new port. ... There are misgivings, however. ...The concerns have been heightened by the prominent role expected to be played by US companies that

have been criticized in the past by US Government auditors and inspectors for overcharging by hundreds of millions of dollars, performing shoddy work, and failing to finish hundreds of crucial projects while under contract in Iraq.[286]

Time for Reflection

On the next page there is a template for readers to evaluate a war they are concerned about. The author recommends that you discuss your completed template(s) with someone else.

Evaluation of War Template

Name(s) of the War

A common perspective for the war (my homeland)

The perspective of the other side (_____)

Background

Were there alternatives to war?

Who benefits?

Costs of the War

Estimated Military Dead _____
Estimated Military Wounded _____
Estimated Civilian Dead _____
Estimated Civilian Wounded _____
Direct War expenditures _____
Moral impact _____

2.16   The "Secret" Wars

There is another category of war involving the United States – war created or carried on in secret through the Central Intelligence Agency (CIA). Many Americans have grown up with the CIA as a part of US Government and aren't especially aware of its history or the drastic change in control of war, and accountability for war, that it brought.

Formed just after World War II, the CIA was established to replace the OSS (Office of Strategic Services) that was created during that war. Fear of communism was intense and growing. Secrecy was maintained as integral and absolutely necessary to the accomplishment of its mission. The CIA avoided most public scrutiny of its actions. In its early years no group or official other than Director of Central Intelligence and the President had the authority to manage or rein in the operations conducted.[287] Accountability for what was done, as well as the means by which these things were accomplished, was largely out of the public view.

Over the years those operations included actions that were blatantly illegal, sometimes in direct contradiction of US law, and generally of international law and the laws of other nations – assassination, the supplying of unauthorized weapons or personnel, conducting a clandestine war, or other actions to overthrow governments determined to be detrimental to US national security or American interests. A 1948 description of the mission of the CIA was defined thus:

> NSC 10/2 [National Security Council] directed CIA to conduct "covert" rather than merely "psychological" operations, defining them as all activities "which are conducted or sponsored by this Government against hostile foreign states or groups or in support of friendly foreign states or groups but which are so planned and executed that any US Government responsibility for them is not evident to unauthorized persons and that if uncovered the US Government can plausibly disclaim any responsibility for them.
>
> The type of clandestine activities enumerated under the new directive included: "propaganda; economic warfare; preventive direct action, including sabotage, demolition and evacuation measures; subversion against hostile states, including assistance to underground resistance movements, guerrillas and refugee liberations [sic] groups, and support of indigenous anti-Communist elements in threatened countries of the free world."[288]

Policies and procedures changed somewhat as the administrations of Truman, Eisenhower, Kennedy, and Johnson came and went, but the basic role of the CIA remained and grew. Outrage over the discovery of the CIA's massive spying on American citizens who opposed the Vietnam War opened up the CIA to heightened public awareness and prompted Congress to investigate. The Church Committee Hearings of 1974 brought much to light that shocked the country and resulted in reform over the next several years.

However, CIA covert actions continued. The wars in Central America and Afghanistan in the 1970s and 80s are examples of the US secret wars that Americans discovered with great effort. The people of Central America knew what most Americans didn't, that the United States had determined who should be in power there and used warfare, without the common knowledge of the American public, to accomplish its goals, deeply impacting the lives and health and the economic and political well-being of the people of Central America, an impact that continues through the present time.

Although the official policy of the US Government in regard to CIA conduct was changed by President Ford's response to public outcry and congressional investigation, including the decision that governmental assassinations would no longer be allowed, they continue under various justifications, one example being the current "War on Terror."

The assassination of six men in Yemen in November 2002 was described in the US media as an escalation of tactics in the War on Terror, as it was a CIA killing of people far from the battlefield: "Defense Secretary Donald Rumsfeld made it clear that the United States was pleased with the outcome of the attack, although he declined to discuss details."[289]

Neither did the CIA discuss details or release any official information. In trying to learn more about this event under the Freedom of Information Act, I received the response that "The CIA can neither confirm nor deny the existence or nonexistence of records responsive to your request," the routine reply given when secrecy is required or desired. Yet multiple assassinations occurred; the men had not been arrested, tried, nor found guilty in a court of law before they were murdered, apparently at the hands of the United States CIA:

> Pentagon officials declined to comment on the bombing, except to say the US military was not involved. CIA officials also refused to comment. But US officials who spoke on condition that they not be identified confirmed the strike was carried out

by a CIA-run Predator aircraft, an unmanned surveillance drone armed with Hellfire antitank missiles.[290]

The rule of law in determining guilt or innocence was ignored. To justify this act as pleasing and necessary because it is a part of the War on Terror, and to say that the prohibition against assassination need not apply during these times, is alarming. The "War on Terror" has been described as global, against an often undefined and unnamed enemy, and for an indeterminate time, thus leaving us with the possibility of eternal "exceptions."

This conduct continues with the expanded approval to assassinate American citizens as well. A February 2010 *Newsweek* article reported:

> The Director of National Intelligence, Dennis Blair, shocked Washington last week when he told a congressional committee that US spy agencies have the authority to assassinate American citizens abroad who are believed to be involved in terrorism.[291]

The shock in Washington seems to have lessened over the months, as drone strikes continue and acknowledgment of the policies that promote them reach the news. But special procedures were required, the article noted, if Americans rather than foreigners are the direct target of the assassination.

No arrest is made; no trial conducted to learn guilt or innocence. The American citizen (or citizen of another nation) is murdered on the spot by assassination at the hands of the US Government, most likely through an unmanned missile strike from a remote location. This is what America stands for?

Ron Mock, in *Loving Without Giving In: Christian Responses to Terrorism and Tyranny*, states:

> Targeted assassination would never be tolerated in any other law enforcement setting. Imagine if your governor began targeted assassinations against various suspected criminals in your neighborhood. Imagine if your state's police carried out these attacks with missiles and bombs, routinely resulting in the deaths of obviously innocent bystanders. Would you tolerate this situation? If not, then why should we expect the families and friends of terrorists, and of the innocents killed in such attacks, to accept them passively? An assassination bears all the hallmarks of terrorism.[292]

The history of the CIA's policy of assassination and the procedures by which the murders can be carried out harkens back to its early days – at least 1954. An instruction manual for use in Guatemala, declassified in 1997, described the means of conducting the murders – screwdriver, hammer, ax, kitchen knife, pushing down a stairwell or out a window (hopefully with a 75 foot drop onto a hard surface), bashing in the skull, use of a baseball bat, timing just right to push the victim in front of a train. The many proposals considered for assassinating Fidel Castro ("Operation Mongoose") also eventually became known; they included poison, explosions, and secret exposure to deadly disease.[293] Other nations' leaders were also targeted, but because of secrecy, the American public was the last to know. Even after the executive order prohibiting CIA assassinations, exceptions became the rule, and today it is said to be a procedure which "pleases" us.

That is an ugly history.

⌒

In November 2009 it was reported that:

When an Italian judge last week sentenced 23 Americans in absentia for the CIA-orchestrated abduction of Hassan Mustafa Osama Masr … [the CIA believing him to be a "terrorist facilitator" after learning he had been preaching violence against American interests from his mosque in Milan] the CIA's top officer in Milan at the time, Robert Seldon Lady, got the harshest sentence (eight years). Nobody expects Lady to serve time. He has long since left Italy.[294]

The article told of the cleric, also known as Abu Omar, being kidnapped by the CIA and taken to Egypt where, he described, he was "hung upside down and had electric prods applied to his genitals". The prosecutor who handled the case commented on the irony of things, saying that had the case against the man been handled through a criminal investigation instead of by kidnapping, he would likely be in jail today. Instead, a gross human rights violation, reportedly at the hands of the CIA, lessened the opportunity for a just resolution. His abduction in 2003 resulted in nearly four years detainment in Egypt, including fourteen months of secret detention, after which he was released without charge.[295] [296]

The violent, secretive acts of the CIA have lessened our security and safety and the opportunity for justice to be served under the rule of law, at the same time they alienate us from other nations. The logic behind exempting the CIA from the rule of law in cases of covert military actions has been explained this way:

> The use of formal military force to conduct a covert military operation amounts to an act of war in terms of international law. If such an operation were undertaken and was somehow discovered and publicized, the President would not only lack plausible deniability, but unless he was prepared to punish severely the military personnel involved (which would be extremely difficult to do if he directed or "permitted" the operation), the Nation would face *de facto* and *de jure* a condition of war that had not been authorized by Congress. By using the CIA, or some other non-military organization to undertake such missions, the President at least fuzzes the legal issue of an act of war. While it is true that CIA covert actions can themselves amount to an act of war, the President can use the CIA to engage in an act of war without U.S. fingerprints. This capability lies in the CIA's lap for a reason.[297]

Presidents "fuzzing the law"? Governments acting so as not to leave fingerprints? Are these the noble American ways we wish to promote and model for the world? Is this how we wish the world to act toward us? Further, in the debate over who should be carrying out covert military operations – the Special Operations Forces (SOF) or the CIA, or both – this concern is noted: "… covert operations can often be contrary to international laws or the laws of war and US military personnel are generally expected to follow these laws."[298] We seem nowadays to take for granted the logic that the CIA is not expected to abide by the law.

The acts of the CIA since its inception in the 1940s and the philosophy and policy that promote such acts need to be challenged. American leaders established the CIA immediately after World War II, in the grip of fear over communist takeover of the world. Its secrecy, renegade conduct, obscured funding and assignments, and our difficulty in holding it accountable should not be blindly accepted as a requirement for running the business of government, nor should it be allowed to become even more deeply entrenched, its mission progressively broadened to include "paramilitary," "warfighting" actions:

> In response to the terrorist attacks on the United States on 11 September 2001, the President – as both Commander-in-Chief and as authorized by Congress in Joint Resolution 23 – ordered our armed forces into combat in order to disrupt and defeat the global terror network. The President concomitantly signed a Presidential Finding directing the Central Intelligence Agency (CIA) to use all necessary means to destroy Osama bin Laden and Al Qaeda. As a consequence of these orders, CIA paramilitary operatives have been performing a warfighting role alongside Special Operations Forces (SOF) in the war against terrorism.[299]

The role of the CIA in America's affairs (both domestic and foreign), its wars and secret wars, and its long term negative impact on America's security should not go unquestioned by the people.

2.17   Reflecting on Our Patterns of War

Whew! Let's see if we can summarize this gallop we've taken through America's wars:

The libraries full of books on America's wars, the seemingly endless websites recounting our history from many perspectives, the media reports on current and past wars, the myriad of films made to keep the stories alive, the people who were there – all these are resources that can both enlighten and over-whelm. Most valuably though, they can lead us to wonder and question what we may have taken for granted. They can raise our awareness of what America's history of war includes. It does not stand up to many people's expectation or assumption of honorable purpose.

This history of war includes example after example of conquest for land and resources through the use of violence, in utter disregard for the people attacked or their rights. War's tendency to devalue human life and place it secondary to perceived benefits, often economic, is recurrent.

War is often launched by messages filled with high and noble words, yet carried out by low and ignoble acts, acts progressively more hideous as technology "advances."

Fear is often used to motivate people to accept war, and is sometimes based on false or incorrect information, presented to the American public by our leaders as flawless fact. Media plays a role in disseminating this information, and war propaganda further limits critical thinking. Opponents of a certain war can be accused of being unpatriotic or even treasonous by those in government who are pushing for war.

War frequently comes when those in power give up pursuing other options or when they are tired of waiting for results. The political future of an individual or political party has regularly been a consideration in the deliberations leading up to war. It seems to depend heavily on the Presidency of the United States, especially when the Executive tries to minimize the role of Congress. Public pressure restrains or nudges forward the decisions of our leaders.

War is often entered into because it is believed to be for the greater good.

In some cases alternatives are found and used and war is prevented or delayed; other times, there seems to be little patience with talk of alternatives or continuing to work for resolution without war.

The wars that have occurred, often had alternatives that, after the fact, are apparent.

The problems that led to war often remain to be solved after the war is over. War and its conclusion have paved the way to more conflict, repeating and launching a cycle of violence.

The moral impact of US wars is unknown in many ways, yet it is clear that involvement in war and the weaponry of war has transformed individual and national morals so that what was once abhorrent is often accepted simply as necessary. US wars have established an incongruity between personal-family-community morality and methods and the governmentally condoned and ordered violence of war, to which each new generation is expected to adapt. The impact of this governmental violence on family and community life has not been defined by this study.

The consequences of war are not predictable when war is begun, but they are often predicted – incorrectly. War holds both known and unknown impact on the present and future.

It has become a pattern, a habit, of America to rely on war as a resolver of problems. The US Government has used it repeatedly in order to accomplish its goals.

America's wars have cost trillions of dollars, killed millions of people, left homelands in rubble, with millions more displaced, injured, or maimed for life. The detriment to the environment has not been calculated, but is acknowledged to be severe.

~

Looking at war, and especially alternatives to war, decades or centuries after the fact sidesteps one big issue. We can rarely give adequate emphasis to the mindset of the people there at the time, or to the emotional climate of the nation. Regardless of what we know now, if they believed there were no alternatives, for them, there appeared to be no alternatives. If they believed Great Britain was so decadent, corrupt, and oppressive that we would be forced to live under cruel tyranny forever unless we went to war, that was their reality. If they believed "little brown men" needed Christianizing and taken over through war, for them, that was exactly the case.

If they believed it was weakness to ask help of other nations or persons to avoid war, then for them it was weakness. If they believed communism would rule the world if they did not intervene militarily, for them, at that time, it seemed true. If they believed they were assassinating evil people or overthrowing socialist governments for the good of others, for them, that was exactly what they were doing. Looking back, however, we see that their "reality" was subjective and often distorted.

We must admit that their choices were limited because of what the people believed to be necessary and possible and how that belief restricted their ability or their desire to act. That does not mean, however, that there were no choices. Nor does it mean that we need to hold their actions up as a pattern to follow, or honor and praise choices that we see now as flawed, just because they thought they were valid then, or because we want heroes to look up to, or long for a spotless and honorable heritage. By doing that we rob ourselves of the opportunity to look carefully at the past and learn from it. If we understand that false information or ignorance led people off the mark in the past, we can humbly and diligently examine ourselves to see where we might be stuck in the same misjudgments or ignorance.

We can grant that people may have held amazingly short-sighted and distorted views of reality even though they were sincere. Sincerity does not equal wisdom. We do not need to remain locked in a history that whitewashes our past. We can acknowledge that our gallop through America's wars has shown us unfortunate and sad sights. From this we can learn to evaluate more closely our present circumstances.

I reviewed American wars; that was the purposeful emphasis of this chapter. It does not mean that others cannot apply the same type of questioning to their nations' pasts. In an "Address on War" made by Alexander Campbell of Virginia in 1848, we find an interesting summary of an investigation into many other wars:

> Some years ago … an elaborate investigation [was undertaken] of the real causes for which the wars of Christendom had been undertaken from the time of Constantine the Great down to the present century. From the results furnished by the Peace Society of Massachusetts it appeared that, after subtracting a number of petty wars … the wars of real magnitude amounted in all to 286.
>
> The origin of these wars, on a severe analysis, appeared to have been as follows: 22 for plunder and tribute; 44 for the extension of territory; 24 for revenge or retaliation; 6 for disputed boundaries; 8 respecting points of honor or prerogative; 6 for protection or extension of commerce; 55 civil wars; 41 about contested titles to crowns; 30 under pretense of assisting allies; 23 for mere jealousy of rival greatness; 28 religious wars, including the Crusades. Not one for defense alone, and certainly not one that an enlightened Christian man could have given one cent for, in a voluntary way, much less have volunteered his services or enlisted into its ranks. …
>
> No one can, indeed, no one will, contend that the decision or termination of these wars naturally, necessarily, or even probably, decided the controversy so justly, so rationally, so satisfactorily as it could have been settled in any one case of the 286 by a third or neutral party.
>
> War is not now, nor was it ever, a process of justice. It never was a test of truth – a criterion of right. It is either a mere game of chance or a violent outrage of the strong upon the weak.[300]

Another article from that general time period (November 18, 1822, *London Observer*) tells about a million bushels of mixed human and horse bones being imported to England from Europe, from "all of the places where, during the late bloody war, the principal battles were fought." They were then shipped to bone grinders who "sold them to farmers to manure their lands."[301]

America is not the only one to have fallen into a pattern of war that raises many questions about its validity.

Surely we can question manure.

Chapter 3
Opening Our Eyes and Our Hearts

One problem in learning about war is that if we're not there, we don't know firsthand what it's like. Even if we are there, we only see a slice of what is happening and why. And what we do see, we may find hard to talk about, at least the nightmarish parts. And so those at home think it's polite not to ask much, or ask at all.

Unlike those in the world who have lived where war is, most Americans haven't seen war first hand. The wars that were fought in America are so far in the past that they no longer create a living picture. Not many Americans pause in our cities and towns and imagine everything around us being reduced to rubble – our bridges and roads blown apart, our buildings simply gone. We don't look at our houses and imagine what it would be to have our own children trapped underneath a pile of debris that had been our home. We don't imagine our food supply, water, power, heat, and transportation all being cut off.

Unless we are among those employed in the military who have left America and traveled to war, we experience it only at a glance – a glance at a TV screen or at words in a newspaper or magazine. And as we glance, we remain surrounded by the comfort of all the little things that make life run beautifully. It is easy to relegate war to some other virtual world that can't upset our schedules or our lives.

We may hear or see stories that touch us, but stories can be set aside and kept for another time, when dinner is over and we've taken the dog for a walk, or after we've picked up the kids from basketball practice. Once read and cried over, they can be mellowed with hot tea and a funny movie. They can be danced around and flown over, and left behind when we go to work … because life goes on, we say.

But for some, it doesn't. Those who have lived through war in their own country, know that truth deeply.

If we're participants or payers or ignorers of war carried out by our government, don't we have a responsibility every once in a while to revisit the stories that make us cry? Cry out? Act? To put ourselves in the shoes of those who were there?

Some of those stories tell more about the warrior than the war. They speak of loyalty and compassion. They tell of friendship, forged by common commitment and struggle, that lasts a life-time. Soldiers return to gatherings of their fellow soldiers decades later, because of the intensity of what they've shared and what they've done for each other. They want to step back into the camaraderie that comes from having lived something together and never forgotten what it was like.

The stories also tell of relationships dropped and contact never attempted because "I had to put all of that behind me." A Vietnam vet talked of having no desire ever to return to Vietnam. A World War II soldier told of not being able to go to the Oregon coast because it hurt too much to see a beach and remember, all those years later. Yet others tell of going back to Vietnam with hope that the journey might erase some of the hate, their own hate of the place where it all happened, and perhaps a stranger's hate, they wonder, for what was done to them there. Others tell of humor and irony and learning and surviving against all odds. They speak of courage and sacrifice unimaginable.

Yet all this happens within the reality of war, and that is another story. That other story may be censored or edited and filtered to let us know what others want us to know, but there are passionate women and men who refuse to be compromised, and they tell it, as best they can, as they saw it. Their stories create a gut feeling, a realization that there is more than the soldier's noble story or the soldier's journey of healing and rebuilding. There is also the story of what it means to carry out war. How war does its work. What it is like to be destroyed by war.

We have little incentive to question or challenge the status quo if we do not open ourselves to hearing and seeing the truth of war, even though it may be hard to do. War is not graphic artistry splashed across the redwhiteandblue big screen TV, with rousing slogans, seconds-long explanations, and musical scores in between ads. We must open ourselves to serious inquiry and seek out those committed to help us understand. It is a fair thing to do. We need to know what we are paying for. We need to know what we are allowing to be done in our names. We need to know the results of our government's actions on others. What are we supporting, really, even if by our silence?

There are some speaking boldly, if we will just listen. Phil Newman, an Oregon physician, joined Linfield College's December 2012 "Legacies of War" panel discussion, part of a year-long, college-wide study of war. He was with others involved in or impacted by the Vietnam War – or resistance to that war – who told of their experiences. Phil was an Army doctor in Vietnam. "We first tended to the amputations," he said, "and then did what we could with what else needed done." He recalled that they were in the unusual situation of having a pediatric ward attached to their unit, but noted that before the war was over, it was closed down to make way for a heroin addiction treatment ward for US soldiers. People weren't happy to see soldiers coming home from war addicted to heroin, he said, but it was the reality for many. Phil said in later reflections:

> The experience for all of us at the 18th was that since we had the only pediatric hospital run by the military in Vietnam and since we also chose to operate on civilians when time allowed, we had, I think, a heightened appreciation of the impact of the war on the civilian population. We had civilian patients on our wards and in the ICU. We had the families of our children camped out on the grounds. We had access to good interpreters so we could interact. My experience gave me a glimpse into the lives of that population and an opportunity to experience them as human beings we could relate to – human beings caught up in this mayhem through chance and with little resources to control their fate.
>
> It seems to me that what we miss in general in this country is representation from the civilian collaterals. They are the ones that can provide consistent focused testimony of the insanity of this kind of endeavor. I think my experience was so searing (and in hindsight so valuable to me) because I had so much access to and involvement in the civilian experience, but still, I was far removed from their actual pain. I did what I could, but in between I could retreat to the officers' hooch for a drink or the mess hall for a meal, and in the end, I always knew my family was safe.
>
> My wife was pregnant when I left for Vietnam. My first case there was a 20-something Vietnamese woman in her last trimester of her first pregnancy who got up in the middle of the night to void. She went out into a field and stepped on a French landmine that had been laying there in wait since the 50s (this was 1970). She came in with both legs gone and multiple abdominal injuries. I operated on her for five hours, but she died on the table along with the fetus. I will never forget her or that family. I would have liked them to

have been there on the panel. I would have told that story, but I didn't think I could share it; maybe next time.

I used to think if everyone got to spend a week in a surgical hospital during an offensive, we would never have to worry about countries going to war.[302]

Phil's wrenching memories echoed those of a nurse who spoke about her Vietnam experience after a college drama some years earlier: "I knew that absolutely nothing was worth this – the mangled bodies we were supposed to fix up. I don't care what the problems were. Nothing was worth this."

An Iraq war veteran told me something of what he had experienced:

"There were times when there were so many dead bodies that we had to bring a bulldozer in and dig a big trench and put the bodies in it."

"US soldiers' bodies?" I asked. It was an extremely stupid question. If I had thought even a moment I would have realized that we most assuredly would not bury US soldiers in a trench in Iraq, but I was surprised and confused by what he had just said – a bulldozer, a trench for bodies?

"Oh, no!" he answered. "That was one thing they told us for sure. 'You don't have to worry about going home. You are going home. We're not leaving you here.' They didn't tell us then that we might be going home all in pieces, but we learned later that they were serious, they were committed to even finding the pieces of the US soldiers' bodies, if that's what happened, and seeing that we got home.

"The bodies I was talking about were Iraqis. We'd give some time for people to get the bodies, but sometimes there was nobody to get them, and if we left them, disease would spread and we'd get disease from the dead bodies, so we had to bury them.

"You know how it is when you have fried chicken," he added, "when the meat just slips off the bones? Well sometimes it was like that. There'd be families there, dead kids, and the whole family dead, and you'd start to pick somebody up to carry them over to bury them in the trench, and the skin and stuff would just slip off the bones in your hands. That was hard. Especially it was like that when they were bombed, because they were cooked."[303]

We must also listen to those who have the courage to write it down for us because they saw it and heard it and understand that their words tell a story we need to know, for many reasons. Those words of truth begin to pry open our eyes, our hearts:

The Observer – "Iraq: the human toll"
Ed Vulliamy – 06 July 2003

It was Rahad's turn to hide. The nine-year-old girl found a good place to conceal herself from her playmates, the game of hide and seek having lasted some two hours along a quiet residential street in the town of Fallujah, on the banks of the Euphrates. But while Rahad crouched behind the wall of a neighbour's house, someone else – not playing the game – had spotted her, and her friends; someone above. The pilot of an American A-10 "tank-buster" aircraft, hovering in a figure of eight. He was flying an airborne weapon equipped with some of the most advanced and accurate equipment for "precision target recognition" in the Pentagon's arsenal. And at 5:30 pm on 29 March, he launched his weapon at the street scene below.

The "daisy-cutter" bounced and exploded a few feet above ground, blasting red-hot shrapnel into the walls not of a tank but of houses. Rahad Septi and 10 other children lost their lives; another 12 were injured. Three adults were also killed.

Juma Septi, father to Rahad, holds a photograph of his daughter in the palm of his hand as he recalls the afternoon he lost his "little flower." A carpenter, Septi had been a lifelong opponent of Saddam Hussein – an activist in the Islamic Accord Party, for which he had been imprisoned, then exiled to Jordan in 1995. Last October, Septi had returned under an armistice to start a new life in his home town, reunited with his family. "I don't really know what to think now," he says. "We have lost Saddam Hussein, but I have lost my daughter. They came to kill him, but killed her and the other children instead. What am I supposed to make of that?"

Jamal Abbas joins the conversation. "I was driving my taxi and heard the noise like thunder, when someone told me, 'Jamal, they've bombed your street!' When I got back here, the smoke was so thick it was like night – children lying wounded and women screaming." Abbas learnt that his niece – 11-year-old Arij Haki, visiting from Baghdad – had been killed immediately. "She was playing a guessing game with her cousins," says the child's father Abdullah Mohammed, "when the top half of her head was blown off."

"But there was no sign of my daughter," says Jamal Abbas, "so I went outside to search in that madness; it was half an hour before I found her, right there, on the ground." Miad Jamal Abbas, aged 11, her body bloody and ripped, was taken to the same hospital ward as Rahad Septi. The two fathers accordingly sat in vigil together. "They died together, just as they had played together, in the same room," says Abbas. "We were close before, now we are bound together."

"It's not easy now to think about what they were like when they were alive," says Septi, making to retreat into the shadows of his home. "I have to think that this was my fate and the will of God. Otherwise, I would go mad. Rahad had a tongue in her head, for sure. She talked too much. She was very little, really, but understood things quickly."

At the cemetery on the edge of the town, where Fallujah dissipates into desert, eleven small mounds of earth have been dug, awaiting proper headstones. The children have been buried together rather than in family plots. Saad Ibrahim whose father, Hussein, was killed in the corner shop he kept, has a few caustic questions for the tank-buster's pilot: "I want to ask him: what exactly did you see that day that you had to kill my father and those kids? Do you have good eyesight? Is your computer working well? If not... well, that's your business. But there was no military activity in this area. There was no shooting. This is not a military camp. These are houses with children playing in the street.

... Ward 114

[In] ward 114 ... separated by a curtain, lie Daham Kassim, aged 46, and his 37-year-old wife Gufran Ibed Kassim. Daham has his arms bound, and a stump where his right leg used to be. Gufran cannot move her arms, wounded by gunshots, and probably never will. But the pain is not in their bodies, it is in their faces.

It is impossible to "interview" Kassim. He dismisses questions, driving his narrative, like a man possessed, towards its conclusion. He speaks in English, an educated man and, until a few months ago, director of the Southeastern electricity board. His torment began on the evening of 24 March, when – after heavy US bombing in his Mutanaza neighbourhood – Kassim told his family to prepare to depart in the morning. They would leave Nasiriyah for the safety of his parents' farm 70 miles away. "We packed anything valuable, and the children were allowed to take a few toys each."

Departure was delayed by a sandstorm, and the family – the four children in the back – set off shortly after noon in Kassim's new car. A few minutes later they reached the American checkpoint at the northern gate to the city. (Significantly, the suicide bomb which killed four US soldiers at a road block and was credited with inflaming American behaviour at check points, occurred a full four days later on 29 March at Najaf. This was the incident described by the Washington Post as, "The first such attack of the war.") "I could see two tanks," recalls Kassim. "They were sand-coloured, with markings on them. I was afraid and stopped my car 60m away. Less than a minute passed. They did not open anything, I saw no one. It was silent." [The American tanks kept their hatches down. The Marines inside would have been looking through their green-tinted rectangular window, at a civilian car carrying a couple and four children.] "I was frozen with fear," continues Kassim. "I could see their guns moving down. Then there was a terrible noise, and my car was buried in shooting."

Kassim's voice begins to crack. "I saw my eldest daughter, Mawra, die. She was nine; I saw it with my eyes: she took the first shot, opened her eyes, and closed them again." Gufran, his second daughter, was also killed immediately. "But my son Mohammed, he was six and in the first year of primary school, he was still breathing. And my Zainab, she is five, was also still alive, although she had been shot in the head."

Two Americans approached the car. "They were called Chris and Joe. They took out my two dead children, then tried to give my son oxygen, but it was no use. He died there, at that moment. I asked for a helicopter to take us to hospital. They refused, but Joe gave us some morphine in exchange for my gold watch. They tied my bad leg to the other, then took us to their base."

There, the Americans had established a field hospital, where they bandaged up the surviving child, father and mother. For two nights, the remains of the family slept in a bed. It appears that the story is reaching an end. "Wait!" insists Kassim, his tears preparing themselves for what is to come, as if his trials could get any worse. "Don't ask me questions. I will tell you what happened."

On the third night, that of 27 March, "there were some Americans wounded that night, in the fighting. Maybe they needed the beds. So they told us we had to go outside. I heard the order – 'put them out' – and they carried us like dogs, out into the cold, without shelter, or a blanket. It was the days of the sandstorms and freezing at night. And I heard Zainab crying: 'Papa, Papa, I am cold, I am cold.' Then she went silent. Completely silent."

Kassim breaks off in anguish. His wife continues the story of the night. "What could we do? She kept saying she was cold. My arms were broken, I could not lift or hold her. If they had given us even a blanket, we might have put it over her. We had to sit there, and listen to her die."

"We'd had trouble having children," Kassim re-enters the conversation. "We'd been trying for six years without success and given up hope. But then God blessed us, and everything went right. Four little flowers - and now four little flowers cut down. What for? For oil and a strategic place for America? Do they know God, these people? Why did they put my Zainab out into the cold? I tell you Mister, she died of cold, she died of cold."

There is urgent business, however. Kassim has still not concluded – indeed he is reaching his purpose. The three Kassim children put to death at the checkpoint had been buried at the site of their shooting, but later taken to the holy city of Najaf for entombment, as is the mandatory custom for Shia Islam. Zainab, however, had been interred inside the US base, "and the question now," pleads Kassim, revived by the urgency of the matter, "is that we must get her to Najaf, where there is a space for her there with her brother and sisters. Please, Mister, I cannot move; you must go and ask how we can take my Zainab to Najaf."[304]

Are we willing to know and feel what happens in war? To real people? On both sides of the battle, or on no side. The "Cost of War" can be shown in a special box, the lives lost written out in numbers, marks on a piece of paper with commas thrown in here and there. But war happens one precious life at a time. Can we hear that truth and put ourselves in the shoes of someone who has lost so much? Can we imagine what that loss is like?

If it no longer hurts deeply, if we no longer have empathy, we have lost our understanding of war.

Chapter 4
Sales Pitches and Rah-Rah Cheers for War

How is it that we buy into war, knowing, even vaguely, war's cruelty and destructive means to an end?

First we have to fear something or someone. Then we must come to believe that war is the best option for dealing with the situation that makes us afraid. Those who are especially reluctant to choose war might even need to be convinced that there is no other way to deal with the problem. And we have to believe that the leaders describing our reasons to fear and making the decisions about our options are truthful and are choosing wisely. Often we need to believe that they know more than we do and that because of their special knowledge, they are able to see clearly what must be done.

The difficulty here is that the situations that cause fear to arise in some leaders and start them on the path to war, would not affect other leaders in the same way. Some are able to look at a difficult situation and see a serious problem, one that needs to be confronted – diplomatically, economically, educationally, politically, multi-nationally, or under the rule of law – and they see other routes being more effective than war. Leaders with little experience or training in options available, can fall into a "default mode" of relying on war to settle a dispute. Those who believe they have the resources to conduct a war are obviously more apt to choose war than those who believe war to be either beyond their resources or too costly in light of other needs or human consequences.

There are questions that can be asked of and about our leaders:

- Why are some leaders drawn to war, as an option, more easily than others?
- How have they been taught or trained to look at war? What has been their personal experience with war?
- What has been their training and experience in interpersonal, inter-group, and international conflict resolution, conflict transformation, and nonviolent action?

We must wonder if our current leaders know well the details of the multitude of nonviolent resolutions of conflict around the world. Do they know thoroughly the work of Martin Luther King Jr. and those whose practices and writings were a foundation of his work in the American Civil Rights movement? Do they know well the principles of nonviolence and the means of accomplishing change and upholding the "peaceful prevention of deadly conflict"?[305]

Psychologist Abraham Maslow has said, "When the only tool you have is a hammer, every problem begins to resemble a nail."[306] How many non-hammer tools do our leaders have in their tool boxes?

We must also ask who it is that advises our leaders and what are the backgrounds, practical experiences, and economic ties of these advisors.

Those questions all deal with the wisdom of placing trust in the decision of a leader who calls for war, and the criteria for choosing leaders. But even before that time comes, we must ask why so many of us buy into war in general. Why do we ignore the absurdity of the destruction and loss, the agony and long-term pain, both in precious human lives and in things we or others have worked years or decades to create, and in the natural world around us? How do we ignore the moral impact on the lives of those who are taught to numb their consciences and sense of moral decency and are then ordered to kill other human beings? How do we push aside the wrenching mental and emotional pain of those who have experienced or watched the destruction?

We don't spent much time pondering why the act of killing another person brings a medal of honor one time and a death sentence another. We seem to ignore the extreme contradiction of violence as normal and necessary in resolution of international disputes while deploring it as criminal and inhumane at a personal level. Furthermore, few of us would really believe that the wisest solution to a conflict or a problem is automatically found in the hands of those capable of destroying the other by war. Nor would we believe that death and destruction; havoc and pain; disruption of food, water, health, roadways, power, markets, and community life; and the provoking of anger, hopelessness, and resentment through war lay the best foundation for the subsequent solving of problems? Yet still, we carry on.

There are clear reasons we push away our doubts and rally for war. They are found in the traditional sales pitches, cheers, and methods of war:

1. We take away the humanity of the "other side."

They become the "enemy," "a dirty yellow Jap," "a kraut," "a gook," "a terrorist." They are no longer a man or woman, a boy or girl, with a name, a story, a past, and a life. They are no longer a nation comprised of people who live and celebrate and struggle. Pictures of their faces at work and play – pouring cement, fighting a fire, building a house, weeding a garden, riding a bike, playing a guitar, tossing a ball, rocking a baby, eating ice cream, giggling over a joke – these don't get passed around when we want to reinforce their nameless enemy status. It's better that we don't see them as people, even flawed people, even people doing wrong. For if they remain vague enough, or stereotyped enough, then they are only the evil we must rid ourselves of.

2. We name ourselves "the good guys."

So what we do must be okay. We are part of a nation which is committed to good in the world. We are good people. Well, the truth is, we are only people. Those who grew up with *Mr. Rogers' Neighborhood* heard him sing:

> "The very same people who are good sometimes, are the very same people who are bad sometimes. It's funny, but it's true. It's the same, isn't it, for me and you."[307]

Common sense tells us that. We know ourselves. We try. We want good. We do good. Sometimes we mess up. We make mistakes. We pick up and go on. Some of us are a little far-fetched on some things; some of us have pretty awful stories. Some of us inspire. Some of us are wise. But not necessarily wise all the time. We're a mix, like other people around the world.

Okay, granted, America says, but isn't our country "the good guy" with our form of government – our freedom, our democracy, our liberty, our justice? Surely we deserve a little credit compared to the injustices people of some other nations have had to go through.

Yes. A lot is right and good about America, and things run pretty well a lot of the time. America gives rise to wonderful people. It's home, and I feel its goodness deep down. It's where the policeman has a stuffed dog in the trunk of his patrol car to give my little boy when he is worried as the ambulance carries his mother away to the hospital after the crash. It's where the kids dance their hearts out in a high school assembly competition, and the principal grabs the big broom to help sweep the floor between acts. And when the jazz choir travels to the coast to perform at a retirement center, the principal drives their bus and cooks the hash browns for their breakfast. It's where the Search And Rescue team meets without pay out at the fairgrounds to be trained and ready when somebody's lost up in the hills.

America is where I can stand on the corner in a vigil, protesting two wars I believe to be wrong, and somebody can give me a thumbs up and somebody else, an obscene gesture. It's where people still have Christmas dinner when their power has been off for four days because of the big snow storm; others invite them in. It's where the volunteer firefighters assure me that it was okay to call when I didn't know where all the smoke was coming from, even though it interrupted their weekly training, and ended up being only a burnt dryer belt.

America is where folks who live along the road get together in the park down by the river once every summer to make sure they know their neighbors, and the kids help each other through the scavenger hunt. It's where the town councils contribute to the community mediation center serving their county because they know it's a good and reasonable thing to do. America is where my kids can go to the same school I went to as a kid, and my mom and dad before me, because sometimes you get to keep your community. It's a community where the kids have teachers they still stop in to see when they come home for a visit.

There are libraries filled with books to check out, parks with trees and a dragonland play structure built during a community work party of all ages, banks with blanket and coat drives every December, and doctors available even on Sunday to put in stitches. There are judges who order a young woman into drug treatment so she'll be better able to mother her children, and sentence a young man to finish high school so he'll find more doors opening. There's a Juvenile Department that grants approval for a first time offender to make amends directly to the victim of her crime and allows four other teens to make restitution by repairing the roof of an abandoned house in their county.

America is a family talent show on the Fourth of July and a hotdog roast at the beach, with three-legged races in the sand, which we have done for decades, even though one sister and brother always team up and claim to be champions – regardless of who crosses the line first. It's National Parks and camping, and coming home to wild blackberries ripe for pies. It's People's Market and Putt's Market, and Erickson's Auto Parts where

Sally runs the parts department and Tim runs the repair shop. Yes, America is surely wonderful! Different for all of us, but full of goodness. Yet America is a mix, like us. America has regrets. We can and have acted selfishly, in fear and ignorance, and committed some deplorable acts that we look back on with deep shame. We are broken in some ways. Our history is enough to cause us to walk humbly, with openness to learn and hold each other accountable. We are not always **The Good Guys**. So it is with all nations, I suspect.

3. We've carefully chosen the words we use to sell war and violent resolution of disputes.

We have marketed it with skill. We refer to military employment as "the service," and joining the military as "going into the service." We talk about our "service men and women" without drawing any distinction between them as persons and the way in which they are asked to carry out this "service" – through destruction and murder. Murder? No. We define it as lawful killing, so we don't use that word, though the deaths have been planned and trained for. More often than not, we don't even refer to the killing. Yet people end up dead all the same. And those who cause that to happen have killed them.

There are other terms we use to market war, or to make it more acceptable, of course, but most of us recognize them as "cleaning it up, whitewashing, selling" or even as manipulative: evil enemy, collateral damage, neutralize, Operation Desert Storm, Shock and Awe, Making the World Safe from Terrorism, Advancing Peace in a Troubled World, Rolling Thunder. We may not realize how we are dulled by their use.

Can we refuse to use those words ourselves, and instead rename them what they are: persons with opposing agenda, persons using violence as a means to an end, a nation we fear, homes and schools obliterated, a massive bombing? Even the term "civilian casualties" is lulling to the brain and heart. Instead of telling the story of a nineteen year old girl whose decapitated body is carried from her home by her weeping mother after a target-missing bomb hit, we label her a "civilian casualty." We don't even know her name.

Wars and battles are given fancy names, and they're repeated over and over so that we begin to wonder if they are fancy. Professional political, advertising, and marketing specialists decide what to call the next one to make it easier to swallow. When we see it done by our adversaries, we call it propaganda. When we do it ourselves, we call it terminology, a slogan, or simply a title.

4. We put on pomp and fanfare for the military that fails to acknowledge the full picture, and that perpetuates violence instead of exploring alternatives to it.

We have town parades and programs, wave flags, and play music. The soldiers march through in uniform or ride on floats, dressed in camouflage. We give speeches full of carefully chosen words about one side of the story. That kind of celebration confuses our appreciation of the person the soldier is with an honoring of the means he or she uses to accomplish the goals, including the horrors of war. These celebrations decrease the likelihood that war will be questioned. Toddlers grow up having watched them every year. Young people, and old, may fail to notice the difference between the war and the warrior and assume it is one and the same, and think we are carrying on to honor both.

War is one of humanity's great failings. If war is honored, it will more easily happen again, requiring more soldiers to be sacrificed and to use the tools of war on others, even when there are alternatives. That gives them neither honor nor respect.

Aiden Delgado, Specialist, US Army, in the film *The Ground Truth*, speaks about honoring veterans:

> If Americans actually listened to the veterans that they claim to respect so much, their attitude would change. But the thing is, Americans want to honor the veterans in ... a very cursory way – you know, putting a yellow sticker on their car, having a little parade or welcome back. But they don't want to honor the veterans by really ... listening to what they have to say.[308]

In order to honor the soldier as a person we must listen to him or her. They don't need to be in uniform. They don't have to march along under a flag. If they've been away, they can be welcomed home with family and neighbors gathering for a potluck and reaching out hands and hugs, telling stories of what happened in times apart, catching up, showing our joy for their safe return. And then we can find the place and time to really listen, as we could do for someone who's been away in the diplomatic corps, or the development workers, the Peace Corps workers, and the many varieties of volunteers, pilgrims, travelers.

It has been said, "If you value your freedom, thank a vet." Standing in a vigil, I have been yelled at, "If it weren't for vets, you couldn't stand there today!" That belief defines our right to free speech and assembly as resulting from military employment. It disregards the heritage of law and of government and those who carry it out, and those who take part to assure its continued functioning. It disregards the impact on our lives and our country made by families, communities, and schools. To narrowly define this freedom as resulting from military action is limited vision, and incorrect thinking. Do our traditions make it appear that those in military employment are doing something more worthy of our praise than our teachers, farmers, builders, health workers, businesses, and faith communities?

A bold, but illuminating question is: How often do we as communities honor the executioners in our prisons? They do a work which I don't condone, but which some who believe in the necessity of war, would also believe is a necessary work. Yet somehow they, and their work, are kept rather anonymous, rather low-key. We don't have parades of gallows, electric chairs, or gas paraphernalia from the past, or executioners marching with lethal injection kits in their hands to the sound of bands playing John Phillip Sousa, or even songs of life-ending quietness. Why is that? And conversely, why are we so insistent that we honor the equipment and the executioners in our international dealings as we do?

I suspect that most who enlist do so because they believe it is an important, needed, and worthy work, available to them, and perhaps one that holds adventure as well as an opportunity for learning and serving. We often think of personal sacrifice and risk of life, which is very real, but there is more that is hard to talk about. The "enemy" soldiers killed by our military are often others like our own, ordered into the role of killer by their governments, or those who want to help their country and believe joining the military is a way to do so. They may be looking for employment when it's hard to find, or wanting to do something that earns them the respect of their families and friends. Still, most of those our soldiers kill are civilians – children who have done nothing wrong, or perhaps folks from a village or in a hospital or shelter who got bombed by accident, or a father carrying his potatoes to market. The person killed may be another soldier of the same company, or an ally, killed by "friendly fire." It is believed that the percentage of war casualties who are civilians is currently ranging from 85 to 90%. Nine of every ten – civilians.[309] [310]

Is it wise to create pomp and fanfare for a system with a bottom line that kills and destroys, and nine of every ten of those killed or injured are civilians and the other one is often quite like our son or friend or daughter – the soldier?

Of course, there are jobs in the military that involve support or planning and training rather than directly carrying out the bottom line. I've seen the recruiting materials. They don't draw much attention to that bottom line, the fact that our military system and war is based on violence, death, and destruction to others, or the threat of it, in order to accomplish its goal. The fanfare ignores that ugly fact.

And the pomp and fanfare start early, with our children. Why do we have third-graders writing letters to vets, thanking them for fighting for our freedom? How much background do we give these very young school children about the multiplicity of reasons for war, the realities of war and what these veterans have experienced and been asked to do, and the effects of war on freedom and liberty (and for whom), before we tell them what to write? And if we don't want them to have this background at eight or nine years of age, what are we teaching them by this exercise?

When school staff encourage our high school youth to dress up in shirt and tie and fancy dress in order to honor and acknowledge the fact that the veterans they are hosting at school that day "have gone into hell to protect our freedom," we must be diligent to separate the intentions and hopes of our guests from the process of war they were a part of. We can ask if the content and style of school program to be held is an honest, valid, and effective way of helping youth learn from the past. Are the stories told and listened to overshadowed by fanfare that glorifies war itself? We can gently, but seriously, invite them to tell of the full impact of war on their lives, the destruction and death they were instrumental in causing others, stories of those whom they fought with, who are now dead, and what they have learned about the long term impact of the war on the lives of the people against whom they fought. And if the vets find it too hard to tell that story, should others fill in? Could there be "enemies" of prior wars who would also be able to come and speak about the war from their experiences?

We must acknowledge that we sell war by pomp and fanfare, and we must question why. What programs do we put on, or watch, or take our children to watch, and what confusion do we spread about honoring the violence of war. By changing our way of celebrating, we can lessen the likelihood that a false appearance of honoring war will lead to its increased and unneeded use, thereby resulting in more soldiers and civilians being sacrificed to the god of war.

We can learn other ways of celebrating. We can return to the early traditions of Armistice Day (which became Veterans Day) observances: "exercises designed to perpetuate peace through good will and mutual understanding between nations" and by "inviting the people of the United States to observe the day in schools and churches, or other suitable places, with appropriate ceremonies of friendly relations with all other peoples."[311] Just imagine what could be done if people weren't afraid that "peace through good will" activities would be considered anti-military and therefore un-American.

We can keep our parades and our programs if we wish, and center them on all the things that have made us a strong and wholesome people, things about our country that we want to honor, and the people who make those things happen – without violence. Our soldiers could slip into their jeans and t-shirts and help others create a float, a parade entry, or street theater that would portray peaceful resolution of conflict and their personal commitment to it. We could stop portraying the execution theme and instead wave flags to our hearts' content as we celebrate our creativity and goodness.

We could encourage more panel discussions like the one held at Linfield College that allow for different perspectives and give the soldiers, their family members, the war protesters, and those who refused to be drafted the opportunity to tell their experiences. We can hear from the vets who were drafted, did not want to go, but felt they had no choice.

Remembering back, I wonder how our community chorus and the local big band, putting on an Old Time Radio Show of 1944, might honor the commitment and sacrifice of a variety of people who found a variety of ways of making our nation strong and our community wholesome. How about highlighting our grandmas? Or our farmers? Our grandpas? Our teachers? Who would stand up, and what songs would bring tears to my eyes?

*5. We also learn to accept war because we live with ethnocentricism
rather than empathy and understanding of others.*

We see our way as the normal, our nation as the model, our history as
valiant, our Founding Fathers as all-wise and wonderful. We talk "regular"
and everybody else has an accent. We live "standard" and everybody else is
a little unusual. Or a lot. We know The Truth and everybody else needs to
learn it. Our faith is the very definition of how everyone else must believe.

It's hard not to think of ourselves and all that is familiar to us as being the
default setting of life. That's how life is, but that contributes to our reluctance
to question the status quo, our way of doing things, our impact on others,
and our "deserved" comforts of life.

If we could learn to put ourselves in the other person's boots or bare feet,
by asking, "How are they seeing this? Why might they act in this way?" we
could begin to move out of the narrow vision of good guys/bad guys. Such
an exercise was made available to Americans early in the recent Iraq War as
a part of the American Friends Service Committee traveling exhibit called
"Eyes Wide Open." The exhibit displayed hundreds of black boots – one pair
for each American soldier killed in Iraq up to that time – and shoes of all
sizes to represent Iraqi civilians killed. It was staggering and heartbreaking.
Nothing more would have been needed, but there was more. A large poster
described what the United States had done in Iraq in "vice versa" terms to
help us ponder how we might have felt if what we did to Iraq had been done
to us by them. Unfortunately, we don't often step out of our own shoes to see
something through another's eyes, unless someone or something brings it
to our attention.[312]

From time to time I drive toward home through Portland, along the
Willamette River, and I glance in awe at the skyline of that beautiful city at
nighttime. The deer on the brightly lit sign that was once *White Stag* and then
Made in Oregon has a red bulb added to its nose every holiday season. The
cables for the lift up to Oregon Health Sciences University cross overhead. I
smile, remembering our ride down from the hospital when we did Portland's
4-T hike – trail, tram, trolley, train. The buildings to my right, across the river,
are a mix of old and new landmarks, many absolutely elegant.

I can't see them from the highway, but I know there are old drinking foun-
tains downtown, bubbling up water, and a sculpted family of bears playing
on the sidewalk. Pioneer Square is there, where people gather for all kinds

of things, including the annual sandcastle carving team competitions. And as I drive, I sometimes wonder if anyone beside me feels the loss it would be, the wrenching of our lives, the senseless waste, if someone treated beautiful Portland like we treated Baghdad when we bombed in March 2003. Even if we had evacuated the city, how could we bear to have to begin again to create all that would be destroyed? But we tend not to wonder in those terms.

Writer and activist Norman Solomon explains it this way:

> When they put bombs in cars and kill people, they're uncivilized killers. When we put bombs on missiles and kill people, we're upholding civilized values. When they kill, they're terrorists. When we kill, we're striking against terror. ... When the mass media in some foreign countries serve as megaphones for the rhetoric of their government, the result is ludicrous propaganda. When the mass media in our country serve as megaphones for the rhetoric of the U.S. government, the result is responsible journalism.[313]

Noam Chomsky, in a speech describing how a journalist from Mars might see our actions in going to war in Afghanistan (showing the similarities between that and our actions in the 1980s in Nicaragua and the on-going US cooperation with Israeli violence) says we ran into too many problems when we tried to use the official definition of terrorism, so we adapted:

> The solution is to define terrorism as the terrorism that *they* carry out against us.... It's only terrorism if they do it to us. When we do much worse to them, it's not terrorism.[314]

Refusing to blind ourselves to our actions or justify our actions through manipulation of words is a beginning point. Then, with awareness of our ethnocentricism, let us accept humbly our place among nations. Perhaps we don't need State of the Union speeches that continue to tell us we are #1 and the best in the entire world, but rather we need to be encouraged to be our best in the family of nations that form our world. That attitude would give us a base from which to work for cooperation and understanding, for learning what the common good even means, and the advantages we gain by becoming a part of an international team of nations. And it might make it harder to buy into war.

6. Making war makes money.

There's profit to be had in war. Who gets it? The weaponry companies gain, and those who are employed by them; the suppliers and transporters of materials; the corporations who get the contracts for supplying other war needs and repairing war destruction, and those who are employed by them; the people in the military who are paid for planning, organizing, and carrying out the wars, though the latter especially often face horrid risks for their benefits – physically, mentally, emotionally, morally.

A shocking – if we weren't numbed to it – aspect of "who gains from war" is the current increasingly broad privatization of war – hiring out war jobs to contractors working at the war site. Making war has been one thing that most Americans have traditionally left to the government, although the supplying of armaments and other materials has, since the beginning, been profitable for individuals and their companies. But today, we are changing even our base assumption – that governments conduct war – by saying the government and its military forces can conduct part of the war and broadly supervise things, but private corporations can take over parts of war-making previously done by the military itself, for a profit, of course.

To wage war for profit is sickness.

I will repeat: To wage war for profit is sickness.

America has become entrenched in that sickness. The more people who benefit directly, economically, by war, the more difficult it becomes to question that which provides their sustenance (and profit).

The impact of profit-making on the likelihood of war itself deserves our concern. After World War I, the Nye Committee of the United States Senate was formed to investigate this very question.

> The committee reported that between 1915 and April 1917, the United States loaned Germany 27 million dollars. In the same period, the U.S. loaned the United Kingdom and its allies 2.3 billion dollars, or about 85 times as much. From this data, some have concluded that the U.S. entered the war because it was in American commercial interest for the United Kingdom not to lose.[315]

The text of the committee report itself describes the nature of munitions companies and their practices at that time (February 1936). Weaponry sales were being conducted all over the world, often arranged through bribery of high officials of purchasing countries, so serious and common a situation that the report couldn't give individual names for fear of causing the unrest or overthrow of some South American countries: "... lies, deceit, hypocrisy, greed, and graft, occupying a most prominent part in the transactions."[316] The committee found that "... not only are such transactions highly unethical, but that they carry within themselves the seeds of disturbance to the peace and stability of those nations in which they take place."

The committee discovered the arms manufacturers not supporting arms limitation agreements; on the contrary, the companies showed contempt for such restrictions and proceeded to ignore or violate them whenever possible. They described in detail how the demilitarization requirements of the Treaty of Versailles toward Germany were totally ignored by chemical and weapons manufacturers in the United States and Britain, as well as American ship-building companies. The influence on the members of Congress and in the War Department by arms suppliers was clear.

The committee found that the munitions manufacturers often released new weaponry to overseas markets, disregarding the protection of secrets, but that the government did not object because they knew it was necessary for munitions companies to make profits that would keep them in business, ready to meet the demands of the next war. They concluded that the commercial interests of the companies took priority over national policy, and that this was a major factor in the rearming of Germany before World War II. US patents were used in German subs that later destroyed US ships and lives. Similarly, at a time when the American government was officially speaking out against Japanese actions in China, US munitions and aviation companies were selling materials and manufacturing processes to Japan. The desire for profits over-rode the desire to help promote or maintain peace, and impacted the future in ways they could never have known at the time. The committee worked between 1934 and 1936, but their findings are still significant for us today:

> While the evidence before this committee does not show that wars have been started solely because [of] the activities of munitions makers and their agents, it is also true that wars rarely have one single cause, and the committee finds it to be against the peace

of the world for selfishly interested organizations to be left free to goad and frighten nations into military activity.[317]

Much has been reported about corruption, abuse, misuse, or inefficiency in the current pattern of awarding contracts for military services. The drive for profits is not an adequate assurance that the conduct of war will be done responsibly; to the contrary, it can be a serious detriment.

There are also those who gain or retain political power and control because they convince people of the need for war and their ability to lead it. They use rhetoric to sway people into believing that war will bring safety and security for all and is the best and only option open to us. When this is done with the use of false and misleading information to turn the situation to their will, they must be exposed and held accountable for their actions.

7. Money spent for war isn't "real money".

We remove the cost of going to war from our lives.

We vote directly on a special bond levy to approve or deny the building of a new classroom at our local junior high school. We vote for the measure to increase or hold the limit on state taxes to fund expansion of children's health insurance. But our vote for war funding is far removed from us. We elect representatives, senators, and a president who make decisions about war, but the funding of war is not translated into real life terms for us. A new classroom at a junior high will mean our property taxes will go up for the next twenty years while the bond is paid off. So people go to the school meeting to hear why the classroom is needed and make sure the investment is wise. We read the papers, listen to a panel discussion, and study the voters' pamphlet to see what kind of health coverage will be provided to children in our state if we increase our state taxes.

But the wars, we are told, will cost this-many-trillion, for these-many-days-or-years-or-so, a figure that means nothing to us except some vague hunch that it's a lot, and we hope it won't get bad for our children or grandchildren if they're stuck paying off our debt. We are not given the choice between the classroom and healthcare or the war (the war that will undoubtedly destroy classrooms and hospitals as well as the kids inside them, as they will be part of that 85–90% civilian category). So we go to the phone and call Washington, D.C., to ask whether we can really afford our wars when there are human needs unmet in our communities. Messages are passed along by some. There is concern and agreement expressed by others. We hope our calls make a difference, yet wonder how they compare to the voices of the lobbyists for the defense industry.[318]

We want to tell our representatives what's happening with money here at home – one of Portland's well-established community high schools is being closed because of funding cuts; the radio just carried news of what school districts around here have done or are looking at doing in the coming weeks to balance their budgets for the next school year – increase class sizes still more; cut PE in the early grades; cut librarians, music programs, and electives; eliminate 14 days from the school calendar in order to save money on staff salaries.[319] News followed that Hood River County libraries closed down because of lack of funding. Through the interview with the head librarian, we learned that after 98 years of service, the main library closed its doors, along with every branch library in the county.[320] (Author note: The libraries remained closed for a year, seeking funding.)

At a recent orientation on services to Oregon's Seniors and People with Disabilities, it was learned that two of their programs will be cut entirely at the end of the month in order to help meet the state budget shortfall and that additional cuts will be made in less than three months, including the program granting delivery of one meal a day to those on Medicaid. Some of the meal providers may be able to stay in operation in spite of the cut funding, we were told, but we should at least expect long waiting lists for Medicaid patients hoping to sign up for meals.[321] I don't know. Maybe the program has fluff. Maybe those people all need to get out and figure out how to make bean soup. But maybe disabilities make it harder to get out. I have to wonder about our priorities and ask if military contractors, weapons manufacturers, military recruiting budgets, and military expenditures in general are under the same strict belt-tightening and program-cutting as our schools, libraries, and disability services.

The Fiscal Times in a February 21, 2010, article put it this way:

> When Defense Secretary Robert Gates presented the Pentagon's whopping $708 billion budget request for 2011, he tried to strike a balance between the military's strategic needs and fiscal discipline.... And yet for all his efforts to boost the relevancy and efficiency of U.S. forces, Gates could not escape a hard budgetary reality: Defense spending continues to spiral upward, even at a time of austerity elsewhere in the federal budget.[322]

National Public Radio reported on July 28, 2010:

> (Renee Montagne, host): We know the wars in Afghanistan and Iraq are costing the U.S. tens of billions of dollars. In Iraq, $50 billion has been spent on rebuilding that country since the war began in 2003. Now a report by the Inspector General for Iraq Reconstruction says that the U.S. government can't account for $8.7 billion of that money.... And this is not the first time we've heard about billions of reconstruction dollars for Iraq being mismanaged.
>
> (Rachel Martin): No, that's right. That same office, the Inspector General for Iraq Reconstruction, found in another audit back in 2005 that the temporary U.S.-led Provincial Authority – the temporary government running Iraq at the time, after the invasion – had essentially lost track of another $9 billion for similar reasons. So bad accounting and poor oversight again.[323]

$50 billion to rebuild the destruction from a US initiated preemptive war? $8.7 billion unaccounted for? $9 billion unaccounted for? Or one meal a day? Who is setting our priorities?

The American Friends Service Committee attempted to make war spending more understandable and "real." In September 2009 they wrote:

> The United States spent $976,121,986,000 on the military in 2008, including budgeted funds and the "special supplements" like the one to pay for the war in Iraq. That's $1.9 million spent *every single minute* for so-called defense.... The total of the U.S. military budget dwarfs the next largest military budget. In fact, the United States spends as much on our military as the combined totals of the next fifteen largest budgets. That's China, Russia, Britain, France, Japan, Germany, Saudi Arabia, South Korea, India, Brazil, Italy, Austria, Canada, Indonesia, and the Netherlands! Why does the United States need to spend so much money on the military when people around the nation and across the world are in such need?[324]

More than the combined totals of the next fifteen largest budgets? Why? $1.9 million a minute? Why?

Our property tax bill came recently. The amount for the new buildings bond levy our school district passed was shown on a separate line, so we knew exactly the cost of our decision to build. It made me wonder what would happen to our motivation to go to war if our next IRS 1040 or 1040EZ automatically added on a separate amount for our family's share of costs of our current wars. We don't have to sit down and budget out how we as a family can pay for this war over the next twelve months. A third now, another third in February, and the final third in May, like our property tax bill? Take money out of the savings account or the IRA? Try to get a part-time job to cover the extra due? Hope nobody gets sick or has to go to the dentist? Let cable and the cell phones go? Wear the old coats another year or two? No. We don't let the cost of war bother us. If we did, we might find alternatives.

The US Department of Defense lists the overseas military sites owned or managed by the Department in its "Base Structure Report – Fiscal Year 2010" and notes: "The Department manages a global real property portfolio consisting of more than 539,000 facilities (buildings, structures and linear structures) located on nearly 5,000 sites covering over 28 million acres. ... Sites are assigned to military installations. An installation is commonly referred to as a base, camp, post, station...."[325] The FY 2008 report stated, "The Department of Defense (DoD) remains one of the world's largest 'landlords'...."[326]

Catherine Lutz, Research Professor at the Watson Institute for International Studies and Professor of Anthropology at Brown University, refers to official numbers of troops, civilian employees, and military facilities in forty-six overseas countries and territories in her report "US Bases and Empire: Global Perspectives on the Asia Pacific," but adds, "These official numbers are quite misleading as to the scale of US overseas military basing, however, excluding as they do the massive buildup of new bases and troop presence in Iraq and Afghanistan, as well as secret or unacknowledged facilities in Israel, Kuwait, the Philippines and many other places."[327] She describes the anti-base social movements rising from groups focusing on the affront such bases are to the national sovereignty and pride of the countries in which they are located. She further states:

> Others focus on the purposes the bases serve, which is to stand ready to and sometimes wage war, and see the bases as implicating them in the violence projected from them. Most also focus on the noxious effects of the bases' daily operations involving highly toxic, noisy, and violent operations that employ large numbers of young males. For years, the movements have criticized confiscation of land, the health effects from military jet noise and air and water

pollution, soldiers' crimes, especially rapes, other assaults, murders, and car crashes, and the impunity they have usually enjoyed, the inequality of the nation to nation relationship often undergirded by racism and other forms of disrespect. Above all, there is the culture of militarism that infiltrates local societies and its consequences, including death and injury to local youth, and the use of the bases for prisoner extradition and torture.[328]

The Department of Defense official listing for FY 2010[329] describes their overseas facilities located in:

American Samoa
Guam
Johnston Atoll
Northern Mariana Islands
Puerto Rico
Virgin Islands
Wake Islands
Antigua
Aruba
Australia
Bahamas
Bahrain
Belgium
British Indian Ocean Territories (Diego Garcia)
Canada
Colombia
Cuba
Denmark
Djibouti
Ecuador
Egypt
Germany
Greece
Greenland
Iceland
Indonesia
Italy
Japan

Kenya
Kuwait
Luxembourg
Marshall Islands
Netherlands
Netherlands Antilles
Norway
Oman
Peru
Portugal
Saint Helena
Singapore
South Korea
Spain
Turkey
United Arab Emirates
United Kingdom

Learning the exact number and location of US military bases and personnel overseas is a challenging task. Adding to those in the Department of Defense inventory listed above, the Military Travel Zone 2013 website includes Afghanistan, Bosnia-Herzegovina, Cyprus, France, Honduras, Hungary, Iraq, Kyrgyzstan, Macedonia, Kosovo, Panama, Saudi Arabia, and Taiwan.[330] The PolitiFact Truth-O-Meter research, evaluating Republican presidential candidate Ron Paul's September 12, 2011, statement that the United States has military personnel in 130 nations and 900 overseas bases, says:

> For the personnel question, we turned to a Sept. 30, 2010, Pentagon document titled, "Active Duty Military Personnel Strengths by Regional Area and by Country." ... We found U.S. military personnel on the ground in a whopping 148 countries – even more than Paul had said. ... However, we should add a caveat. In 56 of these 148 countries, the U.S. has less than 10 active-duty personnel present.[331]

Paul went on to comment, "We're there, occupying their land. And if we think that we can do that and not have retaliation, we're kidding ourselves.

We have to be honest with ourselves. What would we do if another country, say, China, did to us what we do to all those countries over there?"[332]

One must ask why our military has come to be one of the world's largest landlords, spending as much on our military budget as the next fifteen largest country budgets combined. What are we trying to do, and how is it turning out for us?

Chapter 5
"War Is Inevitable. Why Fight It?" Plus Other Common Non-Sense and Un-Common Sense

People say:

"I can't keep up with what's happening."

"Things are way too complicated for me."

"We have to put some trust in our government and our leaders. After all, they're the professionals."

"First you hear one thing, and then another; I can't make any sense out of it."

"I couldn't make a difference if I did try, so why try?"

"The purpose of war is to restore peace and harmony. We must accept it."

"There is a time for everything – including a time to kill and a time for war. There will be wars and rumors of wars. The Bible says so."[333]

"Things will never change. Just look at today's world! War is inevitable. Why fight it?"

"Humans have been waging war as long as we've existed. It's our history and our human nature. We can't stop it if we tried, so why waste the energy. "

"War will make a man out of him – a man of courage, loyalty, self-sacrifice. And the discipline will do him good."

"The church and spiritual leaders long ago showed us how to make war in a moral way. It's called the Just War Theory."

"We can't let another Rwanda happen. Remember Hitler. We need war to stop genocide."

Let's look at those sayings. First of all, things do change. Human sacrifices were once seen as necessary to appease the gods. Cannibalism was an accepted means of dealing with intruders. Andrew Jackson, who became the seventh President of the United States, responded to a rumor about his wife Rachel, by challenging the man who spoke it, Mr. Dickinson, to a duel. Using a "gentlemanly" way to stop a rumor and settle an argument, Jackson shot and killed Dickinson. It was said that the personal honor of men would always demand dueling.[334]

Yes, things change.

~

In response to "Just look at the world! War is inevitable!" one must answer, yes, just look at the world. War is possible. But it is conflict that is inevitable, not war. People can choose how they react to conflict and how to manage it. Most people in many different areas of life – home, work, play, relationships – in a variety of situations simply choose to deal with conflict peacefully and without violence. They have established skills or habits that allow them to manage the conflict. These things are "the norm" so they do not hit the news; violence does, and skews our take on the world.

~

What about putting our trust in the professionals? Yes, if it is reasonable to rely on their training and their experience. But common sense tells us that if individuals have grown up learning war, believing war to be necessary and inevitable, and if at the same time they have not learned about and used a wide variety of effective alternatives, they are NOT in a position to correctly evaluate the options, no matter what their title, age, or position. Their background, if not purposely recognized and broadened, could certainly disqualify them from the role of capable decider.

If the person happens to be the leader of the nation to whom we seem to relinquish so much power in determining whether or not the country will choose war, it is even more imperative that we make certain of his or her knowledge and abilities in the use of effective diplomacy and nonviolent resolution of conflict. We must ask how motivated these leaders are to resolve international disputes nonviolently. What biases do they hold about the inevitability of war? In a world where nobody wants war, that is only common sense.

~

Believing that one person is too insignificant to make any difference is a tempting philosophy to adopt. It takes away some of the pressure to think things out and decide how to respond. But it has repeatedly been proven wrong. People with vision and willingness to take a stand, have and do change things. And every action causes some shift, some ripple, in one direction or another. To do what one believes to be right, without requiring that you also be in control of the results and the timing, allows you to act with purpose and with hopefulness. You are then free to be surprised by good and to become part of the momentum of others' work, perhaps also done against the odds – thereby changing the odds.

~

Those who quote a sacred text as proof that the inevitability of war is assured and thus find no reason to work to eliminate it, must consider the full message of their faith, which will certainly speak of the sacredness of life and the responsibility to act honorably and justly toward others. Those of the Christian faith, for example, who take its radical message seriously – to love enemies and do good to them – and turn it into action in their lives, may find that carrying out their faith involves proactively working against war and the conditions that contribute to it. Fatalistic acceptance of atrocity, human carnage, destruction, and moral and physical damage to so many because of a text, serves faith poorly. To seek to know the limitations of words, as well as their power and inspiration, is worth our time. One must also question the direct applicability of a phrase or sentence to any particular situation, for the range of sacred text is wide, its content contradictory, and its meaning historically and culturally impacted.

Those looking for guidance from the sacred would do well to also look at another "text" readily available – that of creation surrounding them – and learn to read it. We ask how the preciousness of the earth, the absolute wonder to be seen in life all around us (if we learn to see it), and our way of living on and with the earth can influence our thoughts and actions concerning war.

And when the question of faith becomes more than theoretical, and we are asked to serve war or pay for it, or work for its end, and we still don't know what to do with the sacred stories of blessed genocide, perhaps some will echo the words of John Greenleaf Whittier. In his beautiful poem, *Mary Garvin*, he tells the story of parents, now old and finally aware of the deep loss their religious-based banishment of their daughter caused them all, yet who are on the verge of repeating the same mistake. He reflects with them: "Better heresy of doctrine than heresy of heart."[335]

~

That comment about Just Wars, and the criteria invented to answer it (Just War Theory), refers to a series of conditions that must be met in order for a war to be declared "just." We continue to ask: Under what conditions is war acceptable, justifiable, and even morally necessary? But Just War Theory has not worked out very well over several centuries. People seem to see their side and their cause as just and necessary and even holy, and their enemy as entirely wrong and evil, even when that enemy believes itself to be defending the just and holy cause. War seems to have a momentum of its own once it is unleashed, regardless of the conditions we set as guidelines and limits under a theory. It is time we accept that reality: Just War Theory does not control war.

That old question – When is war acceptable, justifiable, and morally necessary? – fools us into thinking there is an answer. It is time, instead, to ask an entirely different question: How can we resolve international conflicts and prevent violence – in ways that uphold basic human rights? Because war does not. Neither do "Just Wars."

~

To say that war will make a man or woman out of a soldier also requires that we know what we mean by the making of a man or woman. Military training often brings together those of diverse geographical, cultural, economic, and racial backgrounds and offers them an intense and deeply shared experience in which they work with, cooperate with, and depend on others as individuals, far beyond limiting stereotypes or prejudiced views they might have once held. It may demand working as a team with others to the point of giving up life for that new brother or sister. They train hard physically, learning what their bodies can do, and what they can accomplish under purposefully strict discipline. The work of war requires an individual to be alert, and as well-trained and as prepared as possible, able to carry out orders, and to move and act in the face of fear for one's self and for others. It can demand unimaginable endurance and perseverance in the face of horrendous conditions.

On the other hand, war also often requires an individual to look out at or down on another human being and destroy that person. War requires using equipment that kills, mangles, dismembers and burns people, and that demolishes and destroys years of work building and creating. It will nearly always result in more innocent deaths than targeted deaths. It requires the development of a deep hate and anger and a willingness to act on those emotions in ways that would never have been acceptable, accepted, or considered in the soldier's life before the war. Sometimes it requires normalizing atrocious and cruel actions as "what must be done" simply to get through the day. For some it means throwing out the moral base of years of life and mutilating, raping, and torturing. It can mean doing what you're told instead of evaluating a situation for complexities, history, mysteries, and possibilities of action. For many it means learning to be overtly racist, nationalist, and verbally abusive, and being left with a deep indoctrination in those traits. Is that what we hope for a man or a woman to become?

Writing about "predictable occurrences among such a huge agglomeration of young military males a long [way] from home," New Zealand professor and South Pacific Islands environmental history researcher Judith Bennett describes circumstances of American military personnel in New Caledonia during World War II: "There were also many incidents of the US forces' drunkenness, brawling, vandalism, and involvement in the manufacture and trade of illicit alcohol, as well as disrespect for, and even rapes of, civilian women."[336] Similar stories abound for other locations, other wars. Are these the experiences that build men and women of character?

The soldiers themselves have to carry on in spite of what they have seen, experienced, and been ordered to do; some don't:

> "Last month [January 2009], suicide took the lives of more Amer-
> ican soldiers than Al Qaeda and the Iraqi insurgency combined.
> According to preliminary numbers, as many as 24 soldiers killed
> themselves in January. That's almost *five times* as many suicides as
> the same month last year. News of this shocking spike in suicides
> comes as no surprise to anyone who has been following this issue.
> 2008 marked the highest rate of military suicide in decades, and
> suicide rates have been rising every year since the start of the Iraq
> war."[337]

But there is even more – the story of what happens to the soldier once he or she has left the military:

> An analysis of official death certificates on file at the State Depart-
> ment of Public Health reveals that more than 1,000 California
> veterans under 35 died between 2005 and 2008. That figure is three
> times higher than the number of California service members who
> were killed in Iraq and Afghanistan conflicts over the same period.

The Pentagon and Department of Veterans Affairs said they do not count the number of veterans who have died after leaving the military. ...

The data show that veterans of Iraq and Afghanistan were two and a half times as likely to commit suicide as Californians of the same age with no military service. They were twice as likely to die in a vehicle accident and five and a half times as likely to die in a motorcycle accident.

"These numbers are truly alarming and should wake up the whole country. ... They show a failure of our policy." [Bob Filner, US Representative, Chairman of House Veterans' Affairs Committee.][338]

Is the failed policy the question of services provided to veterans or a question of what soldiers are asked to witness and carry out in the first place? The earlier "Cost of War" figures given are now seen to be an inadequate accounting of the continuing reality of loss and death.

Referring to the experience of Vietnam veterans this time, a Veteran Health Initiative report comments:

Of course, mortality is not the only health issue associated with PTSD, and other studies have reported that 70 percent to 94 percent of PTSD cases have co-morbid mental disorders, including depression and alcohol and drug dependency. An excess of alcohol and drug use could be related to the reported excess of motor vehicle accidents among Vietnam veterans. Excessive alcohol and drug use, along with depression, could also place veterans at greater risk for accidental poisonings, *i.e.* drug overdoses and suicide.[339]

Leo Tolstoy's 19th century description of training for war holds interest for today:

This result [making men ready to carry out orders of cruelty and brutality] is attained by taking them at the youthful age when men have not had time to form clear and definite principles of morals, and removing them from all natural and human conditions of life, home, family and kindred, and useful labor. They are shut up together in barracks, dressed in special clothes, and worked upon by cries, drums, music, and shining objects to go through certain daily actions invented for this purpose and by this means are brought into an hypnotic condition … submissive to the hypnotizer … armed with murderous weapons, always obedient to the governing authorities and ready for any act of violence at their command….[340]

Tolstoy goes on to describe the outcome of their training:

> At the last moment they will all find themselves in the position of a hypnotized man to whom it has been suggested to chop a log, who coming up to what has been indicated to him as a log, with the ax already lifted to strike, sees that it is not a log *but his sleeping brother*.[341]

Sadly, often the ax is mercilessly and viciously slammed into "the log" before our soldier awakens to the reality of what he or she has done and has to live with for the rest of life. There are surely more humane, life-affirming, spirit-enriching, and respectful ways to experience personal growth, develop self-discipline, and learn to become a man or a woman.

~

And what about the belief that humans have been waging war as long as we've existed? It's our history and our human nature, we say. We can't stop it if we tried, so why waste any energy trying?

Anthropologist Douglas Fry debunks that myth and challenges the danger of an attitude that contributes to self-fulfilling prophecy. When people say, "Why try? We'll never get rid of war" they don't bother to look for, practice, and use alternatives. When they don't bother to look, they don't find. Without alternatives, they accept war and carry on in the belief that it is just human nature.

Fry contends that it is not human nature and brings out the archeological and anthropological research to back his stance. In his book, *Beyond War: The Human Potential for Peace*, Fry explains:

> A careful reevaluation of the evidence will lead our thinking in a new direction. It will reveal how the human potential for conflict resolution tends to be underappreciated, whereas warfare and other forms of violence tend to be emphasized, exaggerated, and naturalized. Exposing this bias has real-world significance. Naturalizing war creates an unfortunate self-fulfilling prophecy: If war

is natural, then there is little point in trying to prevent, reduce, or abolish it. After all, if we can't help being warlike, why should we even bother resisting such tendencies? The danger of assuming that humans are fundamentally warlike is that this presumption may help justify "doing what comes naturally." It also may contribute to an exaggerated fear that naturally warlike "others" are eager to attack us. Harboring such assumptions also can stifle the search for viable alternatives to war: Why attempt the "impossible"?[342]

His research into nomadic hunter-gatherer groups living today as well as those of the past shows that 99% of human existence on the earth has been without war, a very different picture than what bombards us from the media and entertainment worlds today and makes us vulnerable to the "war is human nature" myth. He does not claim the long past was entirely violence free, but describes the significant difference between the individual violence that did exist and that of war, and shows that it was minor in comparison to the highly varied and common processes in place for conflict resolution. He tells of the many bands of non-warring societies that still remain today. It is only within the past few thousands of years (3,000 – 10,000) with the transformation to agricultural, fixed location, higher density, and social and power-grouped societies that warfare emerged, and that the strongest use of war was even more recent than that – having come with the emergence of nation-states.

But Fry does not go on to equate nation-state societies with an inevitability of war. With the "human nature" myth debunked, he shows that the creativity and flexibility of humankind opens unlimited possibilities for resolving conflict nonviolently, even at the international level. He suggests that the incentive for doing so should be very high, and that even though much of society has managed to almost forget the potential damage to our world and the human race that could come from even a "small nuclear war," the stakes today are tremendous. He says, "In an era of nuclear missiles and other weapons of mass destruction, trying to achieve security through the threat or use of military force is like trying to perform heart surgery with a chain saw."[343]

With high resolve and a belief in humankind's past and present ability to find nonviolent means of resolving conflict, we can shake off the "inevitability"-induced apathy and let common sense lead us to put away our chain saws and look at the heart of things clearly.

Those who point to genocide – the remembrance of Hitler or perhaps conditions in Rwanda in 1994 – and use that as justification, or rather as an imperative, for America to go to war in a current situation, tie the prevention of genocide to the call for war in a way that stirs our empathy yet muddles our thinking. The ability to empathize with pain and suffering, to imagine the horror that could come, and be stirred into action to prevent it, is at the very heart of humanity's goodness. We feel the pain within ourselves. We refuse to ignore the injustice that gives rise to it. It is important not to ignore those feelings of compassion. We don't want to turn away with cold hearts and paralyzed hands, and we must not.

Faulty thinking begins when we bind promoting justice and preventing suffering with war-is-our-only-option. We fail to consider every other available means of preventing cruelty. We fail to consider the role of time and timing. We fail to address the roots and conditions that make genocide even a possibility.

Faulty thinking continues when we equate remorse over past inaction, or belated action, with proof that acts of war are required in a specific circumstance at hand. The justification for bombing in Libya in spring of 2011 because of remorse over not stopping genocide in Rwanda in 1994 is an example of this happening, as can be seen in the reports by Evan Harris in two related ABC News articles in March 2011: "Clinton Cites Rwanda, Bosnia in Rationale for Libya Intervention" and "Defense Secretary: Libya Did Not Pose Threat to U.S., Was Not 'Vital National Interest' to Intervene."[344]

Once again, it is tempting to justify war as holy and our drive to go to war or use our weapons of war as a moral obligation. We predict what could happen and announce our determination to stop it, when, in reality, there may be many less worthy, questionable motivations driving our intentions now.

The rationale offered appeared to equate the conditions of both circumstances – Rwanda in 1994 and Libya in 2011. The savagery of Rwanda's murders and abuse was described so graphically by Secretary of State Clinton that we could not bear to think of it happening ever again, to anyone, so when she explained that we must intervene militarily in Libya to stop such a travesty from occurring again, the reaction of many was to rally behind the planes and bombs.

We don't always stop to ask what else is going on, what the history of this situation is, and what our interests and involvement in it are.

Peter Kenyon on NPR reported in November 2011 that:

Westerners looking at the new Libya from afar tend to offer recipes for recovery that feature widespread privatization of state-owned companies and a robust private sector that takes over the tasks of job and wealth generation. ... [A] financial consultant with experience in Iraq and Egypt argued that former leader Moammar Gadhafi's moves to virtually eliminate property rights must be reversed, and that Libya's oil wealth should be used to create venture capital funds.[345]

In the same article, Kenyon tells of a taxi driver who described Gadhafi's attempt to raise gas prices to a "shocking" dollar a gallon and then had to back down when public outrage became so strong. He referenced a proposal that the Libyan laborer had become used to the idea of a having a job for life and was not prepared to enter the "cutthroat" reality of competitive society.

Hmmm ... privatization of resources, wealth generation, property rights, oil wealth, venture capital, jobs for life, cutthroat competition. Could there have been any other concerns on the part of the United States, besides simply protecting the people of Benghazi?

We don't tend to ask what the options besides armed conflict are, nor do we wonder what the nationals of that country could do nonviolently to gain their rights, as they did when they reversed a mandated gas price hike through public outrage and non-cooperation with their government.

We don't tend to ask what *our* killing will do, or talk about the innocent people we will kill. One of our early bombings hit the home of Gadhafi's son, where Gadhafi was at the time. The son and three of Gadhafi's grandchildren were killed.

We just trust that our actions will prevent, not genocide actually, because no one says this meets the definition of genocide, but rather we hope it will prevent possible atrocities that can happen in revolution, civil war, or war.

But there we run into a problem: Once again we slip into a pattern of using violence to stop violence, showing that we believe violence is the most effective way to accomplish our goal. It becomes a pattern for others to follow. We further entrench violence as a tool of choice in those we propose to protect, those whose side we support, and those who may shortly move in to positions of control themselves. The Bad Guys Who Use Violence that we hope to stop, might not see a whole lot of difference between violence and violence.

Several months after NATO's 2011 intervention in Libya began, questions were raised in the United Nations about the extent of civilian casualties from the NATO bombing campaign launched to stop human rights abuses. Amy Goodman of *Democracy Now!* reported on February 21, 2012: "Late last year, the United Nations Security Council rejected a probe into the deaths of civilians during the NATO bombing of Libya. … The United States refused to allow a U.N. Security Council probe into Libyan civilian deaths." She questioned Vijay Prashad, chair of South Asian History and professor at Trinity College in Hartford, Connecticut, for his response. He replied:

> The real question is, why won't NATO allow an evaluation of the Libyan war? What if we discover that the number of civilian casualties, the bombing in places like Marjah, the bombing in places in the center of Tripoli, had indeed cost the lives of a very large number of civilians? What is the harm of NATO coming under an evaluation? It will demonstrate, for instance, the actual commitment to human rights and to responsibility to protect civilians that the United States purports to support. So, the fact that they are not allowing an evaluation causes concern around the world. It means, perhaps, that the bombing campaigns are not going to protect civilians. They might, in fact, exacerbate the danger to civilians.[346]

Prashad went on to explain that the U.N. Security Council required the U.N. human rights officer, Navi Pillay, to give the report on Libya in a closed session. "[I]t seems as if the West and NATO, in particular, does not want to have a discussion about Libya in public, but it wants to utilize human rights as a way to start wars, not a way to evaluate what has happened in a society. Libya is going to suffer from a lack of truth and reconciliation, from a lack of evaluation of the full cycle of human rights investigation to prosecution."

We must ask why it is that the US Government will not allow the light of examination to show the result of the "tools" used. Evaluation is a commonly accepted part of learning from and improving on one's actions. Why not require it of ourselves and our wars?

But we were speaking of genocide – the deliberate mass murder of an ethnic group, race, or minority people – and an assumption that it must be stopped by violence. Genocide is an unimaginable horror, except that we can imagine it because it has happened. The stories are there for us to learn, and they challenge us to make sure it never happens again. But let us be honest: deliberate mass murder of any people is a horror, whether they be of mixed race or one, regardless of the reason for the murder, and whether it be named "genocide" or "war."

Let us also recognize that the US Government is not an innocent bystander in the issue of genocide. We would do well to remember its history with Native Americans, its support of the government of Guatemala during the genocide of the Mayan population, and to ponder the impact of US bombing in Cambodia during the Vietnam War and how that played into later genocide by the Khmer Rouge.[347]

US sale of weaponry around the world makes massive deadly conflict more likely, and our overwhelming reliance on the violence of war throughout our own history up to today, provides the example for those who take it one hideous step beyond what we say is "acceptable consequence of war." And lest we feel too smug, let us ponder how observers would describe the bodies we left behind in our fire bombings in Germany, and our mass murder of the people of Japan in 1945.

Instead of using genocide as an excuse for war, let us face the myth head on: The roots of genocide – both that carried out by Adolph Hitler and in the example of Rwanda by the Hutu perpetrators against the Tutsi – were buried in a complexity of causes. We have already spoken of Hitler. In the case of Rwanda, colonial powers had enacted policies that gave rise to division, privilege and subservience, injustice, and hatred between ethnic groups. Long-endured repression, once the tables were turned and power was taken by the other side, did not end the injustice. It resulted in counter-repression. Education was restricted. Positions of power, with benefits, were granted primarily to those of one ethnic grouping, causing even more inequality and resentment. War and modern weapons of war had been introduced by the colonial powers, and continued to be made available to those who gained their independence and held power. In Rwanda, a campaign to stir hate and instigate mass murder was carried over radio broadcasts, building fear and increasing the likelihood that people would actually carry out the insanity they were being told to do.

What were the means of stopping that genocide that did not have to wait until it was already underway in April 1994? There are foundational, long-term basic means of prevention that include respect for the lands, resources, and people of another area rather than conquest and pillaging, whether done by colonial powers of days past or those grasping power over others and their resources today.

Development of a healthy society – economically, environmentally, and socially – prevents repression of one people by another, and eliminates the conditions that lead to genocide. Making certain that our actions and interactions do not negatively impact the health of another society is a first step. Then, if help is needed, we can work in partnership with the people through aid, technical assistance, and capacity-building for collaboration and problem-solving among all parts of the society. Education counters the ignorance that leads to genocide; just laws, fairly carried out, counter hopelessness that breeds resentment and a "nothing to lose" mindset.

People who have hope, who feel their own contribution of creativity, work, and service to others, are more likely to act with caring toward others, rather than violence, and not succumb to genocidal acts. People who find they can accomplish change that is needed, and who do not feel powerless to act, can be more patient and reasonable in working for change. They will not be trapped in fear that lashes out in violence as the only option.

But these means of stopping genocide are the quieter demands on our hearts and minds. They require involvement and compassion when it doesn't seem to be a life and death matter, when we're busy tending to our own business. Yet these are the very things that bring an end to genocide. This work is being done by a myriad of organizations and individuals around the world, who do not accept the myth of war-is-the-only-option.

David Tegenfeldt, who has lived and worked in Myanmar for over twenty years, and his wife Carol Gowler, are part of a team of strategic peacebuilders there with Hope International Development Agency. They collaborate with civil society partners to create positive social change and apply democratic decision-making for the good of the community.[348]

Another organization, Partners for Democratic Change, was founded in 1989 by Raymond Shonholtz who worked with community and school conflict resolution in California. The vision was to help bolster democratic change around the world. Originally focusing its work through training centers in universities in Eastern Europe, the role of Partners for Democratic Change shifted:

> In its steady expansion, Partners developed future Centers on change and conflict management as independent, in-country, civil society organizations located in: Albania, Argentina, Colombia, Georgia, Jordan, Kosovo, Mexico, Peru, Romania, Serbia, and Yemen. These Centers with their in-country boards of directors

and staff were established with a mandate to build a professional cadre of mediators, negotiators, multi-stakeholder facilitators, and trainers in the government, civil society and private sectors. Partners serves as a support system for the Centers, co-developing programs, providing training and mentoring, and funding in conflict management skills, organizational development, and sustainability.[349]

Committed to long-term involvement, cooperation, and democratic progress, individuals like David, Carol, and Raymond, and the staff and volunteers at the organizations they've worked with, are making violence unnecessary. Skills and processes can be taught that enable people to work constructively through difficult and threatening situations.

Governments are also deepening their recognition of the role of prevention. The Friends Committee on National Legislation (FCNL) reports:

> In August 2011 the Obama administration established a new Atrocities Prevention Board in the National Security Council and mandated an interagency review of government capacities to help prevent atrocities. ... In February the Prevention and Protection Working Group [of FCNL] and the U.S. Holocaust Memorial Museum hosted a briefing on Capitol Hill called 'Preventing Genocide and Mass Atrocities: What More Can Be Done?' The standing room only crowd was packed with House and Senate staffers (representing both sides of the aisle), officials from the Department of Defense and State Department, and many of our friends from other non-governmental organizations. Speakers from the State Department, USAID and the Senate Foreign Relations Committee described the work they are currently engaged in to prevent genocide and identified tools and capacities that would enable the U.S. to halt violence before it starts.[350]

The US Department of State has a key role to play. The establishment of a complex crisis fund and the US Civilian Response Corps in 2008[351] were two means of dealing with serious potential for violent conflict. The "President's Proposal for the Fiscal Year 2011 State Department Budget" included recognition of the importance of civilian efforts to "help bring stability in volatile regions, reverse the spread of violent extremism ... decrease extreme poverty," yet at the same time stated that "lack of adequate State and USAID civilian capacity limits our options in responding to significant global challenges. … These are serious challenges and our preventative efforts cost a fraction of what it costs to fund active military engagement if conditions deteriorate to the point that military action is needed. Military missions are inherently temporary while State and USAID civilians engage with a lasting presence."[352] In 2011 the Bureau of Conflict and Stabilization Operations (CSO) was created within the Department of State in order to deal more effectively with potential violent conflict around the world, focusing on specific prioritized areas and working with local leaders in prevention, innovatively. A key seems to be whether or not we have the will to act preventively and the commitment to finance prevention efforts.

It is of interest to note that the US Peace Corps reported in March 2014, a total of 7,209 current volunteers and trainees and a FY 2014 budget of $379 million.[353] One can compare these numbers with the number of military personnel and military funding to notice the discrepancy in the financial commitment given to this program established to promote world peace and friendship, as compared to attempts at resolution of conflict through the power of violence.

If we choose to wait until things escalate out of control, and the fire is roaring, we must recognize that putting out the fire will be increasingly more difficult and more expensive. Our tendency at that point is to let the Department of Defense take over, shifting emphasis from long-range prevention efforts by agencies which work cooperatively and nonviolently, to the agency of the US Government that works through violence and the threat of violence.

To choose violence to end violence, puts us on a path that not only undermines the honor and passion with which we work, but also leaves us mired in the violence and horror that we accepted only as a means to the end. If we are sincere in crying out against genocide, declaring that we must intervene in order that it not happen again, let us acknowledge that we must be committed to prevention. Further, let us recognize that it is not just genocide that we must stop. It is the cruelty and butchery of violence itself that is the madness. It is our reliance on violence to solve our problems. War is genocide's first cousin.

We can act now to prevent genocide by stopping American weaponry sales, becoming purposeful about disarmament – our own and the world's, modeling determination and a growing ability to live in the world as one nation among many, learning to resolve conflict without violence, living simply with environmental responsibility and human fairness, promoting health, education, adequate water and shelter for all people, and celebrating the richness of a diverse world in creative ways.

We can ask the Secretary of State not to confuse bombing Libyans with preventing genocide in Rwanda, but instead to boldly bring to the attention of the American people the many things the State Department is doing to prevent violence, including in crisis situations. Secretary of State Hillary Clinton could have called together people like David Tegenfeldt, Carol Gowler, and Raymond Schonholtz and asked them to convene a gathering of the world's peacebuilding practitioners to propose three practical, effective, nonviolent alternatives to her proposal to bomb. Even two would do.

War and acts of war are not the way to stop genocide. To say they are, is to fail in our responsibility to act timely, wisely, and justly and with an understanding of the causes of genocide. War causes more death and perpetuates a reliance on violence.

⌒

Having challenged a series of myths about war, what can we learn by turning to good common sense? Common sense tells us that what applies at a personal level has some application to other situations as well, and we can learn from it. What if we applied war methods to our personal conflicts?

For neighboring farmers to settle a dispute over the boundary line between their farms by blowing up the other's farmhouse and killing the other's family doesn't make as much sense as sitting down and discussing what the deeds and survey maps show, where the old fence line was and why, and what each expects and needs now.

Assuming that the contractor is out to rip us off, and buying a fleet of helicopters and guns to mount on the new building to be ready just in case, then getting the neighbors to watch their driveways lest he get them too, will be less effective than visiting with the builder about our expectations and asking him to explain how the project is going.

Opening fire on teens running away from our car with a stereo system in their hands may leave us able to sing along with the songs on our newest CD and listen to the news about dead teens, poverty, drug abuse, and lack of meaningful adult relationships, but it won't solve the problems they live through.

Neighbors accepting the community mediation office's invitation to sit down with mediators to talk over what happened with the fireworks and the call to the police, accomplish much more than a fist fight in the driveway.

Violence has a way of short-changing the progress and the growth that comes with other forms of problem-solving. The use of violence in these examples hits us as ludicrous and extreme. Yet we manage to remove the label of "extreme, ludicrous behavior" from our violent international problem-solving.

If we came upon a group of teens and heard this leader-group chant, we would call for help:

Leader: "What do you wantta do?"

Group: "We want to kill!"

Leader: "Why do you want to kill?"

Group: "Cause killin's fun!"

Yet that was a part of training for US Marines heading to Vietnam.[354] Later, in the Gulf War, they chanted about what makes the grass grow. Troops are led to chant, "Kill! Kill!" and:

"What makes the grass grow?"

"Blood makes the grass grow!"

"Who makes the blood flow?"

"We do! We do! Blood! Blood! Blood!"[355]

When it was learned that too many soldiers fired over the heads of their fellow human enemy, the psychology of killing was incorporated into basic training in order to desensitize soldiers to homicide.

We are requiring that young people who want to do their part to help their country are morphed into beings who learn to hate, learn to de-humanize humans, learn to see things narrowly through vision that eliminates complexity and the need to think and evaluate and respond creatively. They learn to chant for blood and death and define killing as fun. When they come back home, they bring these experiences with them. And those who go through war and have killed, come back to us having lived under the nation's approval and encouragement to murder, and the experience of having murdered. They often are left with emotional and psychological scars that fester, spread, and last a lifetime.

My experience in working with school age youth for over two decades tells me that this is not how we best encourage young men and women to become caring, sensitive, compassionate, creative problem-solvers and participants in the human community. We need to offer them experiences of learning that make them more humane, wiser, and more able to question and evaluate the complexities of life and respond creatively and with empathy.

There has always been a disconnect between "real life" and what happens during war. It was described by a US Marine who was among over seven hundred sailors and Marines on five ships that went into Korea in 1871 on a mission to gain a peace treaty. I doubt that many Americans learned of this happening. "A treaty of amity with Korea appeared necessary in view of her central location amidst the trade routes of the East and the brutal treatment accorded foreigners who were shipwrecked off her coast."[356] America went to get the treaty, in what I would describe as an odd, destructive way.

As US ships moved into Korean waters, they were approached by Korean officials, noted to be of 3rd and 5th rank, not of the 1st rank with whom the Americans wished to negotiate. But the Americans went ahead and reported to them that they would be exploring Korean waters; no resistance from the Korean officials was perceived. However when the ships moved into a protected passage, they were fired upon by Koreans, who then sent word to their king about what had happened. Not even locals were allowed into this passageway without a river pass, the Koreans noted, so they certainly wouldn't allow foreigners coming in on armed vessels to do so. In response to being fired upon, the United States decided to retaliate. But first, they would grant a ten day pause in case the Koreans should come to apologize. No apology came.

After initial problems caused by a landing in the mud, an attack was launched and the forts and many of the Koreans in them were destroyed. Afterward, the ships stayed on another three weeks while attempts to get messages to the king to pursue the peace treaty were made. The Koreans ignored all such efforts, and the US ships finally moved on to China. Should we wonder that our peace initiatives were ignored?

In a letter written to his wife Nan, Lieutenant Colonel McLane Tilton, United States Marine Corps, described the fighting that killed 243 Koreans and 3 Americans during this operation:[357]

> By the bye speaking of sights I witnessed some horrible one's in the Corean [sic] forts. Some of them were burnt coal black and dreadfully mangled by 9 inch shells bursting near them. There were forty heaped in a little place not bigger than our quarter deck, most all shot in the head as they looked over the parapet, and their clothes being white the blood was to be seen in more dreadful contrast

than usual. They all bled like pigs & it is supposed in about one hour we killed 200 of them. I only saw about fifty killed but strange to say at the time it didn't affect me more than looking at so many dead hogs. One of our ship's Quarter-master's came to me with a pitiful expression and asked me if he should put some of the badly wounded out of their misery by shooting them in the head! I told him of course such a thing would be murder, and he must let them remain as they were. This seemed to distress him as he thought it would be a kindness to put them out of their misery by shooting them in the head! I merely mention this little circumstance to show how different things seem from different standpoints. The Qr. Master's motive was kindness doubtless, but surely had he seen anyone injured in a peaceful way, it never would have seemed proper to him to put the sufferer out of his misery by shooting![358]

In the same pamphlet that reprinted Tilton's words to his wife in an earlier century (the Naval Historical Foundation Pamphlet: "Marine Amphibious Landing in Korea, 1871," printed in 1966), General Wallace M. Green, Jr., Commandant of the Marine Corps (1964–67) at the time the pamphlet was published, wrote:

The assault of Marines and sailors on Kangwha Island in 1871 successfully preceded by some 79 years the landing of 1st Marine Division on Inchon, Korea, just 12 miles to the north. As a tactical operation, the earlier assault was an overwhelming success, despite initial landing difficulties....[359]

Introductory comments in the pamphlet echoed Green's evaluation:

It seems appropriate for the Naval Historical Foundation to print this publication as an early example of the proficiency of the Marine Corps in Amphibious operations, and the close cooperation that has always prevailed in such operations.[360]

Tilton described it to Nan in different words:

It is all over now, and as I expected, we have failed to make any treaty with the Coreans [sic]. The local authorities near us return all our communications sent on shore to be forwarded to their

King, and our Expedition so far as a treaty goes has turned out to be fruitless.[361]

The disconnect seems apparent today. "Proficiency" and "overwhelming success" left 246 people dead, others wounded, and a peace treaty certainly more elusive than when they arrived. Perhaps one Marine back in 1871 understood that disconnect when he described for his wife the difference between murder and dead hogs, twisted compassion and fruitless endeavors.

Those who apply violence to domestic or neighborhood disputes are seen as out of touch with reality, and are often labeled "abusers." Those who apply violence to international disputes are – heroes?

⁓

Many people believe the government should not be extensively involved in our personal problem-solving. But when things get out of hand and laws are broken and people stand to be hurt and we need help, most people are glad there is a role government plays in problem-solving. We expect democratic governments to formulate good and just laws and carry them out justly. We grant government that right and responsibility of protection and administration of justice.

Common sense can take us even further. We have granted exclusively to governments the right to wage war, or they have taken it as their exclusive right and we have not refused them. I ask us to question the wisdom of doing so – not the exclusivity of the "right" but the right itself to wage war. Why do we grant governments the right to war? The point is that exclusive rights – or non-exclusive rights, for that matter – do not make something that is horrid, destructive, and immoral okay to do. I contend that the right to wage war is a right no more suited to governments, no more for the good of humanity, and no more an example of effective, just problem-solving, than for us to grant exclusively to physicians the right to poison children. Because governments and physicians are groups that have power and resources to accomplish the named tasks, in no way means that it it is a logical or wise action.

Should school janitors be given the exclusive right to set schools on fire? Should farmers be given the exclusive right to slaughter horses as they are born? Because we can, does not mean we should. We get tied up on the exclusive right part of things and forget to notice that we're talking nonsense. I propose that waging war is an example of non-sense, regardless of who claims exclusive rights.

Tolstoy said, "To destroy another life for the sake of justice is as though a man, to repair the misfortune of losing one arm, should cut off the other arm for the sake of equity."[362]

Let us challenge our own absurdity. Wendell Berry says in his essay, "The Failure of War":

> The most dangerous superstition of the parties of violence is the idea that sanctioned violence can prevent or control unsanctioned violence. But if violence is "just" in one instance as determined by the state, why might it not also be "just" in another instance, as determined by an individual? … If a government perceives that some causes are so important as to justify the killing of children, how can it hope to prevent the contagion of its logic spreading to its citizens – or to its citizens' children?
>
> If we give to these small absurdities the magnitude of international relations, we produce, unsurprisingly, some much larger absurdities. What could be more absurd, to begin with, than our attitude of high moral outrage against other nations for manufacturing the selfsame weapons that we manufacture? The difference, as our leaders say, is that we will use these weapons virtuously, whereas our enemies will use them maliciously – a proposition that too readily conforms to a proposition of much less dignity: we will use them in our interest, whereas our enemies will use them in theirs.[363]

Let us return for a moment to that old question that has so limited our thinking for centuries: "Under what conditions is war acceptable, justifiable, and even morally necessary?" I propose that is not unlike asking the question, "Under what conditions is it acceptable, justifiable, and even morally necessary to beat your wife?" We must not grant the question-creators power over our ability to think and evaluate and to recognize and name this destructive and brutally violent thing called war for what it is – unacceptable, unjustifiable, immoral, and, if we choose to make it so, unnecessary. We must return to the new question and pursue it passionately: "How can we resolve international conflicts and prevent violence – in ways that uphold basic human rights?" It is common sense to ask the question that we really want answered.

Chapter 6
Extra! Extra! Hear All About It!
Nonviolence Raging Success!

That would be nice, wouldn't it? If they were calling out on the street corners and over the TV and radio shows to tell us the many amazing ways people have been cooperating and are now resolving conflicts and preventing war. It might stir our imaginations and raise some hope and some plans of our own. The fact that nonviolent action doesn't hit the news with the same fervor that violence does, leaves us with an impression that it isn't happening or it isn't very significant. That is not true. It may not be seen as "flashy" or "newsworthy" as violence, but nonviolence is in constant use, on big issues.

In both interpersonal and international settings, most occurrences are nonviolent. Ordinary people carry out their work, play, home life, and relationships on a daily basis and manage to work through regular conflict without resorting to violence. Similarly, problems between nations are generally worked out peacefully. With inspiration, determination, and hard work, habits of individuals and of a nation can be changed. We can set aside the fear that change might be too hard or too risky and replace it with an eagerness to become more aware and compassionate, more skilled in cooperation and resolution of differences, and enriched by wisdom gained through the experiences of working together with others. Golda Meir observed, "Orchestras don't mean the end of violins."[364] Common sense and personal experience confirm that. President Harry Truman observed:

> When Kansas and Colorado have a quarrel over the water in
> the Arkansas River, they don't call out the National Guard in each
> state and go to war over it. They bring suit in the Supreme Court
> of the United States and abide by the decision. There isn't a reason
> in the world why we cannot do that internationally.[365]

In an age when weaponry has brought us to the possibility of nuclear annihilation, President Dwight Eisenhower echoed, "The world no longer has a choice between force and law; if civilization is to survive, it must choose the rule of law."[366] Yet we also must acknowledge that Golda Meir, Harry Truman, and Dwight Eisenhower, all with vision of alternatives to war, were unable to avoid the violence of war at least in part because the alternatives of which they spoke had not been adequately implemented. It is time to step up implementation. Familiarity with options is a first step. Let's take a look at what has been done in order to gain understanding of the breadth of possibilities open to us....

~

Chile and Argentina were hours away from war over territory both claimed in the Beagle Channel when Pope John Paul II let both countries know that his representative, Cardinal Samore, was on the way to speak to both sides in search of a solution. Using shuttle diplomacy, mediation with specific stipulations, and direct involvement of the Pope and others from the Vatican, negotiations were carried out over six years, without war, and with an end result satisfactory to both countries.[367]

~

The student movement called "Otpor!" (Resistance!) became a force of national power with a strong role in bringing down the rule of Serbian leader Slobodan Milosevic, whose continued control seemed assured. His hand was on the army, the police force, and much of the media. Freedom of expression and access to open education had been further restricted after the violence in Kosovo. Yet political opposition to him remained fragmented and disorganized. The NATO bombing of Serbia in 1999 (at a cost of approximately $4,000,000,000 plus the $20–30 billion needed to rebuild what had been destroyed[368]) seemed to strengthen, rather than weaken, the hold of Milosevic on the area, leaving the problems of Kosovo and his control unsolved. But the Otpor! students mounted a compelling campaign of resistance using symbols, slogans, humor in the midst of sacrifice and commitment, and effective organization of nonviolent yet forceful tactics that astounded many.

Trained with the writings of Gene Sharp (*The Politics of Nonviolent Action*), the students learned how to organize strikes, avoid arrest, make contacts on "the inside," motivate and train others. They went on to learn how to monitor elections, so that when Milosevic called for an early election, supposing that no strong candidate would be ready to oppose him, Otpor! was prepared.

During this same time, two groups – one governmental and one NGO – offered facilitation for opposition parties to meet. Previously there had been little cooperation and no one was seen as strong enough to challenge Milosevic.

Through a series of face to face meetings, they were able to work together in addressing concerns and selected a candidate to offer the people a choice. Though Milosevic denied the election results that showed his rival Kostunica having won, and refused to step down, the results were made known to the public and a huge demonstration of public disapproval followed, forcing Milosevic's resignation. Otpor! had made Milosevic vulnerable by exposing his weaknesses in dramatic, even playful, ways that made the possibility of his being ousted not only thinkable but probable. With the slogan, "He's finished!" they worked to see that he was, without the need for war.[369]

The story of how singing and holding on tight to their culture saved the nation of Estonia, is told powerfully in the film, *The Singing Revolution*. The determination to carry on their tradition of singing by the tens of thousands in national singing festivals seemed to be the catalyst for reminding the Estonian people of who they were, what they valued, and the power they still held to bring about change, even though they had been taken over politically by others. Film narrator Linda Hunt says:

> In Estonia fairy tale heroes are not brave noblemen who slay dragons and save damsels. Their hero is the shrewd old barnkeeper who sits by the fire, waits, watches, and acts only when the time is right. Patience is a weapon. Caution a virtue.[370]

When their country was overrun by the Soviets in 1940, under a secret pact signed by Hitler and Stalin, Estonian leaders were targets of repression. Many were executed. Ten thousand Estonians were shipped off to Siberian slave labor camps; more than half never returned. In 1941 Hitler broke the pact and moved into Estonia, ousting the Soviets and taking over control. German power held until World War II ended and the Soviets returned. In 1945 Stalin convinced the Americans and the British that he would arrange for free elections in the country. He proceeded to move Russians in to accomplish "Russification" and to establish a communistic government and economy. The percentage of the population of Russian heritage rose from 8% in the 1940s to 40% in the 1980s.

The story of resistance is not entirely nonviolent. Some Estonians were involved in military campaigns during the war; they knew how to fight. An underground armed resistance took to the woods to fight the occupation.

But the majority of the population, perhaps because there was little oppor-tunity for them to arm themselves, or little hope that doing so would result in anything other than hardship or death, had to find alternatives. They took the path of continuing on with life, and if they longed for redress from the conditions around them, they bid their time and watched for opportunity. For many, the carrying on with life included the tradition of folk music. With passion for their heritage ignited by the songs they sang and by the bold steps taken by some determined to make change without retaliation of violence, resistance began to take shape.

The cleverness of the "barnkeepers" took many forms. Though repres-sion at first kept them from openly speaking out against Soviet control or exposing the truth of what had happened during the violent Soviet takeover, the Estonians formed a Heritage Society, a permitted activity, and used it as a forum for keeping the true history of the previous decades alive. When it became illegal to fly the blue, black, and white Estonian flag, they flew three flags – blue, black, and white. When they were prohibited from singing their patriotic songs in their own language, their massive music festivals carried on with other songs, and when the conductor finished, the thousands of singers kept on singing – in their own language, their own songs of national heritage and power.

They met in parks and squares, showing their resistance to outside control. At a rally in September of 1988 the crowd rose to 300,000. They moved to The Tallin Song Festival Grounds (Lauluväljak) to find space, and found that the very grounds inspired their spirits. Later reflecting on what had happened, Estonian artist Heinz Valk said they had started a revolution with a smile and a song.[371] Together with the people of Latvia and Lithuania, the Estonians formed a million-person human chain 600 km long, to show their protest of Soviet occupation.

They denied the legitimacy of Soviet control and set up a national registra-tion for themselves as citizens of Estonia. The registration cards were nick-named "tickets to Siberia," for when this was happening, they had no way of knowing if the act would eventually work to help regain their independence or end up being a cause for harsh punishment, as had been experienced fifty years prior.

Estonia declared a reconfirmation of their independence. The Russian citizenry reacted inside the country, as did the Soviets from outside. There were tense stand-offs, stunning examples of the power of people armed only with moral courage and determination that they were in the right. Their skill in using the political process, in working collaboratively to reach agreement with those in control in Estonia, and in recognizing the power of mass involvement of the people in demonstration, turned the tide. The Soviet Union lost control of Estonia; the people took back their own nation. And immediately thereafter in 1991, the Soviet Union fell, Russia declaring its autonomy and others following. One must ponder the role played by a national tradition of singing, not just in gaining the independence of their own nation through nonviolent action, but in impacting the fate of an empire and the entire world.

I watched the film again and began to wonder what happened next? They had gained independence, but there had to be problems left over. What about all the Russian immigrants living in Estonia? What about those who were born there after 1939 who had grown up only knowing Estonia as their homeland? How did the ethnic Estonians treat them? Did the people lose their commitment to nonviolence?

What I found was an even stronger story of "the barnkeepers' work." The excitement of revolution and working together for justice through a cause that powerfully united the people would have passed. Their focus would have returned to daily life. They would have a new government ready to get on with the work – and difficult problems – before them, not necessarily committed to doing things the way the people had done. The circumstances that followed, many believe, were the very conditions that bring two countries to the brink of violence:

> Following Estonian independence in 1991 a nationalist government came to power and introduced a law that restricted Estonian citizenship to the descendents of only those people who lived in the country before Soviet occupation in 1940. This was soon followed by the introduction of a Law on Aliens, which many Russian speakers feared was a prelude to the mass expulsion of all non-citizens. … Russia, incensed by the new laws, cut off its gas supply to Estonia and declared that the welfare of these disenfranchised people was a Russian national interest. At the same time the continued presence of ex-Soviet troops in Estonia exacerbated already heightened tensions between the two countries.[372]

But war did not follow. Instead the Estonian government contacted the OSCE (Organisation for Security and Co-operation in Europe) and asked for help. The OSCE is an intergovernmental group whose work is to provide for the security and conflict prevention of nations it serves. Its High Commissioner on National Minorities, Max Van der Stoel, immediately went to Estonia to help them resolve the situation. The trust he built enabled President Meri of Estonia to officially ask the opinion of the OSCE on its legislation.

The Commissioner also met with the leaders of the Russian dominant areas who had decided to vote on becoming autonomous zones within Estonia. Though extremist groups had offered armed assistance and paraded in battle dress on the Russian side of the border river, the continued work of the Commissioner and the cooperation of those involved, resulted in resolution without violence. The Alien and Citizenship laws were amended, and those of Russian heritage in Estonia accepted the National Court's decision on the nonlegality of the vote for autonomy. [373]

By seeking out and accepting the help of a neutral third party, even though it may well have been partially motivated by the need to do so in order to strengthen Estonia's bid for entry into the European Union, an alternative to war was found.

Perhaps we can learn something from those who choose to sing, use cleverness and collaboration, turn out by the hundreds of thousands, and ask for help - rather than head off to slay the dragons.

Working to end civil war within Nicaragua in the 1980s, CEPAD (the Council of Evangelical Churches in Nicaragua) supported local peace commissions, often comprised of church leaders, to go between the US funded Contra forces and those of the Nicaraguan Sandanista government. At first they were assumed to be spies for the enemy, but they made personal contact, built trust, and worked on agreements to return kidnapped individuals, assure local farmers safety in planting and harvesting their crops, and eventually enact ceasefires, the laying down of arms, and reintegration of soldiers into their communities. CEPAD and peace commissions carried on after the war and continue to work for basic infrastructure and life-supporting economic, educational, and health conditions for their fellow Nicaraguans.

While the United States saw Sandanista leadership threatening its political and economic interests in Nicaragua and decided to support war, CEPAD instead chose to work for de-escalation and transformation of the conflict. [374]

In 1952 Guatemala elected a president who introduced land reform measures. Two percent of the population owned approximately 70% of the land; 90% of Guatemala's farms were too tiny to support a family. The US corporation, the United Fruit Company, attained the help of the CIA to overthrow the elected government, and civil war broke out with continued US involvement.[375]

In 1981 Paul Wee, a Lutheran pastor, visited Guatemala and made a promise to himself that he would find a way to help end the horrendous conditions he saw and heard about. He later worked with the Lutheran World Federation and began organizing a team there in Geneva to return to Guatemala. Along with Costa Rica's Arias and the Arias Peace Plan's Commissions of National Reconciliation, the Catholic Church, and the Ministry of Defence, the team worked for an end to the civil war.

The Norwegian member of the team suggested Norway was a good location for a meeting of the key figures in conflict. Norway had no colonial past and a foreign policy that officially supported the peaceful resolution of conflict. In a government-owned chalet outside Oslo the dialogue began.

Finally, on the last day of the gathering, as the group began to tell stories of their childhoods and recognized their common past, they shared a vision for Guatemala and its peace, security, and economic well-being. Tears of emotion and recognition of their humanity and kinship launched them into a night-long session to write out their "Basic Agreement on the Search for Peace by Political Means." It was not a peace treaty, but a plan for a way to get to peace. The effort was joined by other religious groups, by the UN, OAS, and the United States. Meetings continued, and in 1996 in Guatemala City, an agreement on peace was signed, ending a 36 year long war. Though many players had a part in the process, both sides noted that without the Lutheran World Federation, it would not have happened. Pastor Wee, remembering the all-night session in Norway, said he felt then that if nothing else happened in his ministry, he would be content.[376] He had responded to his heart's call.

〜

There are many other stories of conditions changed without the use of violence described by Dylan Mathews in *War Prevention Works*. These are a sampling:[377]

- The leadership of a South African businessman facilitating peace between violent factions in a township, launching his efforts with the simple message that violence is bad for business.
- Civil war in Sudan stopped by a peace process that began with each person present listening to the story of pain and suffering the war had brought other participants – three full days of building relationship through the art of listening.
- Peace zones and peace communities established in the midst of areas of violence in Colombia.
- Quakers working with a purposeful neutrality and willingness to keep their role unknown as Nigerian ethnic conflict and potential for peace was explored.
- Peace "secretariats" established at the local, regional, and national levels by a brainstorming "think tank" of opposing parties in South Africa.
- A group of women in Kenya forming their own peace organization, without specific training in conflict resolution, but with a heart for peace, and establishing a forum for elders of different clans to discuss their conflict.
- Women in Somalia physically placing themselves between two warring factions, stopping the fighting as well as forming peacemaking bridges between clans as they marry and leave their own clan to join another.
- ActionAid working together with both Hutus and Tutsis in Burundi who determined their immediate need was to build homes to replace those that had been destroyed, thereby reinforcing the age old traditional values of cooperation that had prevailed before ethnic violence broke out.
- Amnesty International observers documenting and implementing Urgent Action to report human rights violations and situations where individuals are in immediate danger.
- Professor Roger Fisher (co-author, with William Ury and Bruce Patton, of Getting to Yes, 2nd Ed.) of Harvard Law School and the Conflict Management Group, sponsoring a weeklong workshop for key players in the boundary conflict between Ecuador and Peru, surprising the delegates by the emphasis on relationship building, communication and problem-solving skills, solution envisioning and role play, and developing empathy.

- In Burundi: soccer games bringing people together as a community rather than as ethnic divisions; trauma counseling allowing youth to talk about their experiences of violence; employment training offered by NGOs for youth who would otherwise be ripe for militia recruitment and violence; a network of ex-militia and young people at risk forming themselves into "Gardons Contact" (Let's Keep Contact) and, in a powerful example of symbolic power to stop violence, running a "yes to life, no to violence" campaign that included asking people to wear a strip of white cloth on their wrists to stand up against threats of violence and intimidation that told them to remain home or be killed.

The willingness of countries to sell weapons to others across international borders has been shown to affect human rights abuses, the level of conflict and violence around the world, and the repression and control of groups of people. Countries have faced attack by the very arms they have sold to others, now in the hands of those unfriendly to them. In the 1990s "Saferworld" developed a Code for arms transfers. Finding it hard to make progress with countries eager for sales and economic gain, they went to other NGOs and by 1997 had 600 NGOs across Europe signed on in support of the criteria of the Code. The recognition that high profile, popular organizations supported this work resulted in pressure on the governments to respond. Saferworld is still actively pursuing this goal and working toward an international Arms Trade Treaty.

Three years after El Salvador's twelve year civil war came to an end, with 75,000 killed and over a million people displaced, violent crime erupted, resulting in nearly 8,000 violent deaths per year. Modeling after a program in the Dominican Republic, the "Patriotic Movement Against Crime" (MPCD), a group of business leaders, mounted a campaign to give a $100 gift certificate in exchange for a gun which had been left in the hands of the people at the end of the war. They raised $4500, but the first exchange resulted in a needed $60,000 in vouchers. By the second weekend, the total was $103,000 in gift certificates. The impact of the program's success on El Salvadoran life was recognized by the President of the country, who helped with funds to honor all the vouchers and continue the program. In both of these examples, reduction in the availability of weapons eliminated some of the "fuel" for violent outbreaks.

Teachers, religious and political leaders, and others in India have used films, street theater, "myth busting" community gatherings, street parades, daily meetings and prayers by religious leaders of the community, signs and loudspeakers to counter religious and political violence and rioting. The use of the *bund* or general strike of shops or transportation has long been a tool of nonviolent action in India.

Experimentation with nonviolence was refined into a powerful force for change by Mohandas Gandhi in India over the decades that it took to carry out a campaign to gain independence from Britain, without war. Gandhi's work inspired Martin Luther King Jr. who led a nonviolent campaign for the human rights of African Americans in the United States.

The work of resistance and nonviolent action for change came to be known as the force or power of truth and love – *satyagraha*. Gandhi biographer, Louis Fischer, in *The Life of Mahatma Gandhi*, relates how it unfolded.

The Indian Congress announced a renewed campaign for independence from British rule early in 1930. They recognized that their greatest potential for success would not be by armed rebellion against the powerful and entrenched British who would surely have the upper hand with their military might to destroy the resistance. No, the Indian nationalists would use nonviolent action, and they determined that the best person to lead them was Gandhi. But what would the campaign look like? How would it be carried out? What would they do to challenge the injustice and economic and moral exploitation of Britain?

Salt.

Gandhi finally settled on starting the movement by resisting the salt tax. It was illegal at that time for anyone to make salt or use salt other than that under the control of the British authorities. The salt was taxed; the tax affected everyone, rich and poor. Gandhi decided to walk from his ashram to the sea, over two hundred miles away, where he would, in defiance of the law, gather salt and make salt from sea water. He would invite others in his ashram, trained in nonviolence, to accompany him. He expected to be arrested, a signal for others, perhaps thousands of others, to pick up where he would have to leave off. They would refuse to cooperate with British policies and thereby break the power held over their lives.

He wrote to the British Viceroy to describe how the Indian people were suffering from Britain's control, to tell him of Gandhi's plans to lead the resistance, assure him of Gandhi's goodwill toward him, but request that changes be made. In addition to other things, he pointed out that the Viceroy's earnings were over 5,000 times that of the average Indian income, and the heavy military and administrative spending was simply too much of a burden for the people to carry. If the Viceroy chose not to address the needed changes, Gandhi would have to proceed with his plans. His intention was to convert the British people, through nonviolence, to see their unfair ways and the wrong they were doing, and thereby stop the evils.

The Viceroy did not respond, but a short note of reply came from his secretary saying that His Excellency regretted Gandhi's choice that was sure to violate the law and disturb the peace. With careful planning and creativity, and an understanding of the impact of public opinion, Gandhi let the people and the local, national, and international media know that the life and death struggle for justice and independence was underway.

The Salt March to the sea took twenty-four days. Gandhi and the ashram walkers were joined by many others as they passed through villages along the way. Gandhi talked to the large crowds that gathered at every stop, stirring within them the vision for action. On April 6, 1930, at the end of the March, Gandhi defied the British and broke the salt law by gathering salt at the sea. The movement caught fire in the imaginations of the Indian people. Gandhi was arrested the following month. Tens of thousands more were arrested as they too defied the salt law, making salt from the sea and selling it throughout the country. The terms Gandhi had brought to Viceroy Irwin were not soon addressed, but something even more significant had happened. Gandhi had hoped that the resistance would build unity in the people, create a determination to throw off oppression, and bring a recognition of the power they had to do so, even beginning with a symbolic act. The salt tax defiance was not just symbolic, however.

Fischer describes what followed:

> The next act was an insurrection without arms. Every villager on India's long seacoast went to the beach or waded into the sea with a pan to make salt. The police began mass arrests. ... {They] began to use violence. ... Congress volunteers openly sold contraband salt in cities. ... Hundreds were handcuffed or their arms fastened with ropes and led off to jail.[378]

Soon afterward a civil disobedience was carried out by 2500 volunteers at a saltworks factory 150 miles north of Mumbai. It ended in waves of nonviolent resisters being beaten down cruelly and repeatedly. As the injured were carried away, a new batch walked forward to take their place, and they too were beaten until they had to be carried away. The scene was described in detail by an eye-witness reporter, and word was soon carried around the world. Fischer reflects:

> Technically, legally, nothing had changed. India was still a British colony. [Indian writer Rabindranath]Tagore explained the differ-ence. "Those who live in England, far away from the East," he told the *Manchester Guardian* of May 17, 1930, "have now got to realize that Europe has completely lost her former moral prestige in Asia. She is no longer regarded as the champion throughout the world of fair dealing and the exponent of high principle, but as the upholder of Western race supremacy and the exploiter of those outside her own borders. For Europe this is, in actual fact, a great moral defeat that has happened." ...
>
> Gandhi did two things in 1930: he made the British people aware that they were cruelly subjugating India, and he gave Indians the conviction that they could, by lifting their heads and straightening their spines, lift the yoke from their shoulders. After that, it was inevitable that Britain should someday refuse to rule India and that India should someday refuse to be ruled.[379]

I couldn't help but ponder Gandhi's conviction that the means to the end should not corrupt those carrying out the deed, for even if the goal seemed reached, they would have lost rather than progressed. We've read of two very different Marches to the Sea: one led by General Sherman in 1864, in America's Civil War, burning, destroying, creating horror, because war was hell, he said, and the more awful you can make it, the sooner it will be over; another led by Mohandas Gandhi in 1930, stirring a people to act through nonviolent civil disobedience in order to recognize their power to work against injustice and domination and to enlighten the unjust. The first was acknowledged as bringing destruction, anguish, and deeper poverty, and festering more division and resentment that became the aftermath of war and part of a decades' long – if not a century and more – unresolved battle for human dignity. The second March was acknowledged as bringing unity and hope in those feeling wronged, and providing leadership, experience, and confidence in mass nonviolent action as a means of working for change and human dignity.

India gained independence from Great Britain in 1947, remaining in the Commonwealth of Nations. It is an interesting comparison of methods used to bring change, and raises the question of what causes a people to rely on one method or the other.

~

To prevent outbreaks of violence and the targeting of human rights and political activists for assassination, observers act as witnesses and as accompaniers to individuals or groups being threatened with violence, ready to report to the world what they have seen take place. The knowledge that someone is able to focus international attention on an event, is often enough to prevent violence from taking place. Peace Brigades International set up their first office in Bogotá, Colombia, in 1994, and has continued to work in accompaniment and observation-reporting in many other areas.

A similar work is done by Christian Peacemaker Teams, who say they have learned that "Getting in the Way" can bring about change as they practice nonviolent action in order to confront injustice and let the world know what they have seen.[380]

"Witness for Peace" in Nicaragua involved both long term workers and short term teams of US volunteers traveling to Nicaragua to document what they saw in the countryside where locals were subject to kidnapping and killings at the hands of US-supported Contras. Bringing the information back to the United States certainly impacted the public awareness of the extent of otherwise unknown US involvement and the conduct of the Contras.

Another group, "Witness," uses the power of video to record and report incidents of human rights abuses, both filming and then releasing the films to audiences that can make an impact on the situation. They offer training in film production and in human rights campaigns, and make the possibility of being filmed a deterrent to abusers.

Testimonies were printed from interviews of victims of violence in Guatemala; other records of abuse, torture, and death were copied secretly from military records in Brazil and later published and distributed both in Brazil and in the rest of the world. The discovery of what had been hidden from public knowledge and the opportunity to make known the memories that had been repressed for fear of reprisal, became not just a means of healing from the trauma of violence, but a record of the history of those nations that could serve as a warning against repeating such violence.

~

In order to prevent violence in the schools, students in Liberia (nearly half of them in one large state school had been child soldiers), were trained as student mediators and conflict managers. Their training not only included conflict resolution and mediation skills, but trauma awareness and healing, and activities for self esteem development and prejudice reduction. They were taught how to mourn, story-tell, and role play, as well as how to use effective communication and procedures of mediation.[381] Students in Dayton, Oregon, (who weren't used as child soldiers) have for the past twenty years also trained as student mediators and conflict managers in order to prevent violence and to resolve the inevitable conflicts that arise in any setting where people work and play together. Perhaps someday someone from Liberia and someone from Dayton will meet as adults and have the skills, together, to resolve conflicts in the manner they learned as children in school – without war.

Those from Liberia might well tell Americans the story of the thousands of women of their country who created their own "Women of Liberia Mass Action for Peace" and helped end the civil war in 2003 that had killed over 200,000 people. Begun by Christian women who went to their Muslim sisters in a call for unity, the sisterhood of both faiths dressed in white, created t-shirts with their logo, and began sit-ins to force attention on the anguish brought by both sides of the civil war on their families. When peace talks were at last agreed to, they did not stop, but followed the negotiators out of the country and sat in front of the doors where the talks were taking place, finally barricading them in with their bodies until they stopped living the life of luxury "on vacation" and got to work on the conditions for peace. Their story can be seen in the documentary film, "Pray the Devil Back to Hell," an opportunity to watch the grassroots formation of a courageous movement to end war, in the midst of war, through nonviolent action.[382]

~

The film series, "A Force More Powerful," shows dramatically the effectiveness of nonviolent action in bringing about political change and eliminating the injustice and repression of societies or governments who control others to their own benefit. Six separate situations are studied: racial discrimination and injustice in Nashville, Tennessee, in 1959 and 1960; apartheid and violence in South Africa and the boycott of white businesses in 1984–85; resistance against German control over Denmark after Germany invaded the country in 1940 and the Danish response to the German order to arrest all Jews; the 1980 workers strike in Poland that began in a shipyard and moved on to establish a nationwide trade union – Solidarity – during a time of communist rule, a group that won control of the government in national elections of 1989; the 1983 Chilean protests against a decade of dictatorship by the Pinochet government; the Gandhi-led campaign of civil disobedience against British colonial rule over India in 1930–1931.

Explaining the power of nonviolent action in the case of India's noncooperation with British rule, the Study Guide for the film series states:

> But the British showed few signs of bending, and Gandhi turned to more aggressive forms of nonviolent action. He knew the British were vulnerable: they depended on those they ruled. Governments cannot govern if ordinary people do not pay taxes, obey laws or serve in the police and armed forces; wealthy property owners depend on people from the lower classes to pay them rent or work in their enterprises. When the people suspend this kind of cooperation, when they deny their consent to the ruling system, they are using power they intrinsically possess and coercing the government to deal with their demands.[383]

In the case of the Tennessee sit-ins, polite young people refused to leave "whites-only" food counters in the city and were finally beaten and taken to jail. Their treatment brought protest of many others followed by a boycott of the downtown stores. The economic impact of the boycott resulted in changes, including the rights of all to sit at the food counters.

The tactics shown in the film covered a wide range – protest marches, boycotts, deliberate breaking of the law and subsequent penalties for doing so, labor strikes, rent boycotts, evenings of noise making, meetings with those in power, renewed action when necessary, sabotage of orders, hiding Jews and sending them to safety in Sweden, slowdowns. The planning and organization was thorough, and the scope and involvement of people was massive.

The attributes of nonviolent direct action
- thorough and careful planning
- involvement of large numbers of grassroots supporters
- a wide variety of skills and tools
- effective communication
- creative responses
- willingness to risk for the good of the people

222

allow those involved to continue using their experiences to further the cause of democratic and just living even after their original objectives have been accomplished. Had they gained results instead by use of violence and destruction of resources, those people would have moved into positions of leadership experienced in violence and destruction as a means of attaining goals, not very desirable qualities in a democratic, just society.

The examples of committed, skilled, persevering, courageous men and women who chose to use nonviolent methods to effect change – either because of the morality of the methods, or their practicality, availability, and increased potential for success, or both – leave us a legacy for action that we must not brush aside.

~

Just as our gallop through America's wars brought out repeating patterns that our wars had in common, what can we learn from this gallop through nonviolence? These examples, among others, remind us that prevention of war is generally not accomplished by one person or organization alone, but is the result of many efforts combined. However, one individual has often been the visionary or the initiator of action that others joined. Rather than being mechanical and simply a matter of criteria to be met, the success of war prevention depends upon people and their relationships, openness, trust, and compassion and the empathy they spark in and receive from others. The work is often done by people of faith who believe in a power beyond themselves or in a cause greater than their own livelihood.

Those able to work effectively in violence prevention are sometimes those who have already been working in the area of the conflict for a long time and are known to be fair, respectful people. Other times, they are new acquaintances willing to offer third party facilitation.

Getting out of the surroundings of the conflict to another location – be it Norway, or elsewhere – and having informal time together rather than jumping into substance right away, can contribute positively to a satisfactory outcome.

Surprises happen.

Starting with common ground issues or areas of little disagreement can open the way for progress on difficult topics.

Sometimes serving as a potential witness or an accompanying person can be enough to forestall violence.

The work of reconciliation and war prevention is broad and includes education, development, opportunities for meaningful and life-supporting work, health, celebration and tradition, and other long term commitments to a just world. There is room for all to add their good work.

The examples given here indicate that even once conflict is upon us, we still have many ways to respond. We would be unrealistic and naive to think there will not be conflict in the world – serious, difficult, perplexing conflict. That is the reality of life when people of differing views and experiences and habits share a planet! But our response to those conflicts is our choice.

The extensive research of Erica Chenoweth and Maria Stephan presents us with dramatic truths: nonviolent civil resistance works, it works better than violence, and change brought about by nonviolent action more often results in democratic systems. (See www.ericachenoweth.com)

There is no excuse for declaring, "We have no other option but war."

Chapter 7
If Not War, Then What?[384]

Let us begin with words, and the power of words. Words not only reflect thought and describe happenings; they create thought and direct circumstance. Choosing carefully the words we use is an important first step to implementing change.

As individuals and as a nation, we can stop talking the "war is inevitable" line and start talking about options. When someone says, "There will always be wars," we can answer, "That is quite true if that is what we choose." If they say, "War is horrible; there is not one good thing that can be said about it, but sometimes we need it," we can reply, "When exactly is it that war is needed, and what can be done to keep things from getting that far?"

We can refuse to lump the warrior with the war, speaking of them as one. We can tell of our love for the soldier and who we know him or her to be. We can tell of our hate for war, and what we know it to be. We can also begin to hold the warrior accountable for the tool he or she uses – the methods of war – as we hold ourselves accountable for rallying for, asking for, voting for, or paying for its use.

We can refuse to call war noble and name it for what it is – tragic.

We can learn to use powerful words in asking questions that need answered.

First we must ask: What gives us the right?

- Why do we have the right to define who is dangerous and who is not, and use violence to back up our definition?
- Why do we have the right to develop and hold nuclear weapons and then determine who else should and who else shouldn't, and use violence to justify our determination?
- Why do we have the right to decide what leaders should be allowed to remain and what leaders should be destroyed, and use violence to accomplish that?
- Why do we have the right to determine what kinds of economies are workable and fair and good and which must be prevented from taking root, and use violence to do that preventing?

- Why do we have the right to determine what kinds of structures are acceptable and which are not and use violence to overthrow those we don't like?

When it all gets down to it, is it perhaps not that we shouldn't be passionate in our caring about the world? Not that we shouldn't try to create the kind of world we believe in? But doesn't our fault lie in the fact that we have become enamored with the idea that it can all be accomplished through violence, and as long as we have the power, we will use it?

Second, we must ask: What options do we have?

What do "the professionals" in government, to whom our system gives power, say when we ask them: "If war were not a possibility in this situation, what other options would we have?" Undoubtedly, with war drums beating, the answer comes back: "We've tried everything; we have no options left."

We could repeat the question: "But IF war were not an option at all now, what would we be able to try?" We could ask about the long-term impact and costs of those other options and how they might compare to the carnage and destruction of war. We could inquire about the moral and health effects on the participants and the victims in each scenario. We could ask what similar things have happened throughout history and how successful they were.

"But we don't have any other choice!" they repeat, a little louder. "We can't just sit back and do nothing, turn a blind eye, fail to respond."

"Hmmmmm … We seem to be stuck here. The inquiry wasn't about a military strike vs. sitting back and doing nothing. We are looking for a description of the alternatives we might take if military action were not an option."

"Well …"

Third, we must ask: Who else might know?

Is it possible that we're looking for leadership in international conflict resolution in the wrong places? Our political leaders seem to have, at best, a mixed record in dealing with conflict, and yet we allow them to go on using the same structures and resources that have repeatedly led us into war, and somehow hope for different results.

Instead we can let our leaders know that we expect them to seek out other untapped resources that hold potential for resolution, and to do so as a matter of standard procedure when faced with a difficult situation.

One resource is our universities with programs in international conflict resolution, in conjunction with top minds from universities around the world. Another would be the wisdom of our ambassadors worldwide, those who have worked internationally for years, joined by diplomats from other countries who have similar experience. What would Nobel Peace Laureates and leaders in peace and religious organizations say if they were called together to propose a plan to resolve a particular conflict? The US Institute of Peace could work with experts in international conflict resolution both in the United States and from around the world to have crews ready to help determine how best to resolve conflict that has remained unresolved or threatening.

What if we went to the United Nations and eagerly sought to learn from those gathered there, rather than to lobby or barter for their votes to approve our will? The experience and learning of these groups is not routinely utilized.

What if we asked our nation's teachers, doctors, and judges how the world might most effectively deal with conflict, and invited some of them to join their counterparts from around the world to consider the question and make proposals, or to consider a specific situation?

What could musicians tell us? India's Ravi Shankar said:

> It is my strong belief that if only all the political leaders of the world and officers of power in all sectors were a little musical, there would have been less violence and bloodshed and more harmony on this planet. Music is a universal language with no boundaries or prejudices.[385]

Perhaps those who use that other universal language could lead us into deeper dialogue with those we don't bother to hear or seek to understand.

There are conflict resolution practitioners on every continent who work in many circumstances, from the interpersonal to the international. They could be consulted, seriously, for advice.

What might the youth of our nation and the world have to tell us?

And then what would happen if we compared all those ideas, critically, with those of the voices saying that it's time for war?

Fourth, we must inquire: How can we resolve international conflicts and prevent violence, in a way that upholds basic human rights?

Because war does not. What if we chose not to declare those two goals – resolution/prevention and upholding human rights – as mutually exclusive? What if instead we began to ask exactly what we need to do for that to be accomplished? Douglas Fry frames the question this way:

> How can we improve the quality of life for all humanity, reduce the social and economic inequalities that foment hostility, hatred, and terrorism, and create new procedures and institutions for providing justice and resolving differences without war? In short, at the global level, how can we replace the law of force with the force of law?[386]

What if we stopped saying, "There will always be wars," and instead began discussing the alternatives we have or can create?

And finally, with the power of our words, let us ask ourselves and our nation:

What would happen to our perception of the necessity of war if we learned the stories of nonviolence and taught them in our schools and talked about them over supper and remembered them with co-workers and friends? What if communities celebrated them?

To say that war is horrid but necessary to restore peace disregards the many examples throughout history where the seemingly impossible was accomplished by nonviolent, yet determined and courageous, action. Let us renew our commitment to the power of creative, effective, human-rights-sustaining possibilities and the words that describe them.

Then let us look at our actions.

Who are we and how do we want to act as a country, as people who are also caring citizens of the world?

We want to be safe. We want to be respected and have our boundaries honored. We want to be treated fairly, and we want to act fairly toward others. We want to be comfortable and have fun and be healthy. We want to be compassionate and do good. We don't want to be bullies or cruel, insensitive tramplers of others or their rights. We want to lead by example. We want to work for just laws that will promote justice for all, and we want to live in cooperation with others, under the rule of those just laws. We want to replace violence and destruction in and of the earth with creativity and wholeness in and of the earth.

Yet our actions don't necessarily contribute to these desires. The United States has come to rely on military power and military destruction to assure its safety. In March 2003 the United States Government acted on a new policy of "preventive war" by invading and occupying Iraq. The government made a choice, led a choice, to start a war. If we truly want to replace violence and destruction in and of the earth, to lead by example, work for justice for all and live in cooperation with others, we must learn how to make a different choice. How? Helen Keller said in 1916, before the United States had entered World War I:

> You do not need to make a great noise about it. With the silence and dignity of creators you can end wars and the system of selfishness and exploitation that causes wars. All you need to do to bring about this stupendous revolution is to straighten up and fold your arms.[387]

We must learn what it means to straighten up and fold our arms, to stop supporting violence. We could decide to use the rule of law to deal with instances of crime (including the crimes labeled as terrorism). We could work to strengthen international cooperation and law and be willing to use it and be held accountable under it. We need to face American resistance to support international law. Do we believe in governance on the national level but think nothing is beneficial on the international level? Instead of acknowledging, working for, and optimizing justice in and advantages of international law, we have often waved our 6-guns high and called out, "Nobody's gunna tell the mighty old U. S. of A. what's good for our country!" We might learn something if we chose to listen.

What kind of international cooperation and agreements could we support? What do we fear? That we might have to change the way we do business in the world? That we might learn some things that would make us want to live differently? Have we placed our reliance on warfare to accomplish our goals, over the benefits of international cooperation for the common good? Do we believe in the common good?

We must ask how we can support the rule and conduct of just law in international affairs in a way that increases our safety yet does not compromise our ability to work fairly for our own needs.

The United Nations undoubtedly holds a key role in this question. It has had time to see what works and what doesn't work. It has world participation. Yet the U.N. has structures of decision-making in place that reflect inequities in power and control. These can be reexamined for fairness. It would require effort, but the U.S. could choose to be a leader in this endeavor. Individuals could talk about and build ideas for an effective United Nations capable of resolving disputes and offering the world a forum for establishing workable, just laws and a means of guiding the world through disarmament.

Douglas Fry states:

> There is no reason that third-party conflict management options such as mediation, arbitration, and adjudication could not be used in place of war. In an international system that has abolished war, trained mediators and arbitrators, operating under the auspices of the United Nations or other international and regional organizations, could assist with the handling of disputes among nations. International courts could be reserved for more serious cases, especially those dealing with violations of international law or human rights issues. ...
>
> Michael Renner provides some specific redesign proposals for improving the conflict prevention and resolution system of the United Nations. With an eye to prevention, an early warning office could monitor potential conflicts. Early warning reports spanning the globe could allow United Nations mediation and arbitration teams to respond quickly to prevent brewing disputes from escalating. ...
>
> As illustrated by the planned creation of the European Union, humans can exercise foresight and ingenuity to eliminate the threat of war through the design of higher levels of democratic government, complete with built-in conflict management procedures. ... Although more complicated, the same process conceivably could be accomplished at the global level. To argue otherwise is to belittle human ingenuity.[388]

We could immediately begin by referring disputes to international arbitration, knowing how difficult it is for a nation to view its own stance on conflict objectively or to understand any of the merits of an opponent's viewpoint.

Insisting that America seek to resolve disputes based on the merits of the situation rather than on our power to use violence and military might to control an outcome, will require a shift in our thinking and in our policy. Knowing that we can go to war to accomplish our goal cuts short the necessity of dialogue and the hard work of looking at all angles of the problem at hand – what has caused it, what is perpetuating it, what our role in the problem is, what we might be doing to make the situation worse, and what kinds of things could alleviate some or all of the problem. Ron Mock, professor at George Fox University, describes the need for this shift in method in his summary of effective responses to terrorism:

> The War on Terror will never end and the supply of new terrorists will never run out as long as we use the methods of violence to fight terrorist violence. … Others will always be ready to step forward as long as the conditions for terror and tyranny exist. Instead of fighting these scourges with their own tools, we need to create the conditions that keep them from taking root in a community. Democracy, markets, and the rule of law provide the means to get things done, as well as the cultural commitment to decisions on the merits, which make the resort to violence unnecessary and even counterproductive to a community's needs.[389]

We could acknowledge that a wise decision is more likely to be made based on the merits of the case rather than on the basis of who has the most destructive power available and is willing to kill or has already killed the most people, or who is willing to destroy or has already destroyed the most territory. Merit-based decision making is founded on dialogue, negotiation, hearing each other out, working together to reach solutions, and implementation of well-determined law.

We could build the defense of this country and the prosperity and peace of the world through education, health, and elimination of poverty – at home in America and, through our modeling, our personal involvement, and our fair dealings with others throughout the world. We could work to address the underlying causes of violent conflict and support actions that meet basic human needs everywhere.

Nicholas Kristof of the New York Times described education having a better record than military power in neutralizing extremism, adding, "For the cost of just one soldier in Afghanistan for one year, we could start about 20 schools there."[390] We could learn more about the hunches of well-informed journalists who have worked for years to research and bring to our attention realities that we may have overlooked.

We could commit to the attainable goal of safe drinking water for everyone in the world. We could work for the elimination of disease, for equitable and earth-sustaining use of resources. We could stop spending our collective money on destruction and use our money instead to fund things that bring health, understanding, and justice.

In the 1960s students were able to apply for NDSL loans – National Defense Student Loans – to help finance their college education. Education was seen as a key way of making our country strong and being a logical and significant part of any defense program. A broad, yet accurate, vision of "defense" could move our nation and the world away from violence.

We could teach problem-solving to school children, parents, workers, volunteers, political leaders, clergy, and make it common for "continuing education" in this area to be offered at community centers, schools, faith centers, and city halls. We could learn the ways of civility in our public (and private) dealings with others.

Every organization could have in its charter or by-laws or in its acknowledged traditions a recognized and agreed upon way of handling conflict within the organization, so that as its members work with others in many different settings, they become skilled at using effective problem-solving communication and processes, matter-of-factly, as a part of the work and play done there. These same organizations can also help others who might have seen the good work they do and the skill with which their members interact, as happened in the case of the City Montessori School in Lucknow, India, in late 1992.

They were a school, not a community mediation center, and certainly not a city hall or police force, but since they had long held the respect and trust of their community, they became pivotal players in an effort to bring calm and avoid the religious violence that was affecting many other cities at that time. Their willingness to embrace their role as community peacemakers and not opt out of responsibility because they were an educational institution, allowed them to step up to answer need when it arose and their help was requested.

They convened meetings in their school buildings throughout the city to allow people to be heard and to hear each other. Their parents, students, and teachers took the appeal to prevent violence directly to the streets, to the public, and hired jeeps with loudspeakers to carry the message of maintaining peace. They paraded behind the jeeps, carrying posters on which was written: "The name of God is both Hindu and Muslim." The absence of violence in the city was seen as remarkable.[391]

Similarly, individuals can offer their help as third party neutrals (or simply as caring people) as was the case of a woman who was asked to help lead reconciliation and problem-solving efforts for a women's service group that was caught in a time of disagreement and discouragement that made moving forward difficult. She declared that she was not a mediator, but since she was a trusted and respected member of the group and was asked to help, she did the work of one. Her skills and choices of procedures did not include street parades and jeeps with loudspeakers, but rather by a purposeful plan for hearing each person's concern, she helped reopen communication within the group.

But this is not the stuff of war and peace, one might say. To the contrary, it is very much the stuff of war and peace, and it applies directly to human understanding of potential and possibilities, the power of initiative and intervention, and the wide variety of ways people reach accord.

We could begin the shift from being consumers of things to being participants in experiences, and lead our economy, after basic needs, to a shift away from depletable resources to use of unlimited imagination.

Every youth could be given the challenge to serve for a year, in some area of the world. Adventure, service, and seeing ourselves as world citizens could stretch and educate the servers, as it meets needs for the hosts. We could invite youth from other parts of the world to come be of service to American needs.

We could build understanding by learning languages and studying other cultures and visiting other places. We could encourage exchange programs for students, workers, families, retirees, volunteers, around the world. We could expand pen pal, classroom, and video exchange programs.

We could let dreams of peacemaking become realities, as happened for that young man whose story opened this book, who worked as a teacher and saved money to make a world bike journey, in order to connect kids with each other and to classrooms around the world. He asked others to join him, and they created PeaceBike. A woman in her 80s read in a local newspaper about his travels of friendship around the globe. She stayed home, but wanted to journey with him, so followed his route on the Internet, encouraged him with messages, prayers, and small donations to keep him pedaling. Together they built peace – from home and from far away – and young lives were changed.[392] We could encourage more such creative cooperation: Worldsings, World Drama Nights, Host a Country dinners, international games tournaments and play days, "Playing for Change – Peace through Music" activities.[393]

But what about the need to defend ourselves from attack?

What if we do all of these great things and someone still comes after our homeland or the homeland of other innocents?

A deeply caring mother said of her son, soon to leave for the Marines, "Of course, I don't want my boy to have to go to war, but as long as I believe that war may be needed to protect our country, why do I think I have a right to keep my son safe from harm, and ask others' sons to take the risk for me and my family? So, yes, I'm scared for him, and I'm proud of him, all at the same time."[394]

"... as long as I believe that war may be needed to protect," she said. So it's fair to ask, does war protect us and make us safer from attack or invasion? Many believe it does not, and that, in fact, it does the opposite and actually increases antagonism and the potential for violent retaliation in both the immediate and the distant future. The Friends Committee on National Legislation has written in their booklet, "If War is Not the Answer, What Is? Peaceful Prevention of Deadly Conflict":

> Rather than applying the lessons of peaceful prevention that the international community has been gathering, however, the U.S. has reverted to the outdated tools of unilateralism and overwhelming military force – instruments which promise to fuel the threats of weapons of mass destruction and terrorist attacks. Military action may stamp out some elements of a threat, but it cannot remove the roots of conflict and may instead deepen their reach.[395]

The United States leads the world in military spending. We are proving to the world that a country that believes in peace, justice, equality, and liberty, also believes deeply in the efficacy of violence to settle disputes and protect itself from harm. "The Department of Defense is the world's largest employer, directly employing more than three million people.[2006]"[396] There are approximately 210 times more uniformed US armed forces than the combined numbers of our foreign service diplomatic corps and our overseas development workers. "There are substantially more people employed as musicians in Defense bands than in the entire foreign service."[397] With our massive and active military, including the military support of other nations involved in conflict, we invite violence against ourselves simply by setting a pattern to be followed, or to be responded to. It is not convincing to say that war is needed to keep us safe.

The destruction that occurred on September 11, 2001 was not met with a response under criminal law and justice, bringing to trial those responsible for the deeds. The US Government chose to begin the bombing of Afghanistan on October 7, 2001, launching the Afghanistan War. By December 1, 2001, more civilians had been killed in Afghanistan than all the deaths caused on September 11th in the United States. Details of these civilian deaths, carefully gleaned from international news reports and from survivors and eye witnesses, are recorded by Dr. Marc Herold in his "A Dossier on Civilian Victims of United States' Aerial Bombing of Afghanistan: A Comprehensive Accounting." It would be valuable "required reading" for Americans wishing to understand more about the short-term consequences of retaliating for violence with more violence and war. The war and the deaths continue still, over a decade later at the time of this writing.[398] Most Americans know little about the civilians killed in Afghanistan.

What message do we send to the world about violence and response to tragedy? That American lives matter; others aren't so important? That in order to retaliate for lives lost, we will use war, certain to cause more innocent lives lost, rather than restate and act on our belief in the rule of law, in cooperation with other countries?

The war in Iraq, though protested by millions of people around the world before it began, is a pre-emptive war begun by America against another nation.

The example set by the United States over years is echoed over and over again around the world. Of course, America did not invent war. We can honestly say, "We weren't even born yet." But after our birth as a nation, we used war again and again to meet our goals. We chose to see ourselves as new world leaders, yet in this area, we have remained as infants, stuck in the archaic, damaging, inhumane status quo. We have pushed its already horrid limits to the extreme. We have in our hands even deadlier weapons, and the US Government continues to develop still others, including robotic war machines that allow remote control killing by someone at a computer console who fires (or misfires) on a target thousands of miles away.

Such work sets a terrifying and extremely dangerous example to be followed by others. We have no moral basis for challenging those individuals, groups, or governments who rely on violence as well. Whether we call them terrorists or enemy or evil, they are simply following in our footsteps, and we in theirs. We create fear in others, and as we know, fear is often a basis for arming and attacking. We put ourselves in more danger by the very actions we propose will keep us safe. Those in the military who carry out these acts are thus contributing to our decreased safety.

Are there options that could make us safer from attack, avoid violence, and still be able to protect ourselves? Yes.

The United States could do much to reduce its own likelihood of reliance on war and to reduce the world's reliance on weaponry and war by leading the way in dynamic, verifiable, multilateral disarmament.

We could, on a national level, learn from those in the police forces of our cities and counties who have not only committed themselves to prevention, but have attempted to develop and use techniques and tools to stop aggression and harm, without taking human life or causing mass destruction of property. Though the Department of Defense has invested funds and innovation in developing non-lethal weapons and alternatives to violent force, and in training soldiers in their use, we don't hear much about that or Military Operations Other Than War (MOOTW) or similar programs these days.[399]

One must wonder how much money is spent on research and development of non-lethal alternatives vs. lethal weaponry, as well as on the study of methods of conflict resolution and deterrence of violence vs. warfare. Perhaps the contracts for such tools, i.e., those that immobilize opponents, aren't as appealing to corporations currently producing multi-million dollar weaponry that destroys opponents. Perhaps we wouldn't quite know what to do with opponents once they were immobilized anyway. It just might prove to be more productive and cost-effective to find alternatives before needing either the killing machines or immobilization techniques, and research into those alternatives might not take weapons contractors at all! It might require that we fund education, conflict resolution, and diplomacy, and let the weapons manufacturers' contracts go.

If my local power company can retrain meter readers put out of work because remotely-read digital meter systems have come in, and place them in other jobs in the company, surely we can retrain weapons manufacturing folks to move into careers in water resources, wind and solar energy, reasonable housing, sustainable agriculture, health and sanitation, and education. Just for starters.

We must wonder also if war is so entrenched in our military way of thinking that even the vocabulary used limits exploration into alternatives, as when a peace operations training is described as "peace operations wargame."[400] Is it possible that the military is not the arm of government most qualified to keep America safe and healthy? We might note our earlier statistics and ask if it should be turned around: Should the State Department and USAID have more people in their orchestras than the total personnel in our military branches combined ☺?[401] Are we long past due for a Department of Peace?

We could learn from those skilled in nonviolent action who have trained and organized individuals and groups to move into an area of conflict as observers, witnesses, deterring presence, or to act as accompaniers to people in danger. We could work under both governmental and non-governmental leadership, coordinating our efforts to study and develop strategies for nonviolent action on a large scale as an alternative to the large scale destructiveness of our current military strategies. These possibilities present risk, but they also offer an entirely different view of us to the opposing side, especially when accompanied by genuine efforts to open conversation and seek resolution of the situation, asking for the peaceful intervention of others able to negotiate, mediate, or even arbitrate on behalf of both of us.

Any conflicts that are resolved in this manner, mean one less outbreak of violence and one less call for war. President Truman led the United States in one such situation in 1948 when a return to the violence of World War II was very possible. The Soviet Union implemented a blockade of Berlin, cutting off West Berlin from all outside resources. Coal shipments were stopped, as was all electricity from the eastern side. Passenger and freight traffic in and out of Berlin was closed down. Moscow was determined to force the West to abandon the city and leave it to Soviet control. Truman could have asked Congress for power to move in with military force to open the lines of supply;

he certainly was not going to lose Berlin to the Soviets. Instead, he chose to order an airlift of supplies into Berlin:

> During the next eleven months, a massive airlift operation moved some 2,323,000 tons of food, coal, water, and other supplies into the city – with the average daily lift more than enough to supply the needs of the city. By May of 1949 it was clear to the Soviets that the allies could sustain the airlift indefinitely, and that their blockade of Berlin was futile. Moscow came back to the negotiating table, and soon, all restrictions to the city had been lifted. Thus the use of non-lethal airpower achieved the strategic objectives of US national policy in a major crisis without resort to war.[402]

One can readily see how such circumstances, portrayed in the fiery light of American responsibility to protect democracy, fight aggression, save innocents from violation of their human rights, and not-take-no-sass-from-nobody, could have easily led to war. Truman chose a way to address the immediate need, show determination and non-cooperation with the aggressive acts, and when the time was right, he used diplomacy rather than retaliation to reach resolve; war was averted.

~

Any conflict in which war is put on hold long enough to give nonviolence time to work means one less war now.

We can work for the elimination of war, one incident at a time, as it is replaced by alternatives. As the success of those alternatives is seen and more people become skilled in their use, the tide can change and the call for war be continuously diminished. If a cry for war did come, it would immediately be compared to well-known successful alternatives. The reasons for requesting war would be scrutinized and measured against the reasons given for pursuing alternatives. The cost of war would be weighed against the cost of alternatives, and the consequences of war with the consequences of other options. Most importantly, the public would not be taken in by the hype, the smooth, heart-tugging words declaring war as the only option, the words stirring fear within us and assuring us of the high moral uprightness of the government's plan. We would know a deeper story and see the pattern, and we would demand more of our leaders.

The habit of war can be broken.

We would have to give up "historical American patterns of war" – conquest and control of new lands and resources, retaliation by war against individuals' acts of violence, promoting the use of violence to gain power over a situation. We would probe our definition of "national interest" to see what conveniences of life style or economic gain (and for whom?) are the basis for our willingness to go to war, and we would challenge its legitimacy. As was stated in a US Department of Defense Annual Defense Report:

> "These goals [enhancing security, promoting prosperity, promoting democracy] underscore that the only responsible strategy for the United States is one of international engagement. Isolationism in any form would reduce U.S. security by undercutting the United States' ability to influence events abroad that can affect the well-being of Americans. This does not mean that the United States seeks the role of global policeman. But it does mean that America must be ready and willing to protect its interests, both now and in the future."[403]

Have we allowed the few to define America's interests? And determine that we will "protect" them through violence? Have we allowed ourselves to believe there is only a choice between isolationism or international engagement backed by military force?

~

Many in America are already at the point of saying these are needed changes. Many more, if there were alternatives that would be more effective and less costly than war, would easily choose those alternatives. We would make the wasteful and counter-productive level of spending on national defense superfluous and thereby eliminate justification for it. We would turn our own nation and the world away from the destructiveness of war to the creation of a world where war is no longer accepted by the public nor seen as an only option or even the best option by those with the power to carry it out.

Just as slavery was seen as an established American institution in the early days of our nation and is now looked back on with outrage and shame, so one day soon we can look back on the established American institution of war and be relieved that it is gone, a thing of our past, replaced with hard work, courage, and a steadily growing experience of effective means of resolving disputes and conflict without violence.

Other areas of society would transform as well. Instead of 7,029 Peace Corps Volunteers, we could have 70,029 or 700,029.

Instead of medical workers going on two week missions, we could have continuous, rotating health-worker exchanges among countries. Sabbaticals, even half- or quarter-year long, could be built in to the payment schedules and contracts of teachers, construction workers, city administrators, librarians, and others and to the self-employment planning of farmers and other business owners, so that they would have a portion of their earnings set aside to allow them to spend time working with communities in other countries on their most critical needs, learning from them in exchange.

All of these proactive, preventive measures would make the need for military defense much less likely. Young people looking for opportunities for meaningful work, service, or funding for college would not have to compromise their morals by becoming trained killers, nor would billions need to be spent on military recruiting, as war and the preparation for war lessened the need for a large military (and the trillions spent for that).

The brilliance, commitment, vision and leadership abilities of those who question the methods of soldiering or the technology and patterns of current warfare, yet are drawn to the work of their country's defense, could, rather than being recruited to plan and train for war, be challenged to move into careers that tackle the issue of national defense through peaceful means. They could be supported with funding adequate to allow for the research and practice that would be needed to develop a reliably powerful force, respected throughout the nation and the world as its work and methods became known and practiced. They would be the ones helping answer our question: How can we defend our nation, resolve international conflicts and prevent violence – in ways that uphold basic human rights?

Let us describe our vision for what can be:

We can be strong and safe and moral and free and live out our values in international relations as well as at our Fourth of July picnics and PTA meetings, our family reunions and school band concerts. We can be as accountable as a nation as we are as individuals. We can hold our heads high, expecting to use the same kind of fairness and honesty in our dealings in international affairs as we expect at home. We can cooperate with and encourage international resolution of conflict and support of law. We can see the CIA living according to the rule of law and human decency, with the need for secrecy continuously decreased by the openness that comes with working cooperatively and transparently with others.

We can free ourselves from the contradiction, the disconnect, of national promotion of violence in our dealings in the world, and personal striving for nonviolence in our families, schools, workplaces, and communities. We can be courageous and bold and inventive and willing to spend our lives in the declaration and practice of living together without the violence of war.

And until the time comes when our leaders catch up with that potential, we can continue to act. It doesn't have to be as long as one might think if we begin now to include them in our questioning and let them know this is a priority that impacts every other area of our lives. We can let our leaders know that we will support their efforts to resolve conflicts without violence, and that doing so is an evidence of wisdom and strength that we highly honor. We can let them know that we are willing to learn and adapt our lifestyles to a fairer and more just way of living in the world. That is the kind of leadership we need and want from them, to have them use their power and resources at hand to bring these things to the forefront and show us the way. We can echo the words of 19th century French short story writer Guy de Maupassant when he said: "It is as much the duty of anyone who governs to avoid war as it is the duty of the captain of a ship to avoid shipwreck."[404]

We can personally refuse to take part in war. We can personally encourage youth to find employment other than military employment. We can help them see that their military "service" could well make us less safe, and that we don't ask or want that from them. If their work in the military does not keep us and our families safe and protect our nation from danger, but in fact puts us at greater risk, we indeed have a right to challenge their choice, because it affects us.

We would do well to invite them into conversation about recruitment pressure, alternatives more humane and effective than war, and options for employment and other benefits promised as a part of the recruitment. Although the reasons for seeking military employment likely would not include "going into war," it must be recognized that that is the bottom line means to our goals. We can support these youth as they explore options that might seem to them elusive or impossible to reach, and certainly harder to work out than signing their name on the line.

We can share with them the concise, bold, and clearly presented book, *10 Excellent Reasons Not to Join the Military*, because they will have many opportunities to be sold another story, and because taking a few hours to read about the consequences of their decision on the rest of their life is valid.[405]

We can describe many other things they might do that could bring more positive benefits to the world and more safety to our country and our families. We could encourage their desire for adventure, whether it be for overseas travel, service to country or an unexplored opportunity they found compelling right at home. We can let them know we honor them for choices they make to support life and goodness rather than training to destroy life. We can personally refuse to use the "marketing words" for the deception that war propaganda perpetuates.

We could insist that before we perpetuate the notion that wars are fought to protect our freedom, we will learn to finish our sentences. Our freedom to do what, exactly? To do more of what was done through the wars we've been involved with in the past? The study of our history makes that a hollow excuse for war. We need to stop claiming that the military is fighting and wars are being fought to protect our freedom. We are deceiving ourselves.[406]

We can immediately establish our own personal plan for getting information of a more balanced nature, identifying resources with a broader perspective than that of the official government stance. Then, should a crisis mount, we will already be in the habit of information input from sources giving various perspectives on the issue. We can recognize that it is simply illogical to think that our governments are not biased. The American government, for example, is comprised of American structures, policies, experiences, and goals, and it would be expected to see things in that American light. We have already seen that there are patterns of official propaganda, partial or incorrect information given as fact, secrecy, cultural and economic bias, greed and power, misinterpretation, impatience, and short-sightedness in governmental information about conflict and war. Thus even without saying a purposeful misleading of the public could be expected, one must recognize that the information given us is limited in its ability to inform us well and fully about an issue.

Unless we wish only to know one viewpoint – that which our government is giving out at the time – we must look further. We can especially challenge what we are being told we must fear. Fear sells. It tends to override doubt, reluctance, and curiosity. Knowing that patterns of creating fear, for whatever reason, have been a part of our history and a clearly recognized means of getting a populace behind the call to go to war, we can push through the rhetoric and the emotion to inquiry.

We can note the tendency of media to rely on official government information as its source. It also is influenced by its own financial needs and advertisers. Rather than assume it has no bias or misinformation, and that it will tell us what we need to know, we can encourage the media to report on what concerns us. We can let them know we honor the importance of speaking the truth as it is seen and heard. We can establish international friendships and ask their perspective on what's happening. We can seek out news from other countries to find varying viewpoints. It is wise and necessary to establish a variety of sources of input. It doesn't have to be a constant bombardment by multitudes of media, but a personal plan that works to gain insight from differing perspectives.

We can teach our children and grandchildren that there are choices other than war, even if we took part in war ourselves, even if we are not personally sure that a certain alternative will always work. We can teach them that war happens because people choose it and people start it. We can learn and tell them the stories, show them the movies, and read with them the examples of nonviolent action that brought about social change or change in governments.

We can help children learn and experience themselves as world citizens as well as children of their homeland. We can personally head to the library and find the books, the stories that tell of others from around the world and their experiences. We can celebrate the fun it is to travel through a book into other lands, as described in the words of a little poem titled *Corremos*:

> *Para comprender la vida de otros*
> *Es bueno ir y bueno ver.*
> *Pero si no tenemos aviones,*
> *Corremos a los libros – para leer, leer.*[407]

We can study a language or languages other than our "mother tongue" or at least not be irritated when we encounter a language different from our own, or expect everyone else to learn my language rather than making the effort to learn theirs. (We might even be curious enough to check a footnote to see if there might be a translation in the back of the book.) A librarian friend, and master champion of books and reading, also reminded me that sometimes we can skip both the planes and the library and go directly to "other lands" folks who often live just down the street.

We can encourage children to learn to be better problem-solvers than we have been, and then learn from them, so that their confidence in what they find to work helps dispel our doubts.

⌒

We return to the question that opened this book. Carved into stone in the Franklin Roosevelt Memorial in Washington, D.C. are his words: "More than an end to war, we want an end to the beginnings of all wars." That excerpt is from a speech he wrote the night before he died of a cerebral hemorrhage:

> We seek peace – enduring peace. More than an end to war, we want an end to the beginnings of all wars – yes, an end to this brutal, inhuman, and thoroughly impractical method of settling the differences between governments. … The work, my friends, is peace, more than an end of this war – an end to the beginning of all wars, yes, an end, forever, to this impractical, unrealistic settlement of the differences between governments by the mass killing of peoples.[408]

Even though Roosevelt declared war impractical, brutal, and unrealistic, he also showed us by example that patterns are hard to break. We have to want change passionately, and then act consistently with that desire. Roosevelt was not able to do that. We must learn about the conditions that allow a beginning of war to happen, and work to prevent that condition. We can realize that being on the brink of war is a dangerous stance. We can encourage statesmanship over "brinkmanship."

We can learn communication skills and problem-solving skills and put them to use in our own families, organizations, and places of work. We can practice how to listen and "bounce back" what we've heard, in family meetings or around the dinner table when things don't seem absolutely critical, so that when they are critical, we will know how to use these skills. The next time we are criticized, we can pause, and instead of defending ourselves or explaining why the other person is wrong, we can sincerely "bounce back" what we've heard them say, in order to learn if we have understood right and to give them a chance to explain more. Once we have listened and learned all we can from them, only then we might ask to explain something from our perspective. It's harder to do than it sounds. But it can help establish a pattern of intentional effective listening, one of life's most important communication skills.

We can recognize that the experiment in personal liberty and representative government that became the United States of America is not to be taken for granted, and that for it to be carried on, it must have the involvement of its people. We can discover the ways of involvement that bring about awareness, change, and action, and that hold our elected officials accountable.

If we concur with Abraham Lincoln's stance regarding the Mexican-American War, that it is not for the "King" to decide if we go to war, but a matter so grave and so oppressive, so likely to impoverish people while pretending that their good is the object, that it requires the decision of Congress – the representatives of the people of the United States – we must be the people who let Congress know what we expect and require. They are to deliberate on what war is as a way of settling disputes in today's world, on the complexities of conflict that are not resolved by war, on the costs and consequences of war-making, and on the many more effective and humane options that could be pursued. And we speak out and act on our expectations and our requirements.

We can celebrate the work of our patriot-peacemakers in many walks of life for holding a light by which we come to see more clearly what we are doing, and for finding ways of creating change and making justice a reality.

We can find ways to use the flag or songs or words to promote wholesome American values and recognition of our role as caring world citizens, and refuse to wave or display the flag to promote violence or war or to add to a rage that calls for violence.

We can find answers that will stop the beginnings of war.

John Horgan, in his book, *The End of War*, challenges us to begin by living and acting honestly:

> We claim to revere peace and human rights – and yet we keep embarking on unnecessary wars, in which we treat alleged enemies and even civilians cruelly. We pay lip service to the principles of national sovereignty and international law while secretly carrying out deadly commando raids and drone attacks around the world. We sell weapons to other nations, and to their adversaries. We prop up dictators if they let us build military bases on their land, exploit their cheap labor, or sell us their oil and other resources at low prices. We are guilty of shameful hypocrisy. If we practiced what we preached – if we showed through our actions that we

recognize how wrong war is – we Americans could lead the entire world to an enduring peace.[409]

Horgan looks toward the time when war between nations will be inconceivable, a time of "imaginative, courageous leadership."[410]

We would do well to become imaginative, courageous citizens, probably the surest way of creating within leadership the vision and hope they need to act courageously. Each of us does not have to do it all. But we can each start by doing one thing.

⌇

After speaking of the end of war, the beginning I suggest may at first sound minuscule, but there is a reason behind it. I suggest we begin by choosing one way to communicate better, a plan written down and referred to over and over again until we have learned and practiced the skill, making it a habit. Second, I challenge us each to name one thing we want to learn about and find a book or some other resource on it, and then ask somebody else their opinion about what we've read or learned. We can try out our newly designed plan for information input on this topic. Next, we can choose one thing to stop doing or saying. These three things can be the base for a personal shift in our habits, causing an awareness of our power to act positively and to change.

Then, and soon, we can do one thing about war itself. It can be defined as broadly as we wish, as long as we do something. For it's been said: "It's easier to act your way into a new way of thinking than to think your way into a new way of acting."[411] So we must determine one thing we can do to act against war. And then join someone or some group of people who will act with us, so that we may learn from them and take encouragement from working together, as we in turn inspire others by our commitment and hopefulness.

We must refuse to be directed or manipulated by those who cannot or will not move away from a reliance on war. We must continue to question, learn, and discover the answers.

As author of this book, I do not need to have or propose all the answers. I am one person. I have become passionate about the insanity of war as a method of national security and defense and for attaining our "national interests" or doing good in the world. Yet it is not for me to describe all that each one of us can do.

Yours is the challenge too. You may spark an idea that grabs the imagination of your community – or of the world. You may find ways of telling your own story of hope that will cause someone else to see things in a new way. You can join with millions of others who choose to do something to challenge America and this world to stop and take a new path.

~

This book was finished, though not yet published, when my husband and I heard a radio interview with author and visionary for a better world, David Swanson. He was to speak in Portland, Oregon, that night. We looked at each other and said, "Let's go." I am still startled by what I learned that evening. For the past few years I had been pouring over materials about America's wars. I'd been studying history books, articles, websites, news reports, and commentary on both current affairs and our past. But as David spoke, I realized how fully, even with this research, I remained a part of *What America Missed in U.S. History Class*. His topic held great significance.

David told how the nations of the world renounced war as an instrument of national policy in their relations with one another and agreed to settle all disputes – of whatever nature or origin – by peaceful means. And it wasn't thousands of years ago; it was 1928, when the reality of what happens when the world goes to war was still so vivid in their lives. The Kellogg-Briand Pact is a work initiated by the French and the Americans and joined by many other nations. The American people not only rallied behind its adoption by US political leaders, but were instrumental in this effort to outlaw war. Governments around the world acknowledged the will and determination of their people to move beyond war, and responded with this commitment to a new beginning, a "sacred promise," as Frank Kellogg, US Secretary of State, was to describe it. The story is recorded in Swanson's book, *When the World Outlawed War*.

I checked the 1,052-page US History textbook I had recently purchased. Yes, it was there, all two sentences. Two sentences.

David explained that the treaty is still on the books. It was ratified by the US Senate. It is officially the law of the land. It was used in the Nuremberg trials after World War II, against defendants charged with "Conspiracy to Commit Crimes Against Peace." Swanson continues,

> The Chief Prosecutor at Nuremberg, US Supreme Court Justice Robert H. Jackson, said in his opening statement:
> "And let me make clear that while this law is first applied against German aggressors, the law includes, and if it is to serve a

useful purpose it must condemn aggression by any other nations, including those which sit here now in judgment."[412]

During a time when people would not accept war as "just the way things are and ever will be," there was a mass movement to do away with it entirely. That movement included farmers, churches, businesses, academics, peace organizations, parent-teacher groups, editors, youth, veterans, politicians, people with a passion to end war. Swanson's listing is impressive, and includes the National Committee on the Cause and Cure of War, a coalition of women's groups with five million women, who organized locally and nationally, relentlessly pressing for the treaty and its ratification by the Senate in January 1929. It passed, and was signed into law by President Coolidge on January 17, 1929.

Yet patterns are hard to break, and governments with power and the will to use war, notwithstanding the Pact, did so and do so, including the United States Government. That does not mean that the power of the people failed to light the way to what could be. Nor does it mean that we should abandon the law, any more than we should remove all stop signs because someone failed to stop. The largely forgotten story of the millions who carried this light of peace needs to be re-told and re-learned. When the masses once again come to believe that war should be stopped, and determine that they will find, develop, and use alternatives, it can happen.

But the masses aren't just the other guy.

What will be your first step?

_____

_____

_____

_____

_____

_____

This I know:

We must speak the truth about war, boldly.

War is destructive.

War is wasteful.

War is cruel.

War carries within it the seeds of resentment and retaliation.

War reinforces the use of violence and power over others

as a basis for making decisions.

Power is not a substitute for wisdom or for justice.

War is unworthy of humankind.

We can build new habits if we choose to do so.

We can find alternatives.

Many are here now, ready to be used.

One conflict resolved without violence

builds potential for another.

And another. And another.

It is time. It's time!

For a world beyond war.

Sometimes, one just needs to speak up. – Wisdom from
The Emperor's New Clothes by Hans Christian Andersen

Endnotes

1   Roosevelt, Franklin D. These words are written into the stone at the Franklin Roosevelt Memorial in Washington, D.C. The phrase is excerpted from an address written the night before he died. It was to have been delivered to the nation by radio in honor of Thomas Jefferson on Jefferson Day, April 14, 1945. The complete sentence is used on page 244.

2   Beckwith, Tad. "On the Trail: Journals from the Road, Sunday, October 7, 2001 – Tuesday, October 9, 2001." PeaceBike, First Expedition. www.peacebike. org. Web. 26 Nov 2012. Also see www.peacebikejourney.org.

3   Reference was to the assassination of Sheikh Ahmed Yassin as he was leaving a mosque after morning prayers on March 22, 2004, an attack that also killed two of his body guards and five bystanders and injured others. Wright, George and agencies. "Israel assassinates Hamas leader." *guardian.co.uk*. N.p., 22 Mar 2004. Web. 16 Apr 2010. http://www.guardian.co.uk/world/2004/mar/22/israel1.

4   Iraq War Veteran. Yamhill Valley Peacemakers. Linfield College, McMinnville, OR. 06 May 2009. Address.

5   Chapter title is borrowed from Professor Ralph Beebe, George Fox University, Newberg, Oregon, and his class syllabus for "War and Conscience in United States History," Fall 2009.

6   Jackson, Matthew O. and Massimo Morelli. "The Reasons for Wars – an Updated Survey." Pg. 6. Dec 2009. Web. 28 Apr 2010. http://www.stanford. edu/~jacksonm/war-overview.pdf.

7   "Pig War," and "War of the Golden Stool." Web. 28 Apr 2010. http:// en.wikipedia.org/wiki/Pig_War; http://en.wikipedia.org/wiki/War_of_the_ Golden_Stool.
Sweet, Julie Ann. "The War of Jenkins' Ear," History & Archaeology: Colonial Era, 1733–1775, New Georgia Encyclopedia, Georgia Humanities Council and the University of Georgia Press, 13 Feb 2003, edited 04 Mar 2013. Web. 03 Sep 2013. http://www.georgiaencyclopedia.org/articles/history-archaeology/war-jenkins-ear
"The Northern War," NZ History, History Group of the New Zealand Ministry for Culture and Heritage. Web. 03 Sep 2013. http://www.nzhistory.net.nz/war/ northern-war. ("This conflict has also been called the 'Flagstaff War' and 'Hone Heke's Rebellion.'")

8   "The Pig War: San Juan Island National Historic Park." *National Park Service, Department of the Interior.* N.p., n.d. Web. 12 Jul 2010. http://www.nps.gov/sajh/historyculture/the-pig-war.htm.

9   "Pig War." Web. 28 Apr 2010. http://en.wikipedia.org/wiki/Pig_War

10   In 1871 the question of ownership of the San Juan Islands was referred to arbitration by the British and the Americans. Arbitration was directed by Kaiser Wilhelm I of Germany and was carried out by three men working for nearly a year to reach a decision. War in the San Juans was successfully avoided. (See http://www.nps.gov/sajh/historyculture/the-pig-war.htm)

11   Hall-Quest, Olga. *From Colony to Nation.* New York: Dutton, 1966. 28. Print.

12   Lossing, Benson, J. "A line by line analysis of the accusations of the Declaration of Independence ." *ColonialHall.com.* N.p., 21 Aug 2008. Web. 18 Mar 2010. http://colonialhall.com/histdocs/declaration/declarationanalysis05.php

13   "George Mason and the American Revolution." *Gunston Hall, Home of George Mason.* [citing: Robert A. Rutland, ed. The Papers of George Mason (Chapel Hill, NC: The University of North Carolina Press, 1970) 1:127–30.], n.d. Web. 18 Mar 2010. http://www.gunstonhall.org/georgemason/essays/revolution.html.

14   Wells, Ronald A., Ed. *The Wars of America - Christian Views.* (2nd ed.) Macon, Georgia: Mercer University Press, 1991. 14–15. Print.

15   Stewart, Gail B. *America's Wars: The Revolutionary War.* San Diego, CA: Lucent Books, 1991. 64–65. Print.

16   Ibid., 86.

17   Ibid., 104–105.

18   Hall-Quest, Olga. *From Colony to Nation.* New York: Dutton, 1966. 96. Print.

19   "Principal Wars in Which the United States Participated: U.S. Military Personnel Serving and Casualties (Military Casualty Information, DoD Principal Wars)." *U.S. Department of Defense.* N.p., May 2008. Web. 25 Mar 2010. http://siadapp.dmdc.osd.mil/personnel/CASUALTY/WCPRINCIPAL.pdf

20   Stewart, Gail B. *America's Wars: The Revolutionary War.* San Diego, CA: Lucent Books, 199. 75. Print.

21   White, Matthew. "Statistics of Wars, Oppressions and Atrocities of the Eighteenth Century." *Historical Atlas of the Twentieth Century.* N.p., Jun 2005. Web. 25 Mar 2010. http://users.erols.com/mwhite28/wars18c.htm.

22   Daggett, Stephen. "CRS Report for Congress: Costs of Major U.S. Wars." *Federation of American Scientists.* Congressional Research Service: Library of

Congress, 24 Jul 2008. Web. 24 Mar 2010. http://www.fas.org/sgp/crs/natsec/ RS22926.pdf. (Daggett explains the methods by which costs have been estimated, noting that figures are only for the specific military operation costs and do not include any expenses of veterans' benefits, interest on war debt, assistance to allies, cost of reconstruction, diplomatic security, or costs of "recruiting, paying, training, and equipping standing military forces." He further notes that the conversion from original costs to 2008 dollar equivalency is problematic for several reasons and results in "a rough exercise."

23   Small, Melvin. *Was War Necessary?* Beverly Hills, CA: Sage Publications, 1980. 44. Print.

24   Ibid., 53–54.

25   Wells, Ronald A., Ed.. *The Wars of America - Christian Views.* (2nd ed.) Macon, Georgia: Mercer University Press, 1991. 1. Print. Quoting Maldwyn A. Jones, "American Wars," *The United States: A Companion to American Studies,* ed. Dennis Welland, London: Methuen, 1974. 45.

26   "Battle of New Orleans." *Wikipedia.* N.p., Web. 25 Mar 2010. http://enwiki-pedia.org/wiki/Battle_of_New_Orleans.

27   "Principal Wars in Which the United States Participated: U.S. Military Personnel Serving and Casualties (Military Casualty Information, DoD Principal Wars)." *U.S. Department of Defense.* N.p., May 2008. Web. 25 Mar 2010. http://siadapp.dmdc.osd.mil/personnel/CASUALTY/WCPRINCIPAL.pdf

28   White, Matthew. "Statistics of Wars, Oppressions and Atrocities of the Nine-teenth Century." *Historical Atlas of the Twentieth Century.* N.p., Jun 2005. Web. 25 Mar 2010. http://users.erols.com/mwhite28/wars19c.htm.

29   Taylor, R. "Summary of the End of the War of 1812." *The War of 1812 Website, MilitaryHeritage.com.* Web. 25 Mar 2010. http://www.warof1812.ca/summary.html.

30   Daggett, Stephen. "CRS Report for Congress: Costs of Major U.S. Wars." *Federation of American Scientists.* Congressional Research Service: Library of Congress, 24 Jul 2008. Web. 24 Mar 2010. http://www.fas.org/sgp/crs/natsec/RS22926.pdf.

31   The official US date set for listing veterans of Indian Wars is January 1, 1817, through December 31, 1898 (Torreon, Barbara Salazar. "U.S. Periods of War," *Congressional Research Service.* 25 Mar 2010. Web. http://assets.opencrs.com/rpts/RS21405_20100107.pdf). However, using those dates is not to suggest that war against Native Americans did not occur before 1817. Also, Native Americans were involved in early U.S. declared wars, both the Revolutionary War and the War of 1812, on both sides of the conflict.

32   O'Donnell, Terence, *An Arrow in the Earth: General Joel Palmer and the Indians of Oregon*, Portland, OR: Oregon Historical Society Press, 1991. 291. Print.

33   Ibid., 129, 151, 159, 166, 169.

34   Quoting the words of the Indian leader Stickus to Joel Palmer and Governor of Washington Territory, Isaac Stevens, in a council at which thousands of Indians were expected at Walla Walla, Washington, in May 1855: O'Donnell, Terence, *An Arrow in the Earth: General Joel Palmer and the Indians of Oregon*, Portland, OR: Oregon Historical Society Press. 1991. 196, 201. Print.

35   Beckham, Stephen Dow. *Oregon Indians: Voices from Two Centuries.* Corvallis, OR: Oregon State University Press, 2006. 82. Print.

36   Ibid., 265.

37   Ibid., 131.

38   O'Donnell, Terence, *An Arrow in the Earth: General Joel Palmer and the Indians of Oregon*, Portland, OR: Oregon Historical Society Press, 1991. 48. Print. Quoting : B.F. Dowell to Frances Victor, H.H. Bancroft microfilm, reel 3, Bancroft Library, University of California, Berkeley, 4 (Oregon Historical Society Microfilm 176).

39   Ibid., 165–66.

40   O'Donnell, Terence, *An Arrow in the Earth: General Joel Palmer and the Indians of Oregon*, Portland, OR: Oregon Historical Society Press, 1991. 169. Print.

41   Ibid., 214.

42   "Text of the Northwest Ordinance (1787)." *Archiving Early America.* N.p., n.d. Web. 26 Mar 2010. http://www.earlyamerica.com/earlyamerica/milestones/ordinance/text.html

43   Stephens, Joe K. "Oregon Judicial Department History: History Pre-Statehood, Oregon." *State of Oregon Law Library.* N.p., n.d. Web. 26 Mar 2010. http://www.oregon.gov/SOLL/OJD_History/HistoryOJDPart1.shtml.

44   O'Donnell, Terence, *An Arrow in the Earth: General Joel Palmer and the Indians of Oregon*, Portland, OR: Oregon Historical Society Press, 1991. 176. Print.

45   Beckham, Stephen Dow. *Oregon Indians: Voices from Two Centuries.* Corvallis, OR: Oregon State University Press, 2006. 219. Print.

46   Ibid., 140.

47   "Historical Value of U.S. Dollar (Estimated)." Web. 28 Apr 2010. http://mykindred.com/cloud/TX/Documents/dollar/

48   O'Donnell, Terence, *An Arrow in the Earth: General Joel Palmer and the Indians of Oregon*, Portland, OR: Oregon Historical Society Press, 1991. 201. Print.

49   Ibid., 141.

50   Ibid.

51   Ibid., 168.

52   Kentta, Robert. "A Siletz History." 2000. *Siletz Tribal Newspaper* (Parts 1 – 15). Part 7. Print. Also located on the website of the Confederated Tribes of Siletz Indians at: http://www.ctsi.nsn.us/chinook-indian-tribe-siletz-heritage/our-history/part-i.

53   O'Donnell, Terence, *An Arrow in the Earth: General Joel Palmer and the Indians of Oregon*, Portland, OR: Oregon Historical Society Press, 1991. 251–252. Print.

54   Kentta, Robert. "A Siletz History." 2000. *Siletz Tribal Newspaper* (Parts 1 – 15). Part 8. Print. Also located on the website of the Confederated Tribes of Siletz Indians at: http://www.ctsi.nsn.us/chinook-indian-tribe-siletz-heritage/our-history/part-i.

55   Beckham, Stephen Dow. *Oregon Indians: Voices from Two Centuries.* Corvallis, OR: Oregon State University Press, 2006. 259. Print.

56   Ibid., 259–270.

57   "Treaty with the Middle Oregon Tribes, November 15, 1865." *First People.* N.p., n.d. Web. 12 July 2011. http://www.firstpeople.us/FP-Html-Treaties/TreatyWithTheMiddleOregonTribes1865.html. Also found: Ibid., 208–210.

58   Beckham, Stephen Dow. *Oregon Indians: Voices from Two Centuries.* Corvallis, OR: Oregon State University Press, 2006. 234. Print.

59   O'Donnell, Terence, *An Arrow in the Earth: General Joel Palmer and the Indians of Oregon*, Portland, OR: Oregon Historical Society Press, 1991. 129. Print.: Quoting Peter H. Burnett, *An Old California Pioneer*, Oakland, CA, Biobooks, 1946. 89–90.

60   White, Matthew. "Statistics of Wars, Oppressions and Atrocities of the Nineteenth Century." *Historical Atlas of the Twentieth Century.* N.p., Jun 2005. Web. 25 Mar 2010. http://users.erols.com/mwhite28/wars19c.htm.

61   O'Donnell, Terence, *An Arrow in the Earth: General Joel Palmer and the Indians of Oregon*, Portland, OR: Oregon Historical Society Press, 1991. 155. Print.

62   "Historical Value of U.S. Dollar (Estimated)." Web. 30 Apr 2010. http://mykindred.com/cloud/TX/Documents/dollar/

63   Fisher, Louis, Specialist in Constitutional Law. "The Mexican War and Lincoln's 'Spot Resolutions.'" (Referring to words of Rep. Garrett Davis in the U.S. House of Representatives.) *Library of Congress.* The Law Library of Congress, James Madison Memorial Building, 18 Aug 2009, 2–3. Web. 12 Jul 2010. http://www.loc.gov/law/help/usconlaw/pdf/Mexican.war.pdf.

64   Goodell, William. "This Is a War for Slavery." 1852. *We Who Dared to Say No to War: American Antiwar Writing from 1812 to Now.* Murray Polner and Thomas E. Woods, Jr.. Philadelphia: Basic Books (Perseus Books Group), 2008. 33–45. Print.

65   Fisher, Louis, Specialist in Constitutional Law. "The Mexican War and Lincoln's 'Spot Resolutions.'" *Library of Congress.* The Law Library of Congress, James Madison Memorial Building, 18 Aug 2009. Web. 12 Jul 2010. http://www. loc.gov/law/help/usconlaw/pdf/Mexican.war.pdf.

66   Ibid.

67   Ibid.

68   "The Treaty of Guadalupe Hidalgo; February 2, 1848." *Yale Law School, Lillian Goldman Law Library, The Avalon Project – Documents in Law, History, and Diplomacy.* Treaties and Conventions between the United States of America and Other Powers Since July 4, 1776, Washington, DC: Government Printing Office, 1871. Web. 18 Mar 2010. http://avalon.law.yale.edu/19th_century/guadhida.asp.

69   Grant, Ulysses S. "Personal Memoirs of U.S. Grant, Volume 1." Jul 1885. *North Central Washington Portal.* N.p., 18 Jul 2006. Web. 13 Jul 2010. http:// ncwportal.com/community/ulysses_simpson_grant.

70   "Principal Wars in Which the United States Participated: U.S. Military Personnel Serving and Casualties (Military Casualty Information, DoD Principal Wars)." *U.S. Department of Defense.* N.p., May 2008. Web. 25 Mar 2010. http://siadapp.dmdc.osd.mil/personnel/CASUALTY/WCPRINCIPAL.pdf

71   White, Matthew. "Statistics of Wars, Oppressions and Atrocities of the Nineteenth Century." *Historical Atlas of the Twentieth Century.* N.p., Jun 2005. Web. 25 Mar 2010. http://users.erols.com/mwhite28/wars19c.htm.

72   Daggett, Stephen. "CRS Report for Congress: Costs of Major U.S. Wars." *Federation of American Scientists.* Congressional Research Service: Library of Congress, 24 Jul 2008. Web. 24 Mar 2010. http://www.fas.org/sgp/crs/natsec/ RS22926.pdf.

73   "The Constitution of the Confederate States of America." Civil War Preservation Trust. 18 Aug 2009 http://www.civilwar.org/education/history/primarysources/csconstitution.html

74   Wells, Ronald A., Ed. *The Wars of America – Christian Views.* (2nd ed.) Macon, Georgia: Mercer University Press, 1991. 104. Print.

75   Rob Lopresti, "Which U.S. Presidents Owned Slaves." Web. 1 Oct 2009. http://www.nas.com/~lopresti/ps.htm.

76   "Highlights of Percy Skuy History of Contraception Gallery – The Civil War: Sex and Soldiers." Case Western Reserve University. Web. 15 Jul 2013. http://www. case.edu/affil/skuyhistcontraception/online-2012/Civil-War.html

77   Biel, Timothy Levi. *The Civil War (America's Wars* series). San Diego, CA: Lucent Books,1991. 8, 121. Print.

78   Ibid., 126.

79   Grant, Ulysses S. "Personal Memoirs of U.S. Grant, Volume 1." Jul 1885. XVI. *North Central Washington Portal.* N.p., 18 Jul 2006. Web. 13 Jul 2010. http:// ncwportal.com/community/ulysses_simpson_grant.

80   Hill, Samuel S. Jr. "Could the Civil War Have Been Prevented?" [Originally published in *Christian Century,* 31 Mar 1976. 304–308.] Web. 1 May 2010. http:// www.religion-online.org/showarticle.asp?title=1833

81   Grant, Ulysses S. "Personal Memoirs of U.S. Grant, Volume 1." XVI. July 1885. *North Central Washington Portal.* N.p., 18 Jul 2006. Web. 13 Jul 2010. http:// ncwportal.com/community/ulysses_simpson_grant.

82   "War of 1812 – Course of the War," Wikipedia. Web. 17 Jul 2013. http:// en.wikipedia.org/wiki/War_of_1812

83   "James Buchanan: Fourth Annual message to Congress on the State of the Union." (December 3, 1860) *The American Presidency Project.* americanpresidency. org. University of California at Santa Barbara. 19 Aug 2009 http://www.presidency. ucsb.edu/ws/index.php?pid=29501.

84   Mock, Ron. *Loving Without Giving In: Christian Responses to Terrorism & Tyranny.* Telford, PA: Cascadia Publishing House, 2004. 190. Print.

85   Leland, Ann, and Mari-Jana "M-J" Oboroceanu. "American War and Military Operations Casualties: Lists and Statistics." *Federation of American Scientists.* Congressional Research Service: Library of Congress, 26 Feb 2010. Web. 24 Mar 2010. http://www.fas.org/sgp/crs/natsec/RL32492.pdf (Congressional Research Service estimates Civil War deaths to be 524,332 to 529,332, based on incomplete returns from Confederate sources regarding the number of Confederate soldiers who died in Union prisons – between 26,000 and 31,000.)

86   White, Matthew. "Statistics of Wars, Oppressions and Atrocities of the Nineteenth Century." *Historical Atlas of the Twentieth Century.* N.p., Jun 2005. Web. 25 Mar 2010. http://users.erols.com/mwhite28/wars19c.htm.

87   "Americans Killed in Action, Numbers, American War Library." 22 Mar 2007. The American War Library. Web. 25 Apr 2008. http://members.aol.com/usregistry/allwars.htm.

88   Daggett, Stephen. "CRS Report for Congress: Costs of Major U.S. Wars." *Federation of American Scientists.* Congressional Research Service: Library of

Congress, 24 Jul 2008. Web. 24 Mar 2010. http://www.fas.org/sgp/crs/natsec/
RS22926.pdf.

89   Morgan, H. Wayne. *America's Road to Empire: The War with Spain and Overseas Expansion*. New York: Wiley, 1965. 41. Print.

90   Ibid., 13.

91   Ibid., 53.

92   Wells, Ronald A., Ed. *The Wars of America – Christian Views*. (2nd ed.) Macon,
Georgia: Mercer University Press, 1991. 145. Print.

93   Morgan, H. Wayne. *America's Road to Empire: The War with Spain and Overseas Expansion*. New York: Wiley, 1965. 13–14, 28, 34–35, 47, 51–52, 55–61, 65.
Print.

94   Ibid., 61.

95   McEnroe, Sean, "Painting the Philippines with an American Brush: Visions
of Race and National Mission among the Oregon Volunteers in the Philippine
Wars of 1898 and 1899." *Oregon Historical Quarterly 104.1 (2003)*: 60 pars. 7 May
2010 http://www.historycooperative.org/journals/ohq/104.1/mcenroe.html.

96   Powell, Anthony L. "An Overview: Black Participation In The Spanish American War." (Quoting Chaplain Plummer) *The Spanish American War Centennial
Website*. N.p., n.d. Web. 26 Mar 2010. http://www.spanamwar.com/AfroAmeri-
cans.htm.

97   Ibid., 93. (quoting Day to McKinley, September 30, 1898, McKinley papers,
Library of Congress, Manuscripts Division, Washington, D.C.)

98   Fisher, Louis. "Destruction of the Maine (1898)." 04 Aug 2009. The Law
Library of Congress. Accessed 21 Mar 2010. http://www.loc.gov/law/help/
usconlaw/pdf/Maine.1898.pdf

99   "The Destruction of the U.S.S. Maine." *Naval Historical Center*. Department
of the Navy – Naval Historical Center, 13 Aug 2003. Web. 19 Mar 2010. http://
www.history.navy.mil/faqs/faq71-1.htm.

100   Wells, Ronald A., Ed. *The Wars of America – Christian Views*. (2nd ed.) Macon,
Georgia: Mercer University Press, 1991. 152–153. Print.

101   Dyal, Donald H. *Historical Dictionary of the Spanish American War*. West-
port, CT: Greenwood Publishing Group, 1996. viii. Print. Accessed 25 Mar 2010
at: http://books.google.com/books?id=PvxFKPI6q_oC&pg=PA20#v=onepage&q
=&f=false

102   "Principal Wars in Which the United States Participated: U.S. Military
Personnel Serving and Casualties (Military Casualty Information, DoD Principal

Wars)." *U.S. Department of Defense*. N.p., May 2008. Web. 25 Mar 2010. http://siadapp.dmdc.osd.mil/personnel/CASUALTY/WCPRINCIPAL.pdf

103 Daggett, Stephen. "CRS Report for Congress: Costs of Major U.S. Wars." *Federation of American Scientists*. Congressional Research Service: Library of Congress, 24 Jul 2008. Web. 24 Mar 2010. http://www.fas.org/sgp/crs/natsec/RS22926.pdf.

104 "Little brown brothers" was a term used by William Howard Taft, America's first civilian chief administrator in the Philippines (1901–1904).

105 Morgan, H. Wayne. *America's Road to Empire: The War with Spain and Overseas Expansion*. New York: Wiley, 1965. 72. Print.

106 Ibid., 74–75. (Quoting Senator Frye's letter to James Wilson, June 6, 1898, Wilson papers, Library of Congress, Manuscripts Division, Washington, D.C.)

107 Ibid., 75.

108 McKinley, William. "Manifest Destiny, Continued: McKinley Defends U.S. Expansionism." *History Matters*. Web. 23 Jun 2014. http://historymatters.gmu.edu/d/5575/.

109 Wells, Ronald A., Ed. *The Wars of America – Christian Views*. (2nd ed.) Macon, Georgia: Mercer University Press, 1991. 159. Print.

110 McEnroe, Sean, "Painting the Philippines with an American Brush: Visions of Race and National Mission among the Oregon Volunteers in the Philippine Wars of 1898 and 1899." *Oregon Historical Quarterly 104.1 (2003)*: 60 pars. 7 May 2010. http://www.historycooperative.org/journals/ohq/104.1/mcenroe.html.

111 Zinn, Howard. *A People's History of the United States*. New York, NY: Harper & Row, Publishers, Inc., 1980. 308. Print.

112 McEnroe, Sean, "Painting the Philippines with an American Brush: Visions of Race and National Mission among the Oregon Volunteers in the Philippine Wars of 1898 and 1899." *Oregon Historical Quarterly 104.1 (2003)*: 60 pars. (Interview quoted from: Henry F. Graff, ed., *American Imperialism and the Philippine Insurrection: Testimony Taken from Hearings on Affairs in the Philippine Islands before the Senate Committee on the Philippines – 1902*, Boston: Little, Brown, 1969. 64–5). 7 May 2010. http://www.historycooperative.org/journals/ohq/104.1/mcenroe.html.

113 McEnroe, Sean, "Painting the Philippines with an American Brush: Visions of Race and National Mission among the Oregon Volunteers in the Philippine Wars of 1898 and 1899." *Oregon Historical Quarterly* 104.1 (2003): 60 pars. 7 May 2010 http://www.historycooperative.org/journals/ohq/104.1/mcenroe.html.

114 Cleveland, Grover. "Ex-President Grover Cleveland on the Philippine Problem. Boston: New England Anti-Imperialist League, 1904."

Humanities Web. Web. 1 May 2010. http://www.humanitiesweb.org/human. php?s=h&p=c&a=p&ID=23005.

115 *American Experience: Hawaii's Last Queen: The Embattled Reign of Queen Lili'uokalani.* Public Broadcasting Service (PBS), 1997. Film.

116 Sforza, Teri. "Hawaii's Annexation a Story of Betrayal." *Orange County Register* 9 Nov 1996: n. p. Web. 10 May 2010. <www.hawaii-nation.org/betrayal. html.

117 "Native Hawaiians blockade historic palace." *CNN.com/US.* CNN, 1 May 2008. Web. 10 May 2010. http://www.cnn.com/2008/US/05/01/hawaii.palace. takeover/index.html.

118 "US Public Law 103–150, Nov. 23, 1993: 103d Congress Joint Resolution" and "Congressional Record – Senate, Wednesday, Oct. 27, 1993, 103rd Congress 1st Session, Reference: Vol 139 No 147; Title 100th Anniversary of the Overthrow of the Hawaiian Kingdom." *Hawaiian Constitutional Convention 2008.* N.p., 10 May 2010. Web. 10 May 2010. http://hawaiianconstitutionalconvention.com/ Public_Law_103-150_931123.pdf and http://hawaiianconstitutionalconvention. com/senate_congressional_record_931027.php

119 Morgan, H. Wayne. *America's Road to Empire: The War with Spain and Overseas Expansion.* New York: Wiley, 1965. 76. Print.

120 Gibney, Frank. "Is President Bush Repeating McKinley's Mistake in the Philippines?" *George Mason University's History News Network.* N.p., 28 Jul 2003. Web. 13 Jul 2010. http://hnn.us/articles/1595.html.

121 White, Matthew. "Source List and Detailed Death Tolls for the Man-made Megadeaths of the Twentieth Century." *Historical Atlas of the Twentieth Century.* N.p., Jun 2005. Web. 25 Mar 2010. http://users.erols.com/mwhite28/warstats.htm.

122 Dumindin, Arnaldo, "Philippine-American War, 1899–1902." Web. 7 May 2010. http://philippineamericanwar.webs.com/treatyofparis.htm

123 Plante, Trevor K. "Researching Service in the U.S. Army During the Philippine Insurrection," *Prologue Magazine,* Summer 2000, Vol. 32. No. 2. The National Archives. Web. 7 May 2010. http://www.archives.gov/publications/prologue/2000/ summer/philippine-insurrection.html

124 Couttie, Robert. "The War in the Philippines." *The Spanish American War Centennial Website.* Web. 1 May 2010. http://www.spanamwar.com/Philippines. htm

125 2008 Dollar figure is based on comparative values as given for dollar conversion in Spanish-American War (see Daggett, Reference #143).

126 The exact words recorded for Wilson are, "So far as I can learn, such wrongs and annoyances have been suffered to occur only against representatives of the

United States. I have heard of no complaints from other governments of similar treatment." (See reference following.)

127 "Woodrow Wilson: The Tampico Affair, Woodrow Wilson, 1914, U.S., Department of State, Papers Relating to Foreign Affairs, 1914, 474–76." *TeachingAmericanHistory.org*. Ashbrook Center for Public Affairs at Ashland University. 19 Aug 2009 http://teachingamericanhistory.org/library/index. asp?documentprint=678.

128 Ibid.

129 Yockelson, Mitchell. "The United States Armed Forces and the Mexican Punitive Expedition: Part I." *U.S. National Archives & Records Administration* 29.3 (Fall 1997): Web. 20 Jun 2008. http://www.archives.gov/publications/prologue/1997/ fall/mexican-punitive-expedition-1.html.

130 "The First World War: Combatant States." *Channel4.com – The First World War – text only*. Channel 4 TV – London. 19 Aug 2009 http://www.channel4.com/ history/microsites/F/firstworldwar/index_comba_t.html.

131 Link, Arthur S., *Wilson the Diplomatist*. Baltimore: John Hopkins Press, 1957. 34. Print.

132 Wells, Ronald A., Ed. *The Wars of America – Christian Views*. (2nd ed.) Macon, Georgia: Mercer University Press, 1991. 174. Print. (Quoting Ray S. Baker, *Woodrow Wilson: Life and Letters*, Potomac ed., 7 vols. [New York: Charles Scribner's Sons, 1946], 5:399.)

133 Ibid., 171.

134 Wells, Ronald A., Ed. *The Wars of America – Christian Views*. (2nd ed.) Macon, Georgia: Mercer University Press, 1991. 174–75. Print. (Quoting Arthur S. Link, *Wilson: Campaigns for Progressivism and Peace*. Princeton, NJ: Princeton University Press, 1965. 399)

135 Link, Arthur S., *Wilson the Diplomatist*. Baltimore: John Hopkins Press, 1957. 89. Print.

136 Richman, Sheldon. "The Roots of World War II." Feb 1995. Freedom Daily: The Future of Freedom Foundation. Web. 22 Mar 2010. http://www.fff.org/ freedom/0295d.asp

137 Wells, Ronald A., Ed. *The Wars of America – Christian Views*. (2nd ed.) Macon, Georgia: Mercer University Press, 1991. 186–87. Print.

138 Buckley, Ian. "Articles: Australia's Foreign Wars: Origins, Costs, Future?!; Ch 7, Part C(f) US Presidential Initiative – the Hoover Plan." *The British Empire*. Stephen Luscombe. 21 Aug 2009 http://www.britishempire.co.uk/article/australiaswars7.htm. or Buckley, Ian. "Australia's Foreign Wars: Origins, Cost, Future?!: Chapter 7 C(f)." *ibuckley*. 22 Aug 2009 http://users.cyberone.com.au/ibuckley.

139 Dellinger, David. "Why I Refused to Register in the October 1940 Draft and a Little of What It Led To." *We Who Dared to Say No to War: American Antiwar Writing from 1812 to Now*. Murray Polner and Thomas E. Woods, Jr.. Philadelphia: Basic Books (Perseus Books Group), 2008. Print. (Also in: Gara, Larry and Lenna Mae Gara, *A Few Small Candles: War Resisters of World War II Tell Their Stories*. Kent, Ohio: Kent State University Press, 1999.)

140 "Principal Wars in Which the United States Participated: U.S. Military Personnel Serving and Casualties (Military Casualty Information, DoD Principal Wars)." *U.S. Department of Defense*. N.p., May 2008. Web. 25 Mar 2010. http://siadapp.dmdc.osd.mil/personnel/CASUALTY/WCPRINCIPAL.pdf

141 White, Matthew. "Source List and Detailed Death Tolls for the Man-made Megadeaths of the Twentieth Century." *Historical Atlas of the Twentieth Century*. N.p., Jun 2005. Web. 25 Mar 2010. http://users.erols.com/mwhite28/warstats.htm.

142 Hanlon, Michael F. "Special Feature: The Great War in Numbers." *World War I, Trenches on the Web*. N.p., n.d. Web. 26 Mar 2010. http://www.worldwar1.com/sfnum.htm.

143 Daggett, Stephen. "CRS Report for Congress: Costs of Major U.S. Wars." *Federation of American Scientists*. Congressional Research Service: Library of Congress, 24 Jul 2008. Web. 24 Mar 2010. http://www.fas.org/sgp/crs/natsec/RS22926.pdf.

144 John I. Woolley and Gerhard Peters, *The American Presidency Project* [online]. CA: University of California (hosted), Gerhard Peters (database). Available from World Wide Web: http://www.presidency.ucsb.edu/ws/index.php?pid=16053: "Franklin D. Roosevelt – Address to Congress Requesting a Declaration of War with Japan, December 8, 1941." Web. 5 Sep 2009.

145 "Japanese Note to the United States December 7, 1941 (Generally referred to as the 'Fourteen Part Message.')." *Yale Law School, Lillian Goldman Law Library, The Avalon Project – Documents in Law, History, and Diplomacy*. 17 Dec 1941. United States Department of State Bulletin, Vol. V, No. 129, Dec. 13, 1941, Web. 8 Feb 2010. http://avalon.law.yale.edu/subject_menus/wwii.asp.

146 "Events Leading to the Attack on Pearl Harbor." Wikipedia. http://en.wikipedia.org/wiki/Events_leading_to_the_attack_on_Pearl_Harbor, referencing: Maechling, Charles. "Pearl Harbor: The First Energy War." *History Today, Vol. 50, Issue 12*. 41–47. Dec 2000. Web. 22 March 2010.

147 "National Affairs: Pearl Harbor: Henry Stimpson's View." *Time Magazine* 01 Apr 1946: n. pg. Web. 23 Mar 2010. http://www.time.com/time/magazine/article/0,9171,792673-1,00.html.

148 "A Brief History of U.S. Navy Destroyers." *Navy.mil.* United States Navy, n.d. Web. 23 Mar 2010. http://www.navy.mil/navydata/navy_legacy_hr.asp?id=142.

149 "A Brief History of the Army in World War II." *U.S. Army Center of Military History.* N.p., 3 Oct 2003. Web. 23 Mar 2010. http://www.history.army.mil/brochures/brief/overview.htm.

150 Richman, Sheldon. "The Roots of World War II." Feb 1995. Freedom Daily: The Future of Freedom Foundation. Web. 22 Mar 2010. http://www.fff.org/freedom/0295d.asp

151 Student interview, Dayton, Oregon, June 2009.

152 "Auschwitz: Inside the Nazi State – The North Carolina Connection: St. Louis Refused Entry." Teacher's Resource Guide. UNC TV. UNC TV ONLINE – North Carolina's Statewide Television Network. N.p., n.d. Web. 10 May 2010. http://www.unctv.org/auschwitz/bystanders.html.

153 Friedman, Saul S. *No Haven for the Oppressed,* Wayne State University Press, Detroit, 1973. 172.

154 Ibid., 196.

155 Ibid., 174.

156 Ibid., 195, 228.

157 Ibid., 222.

158 Kalb, Marvin, "The Journalism of the Holocaust," http://www.wshmm.org/lectures/kalb.htm, February 27, 1996.

159 "With Dignity and Humanity, Bulgaria saved the lives of 49-thousand Jews." Web. 13 Apr 2004. http://www.abvg.net/Sacred/Kiril.html

160 President Parvanov of Bulgaria in a speech delivered at the Special Session of the National Assembly of Bulgaria on the occasion of the Day of the Holocaust and the 60th Anniversary of the Rescue of Bulgaria's Jews, recounting the circumstances of this happening. 11 Mar 2003. Web. Accessed at "The Unifier King and The Rescue of the Jews from Unified Bulgaria: On the Role of King Boris III of the Bulgarians during the years of the Holocaust." *Geocities.com.* 13 Apr 2004. http://www.geocities.com/boris3jews/.

161 Gruber, Ruth E. "Bulgarian, Macedonian Jews Eye Shoah." *Baltimore Jewish Times.* 06 Mar 2003. Web. 13 Apr 2004. http://fido.seva.net:8090/pipermail/holocaust/2003-March/000761.html.

162 Boyadjieff, Christo. Excerpt from "Saving the Bulgarian Jews in World War II." Web. 13 Apr 2004. http://www.b-info.com/places/Bulgaria/Jewish/Boyadjieff.shtml

163 Smykla, Margaret. "South Neighborhoods: Bulgarians' efforts to save Jews is topic for Scott Holocaust observance." 30 Apr 2003. *Post-Gazette.com*. Pittsburgh, PA. Web. 13 Apr. 2004.
http://www.post-gazette.com/neigh_south/20030430s19holocaust0430p4.asp

164 Small, Melvin. *Was War Necessary? National Security and U.S. Entry Into War.* Beverly Hills, CA: Sage Publications, 1980. 21. Print.

165 Churchill, Winston. *The Second World War: The Gathering Storm*. Boston: Houghton Mifflin Company, 1948. iv. Print.

166 Small, Melvin. *Was War Necessary? National Security and U.S. Entry Into War.* Beverly Hills, CA: Sage Publications, 1980. 247. Print.

167 Ibid., 247–248.

168 Ibid., 300.

169 Ibid., 232–233.

170 Ash, Barbara. "The Day Hitler Blinked." *Research in Review,* Fall & Winter 1997, Florida State University. Web. 5 Nov 2014. [Referencing the work of Dr. Nathan Stoltzfus]. http://www.rinr.fsu.edu/fallwinter97/features/hitler.html

171 Beebe, Ralph, Professor Emeritus, George Fox University. Newberg, OR. October 22, 2009. Class discussion.

172 Beevor, Antony. "They Raped Every German Female from 8 to 80," *The Guardian*. 01 May 2002. Web. 28 Oct 2009. http://www.guardian.co.uk/books/2002/may/01/news.features.

173 "STARBASE: A Department of Defense Youth Program." Web. 13 Mar 2010. http://www.starbasedod.org/.

174 "Principal Wars in Which the United States Participated: U.S. Military Personnel Serving and Casualties (Military Casualty Information, DoD Principal Wars)." *U.S. Department of Defense*. N.p., May 2008. Web. 25 Mar 2010. http://siadapp.dmdc.osd.mil/personnel/CASUALTY/WCPRINCIPAL.pdf

175 White, Matthew. "Source List and Detailed Death Tolls for the Man-made Megadeaths of the Twentieth Century." *Historical Atlas of the Twentieth Century*. N.p., Jun 2005. Web. 25 Mar 2010. http://users.erols.com/mwhite28/warstats.htm.

176 Daggett, Stephen. "CRS Report for Congress: Costs of Major U.S. Wars." *Federation of American Scientists*. Congressional Research Service: Library of Congress, 24 Jul 2008. Web. 24 Mar 2010. http://www.fas.org/sgp/crs/natsec/RS22926.pdf.

177 Wells, Ronald A., Ed. *The Wars of America: Christian Views*, Mercer University Press, Macon Georgia, 1991, 209. Print. (Quoting Robert C. Batchelder, The Irreversible Decision. Boston: Houghton Mifflin, 1962. 178.)

178 Ibid., 209. (Quoting Robert C. Batchelder, The Irreversible Decision, Boston: Houghton Mifflin, 1962. 179.)

179 "Strategic Bombing During World War II." *Wikipedia*. Web. 8 Feb 2010. http://en.wikipedia.org/wiki/Strategic_bombing_during_World_War_II.

180 White, Matthew. "Source List and Detailed Death Tolls for the Man-made Megadeaths of the Twentieth Century." *Historical Atlas of the Twentieth Century*. N.p., Jun 2005. Web. 25 Mar 2010. http://users.erols.com/mwhite28/warstats.htm (referencing studies by Michael Clodfelter: Warfare and Armed Conflict: A Statistical Reference to Casualty and Other Figures, 1618–1991.)

181 Harris, Jonathan. *Hiroshima: A Study in Science, Politics, and the Ethics of War*. Menlo Park, CA: Addison-Wesley Publishing Co., 1970. 68. Print.

182 Ibid., 25.

183 Ibid., 22.

184 Ibid., 29.

185 Ibid., 30.

186 Ibid., 33.

187 Ibid., 33–34.

188 Garner, Dwight. "Books of the Times: After Atom Bombs' Shock, the Real Horrors Began Unfolding (book review of: *The Last Train From Hiroshima: The Survivors Look Back*, by Charles Pellegrino)." *The New York Times*. 20 Jan 2010. Web. 22 Feb 2010. http://www.nytimes.com/2010/01/20/books/20garner.html?pagewanted=print

189 Gary E. Weir, "Silent Defense: One Hundred Years of the American Submarine Force," U.S. Naval Historical Center, April 27, 1999, Chief of Naval Operations, Submarine Warfare Division, Submarine Force History; 28 Oct 2009. http://www.navy.mil/navydata/cno/n87/history/fullhist.html.

190 Ibid.

191 "ICRC in WWII: German prisoners of war in Allied hands", ICRC (International Committee of the Red Cross). 28 Oct 2009. http://www.icrc.org/web/eng/siteeng0.nsf/html/57JNWX,

192 "Ike's Revenge?" *Time Magazine*, October 2, 1989. Web. 28 Oct 2009. http://www.time.com/time/magazine/article/0,9171,958673,00.html.

193 Wells, Ronald A., Ed., *The Wars of America: Christian Views*, Mercer University Press, Macon Georgia, 1991. 222. Print.

194 "Powers of Persuasion: Poster Art from World War II," The National Archives. Web. 30 Oct 2009. http://www.archives.gov/exhibits/powers_of_persuasion/powers_of_persuasion_intro.html#.

195 "Powers of Persuasion: Poster Art from World War II," The National Archives. Web. 30 Oct 2009. http://www.archives.gov/exhibits/powers_of_persuasion/warning/warning.html

196 Harry S. Truman, President of the United States, quoted in "U.S. & THE WORLD: Awful Responsibility" Monday August 20, 1945, *Time Magazine*. Web. 4 Nov 2009. http:www.time.com/time/magazine/article/0,0171,797659.00.html.

197 Matray, James I. "Review Essay – Korea's Partition: Soviet-American Pursuit of Reunification, 1945–1948." 1998. Web. 9 Feb 2010. http://www.mtholyoke.edu/acad/intrel/korpart.htm

198 Small, Melvin. *Was War Necessary? National Security and U.S. Entry Into War.* Beverly Hills, CA: Sage Publications, 1980. 272. Print.

199 Bachrach, Deborah. *The Korean War (America's Wars Series).* San Diego, CA: Lucent Books, 1991. 21. Print.

200 Small, Melvin. *Was War Necessary? National Security and U.S. Entry Into War.* Beverly Hills, CA: Sage Publications, 1980. 287. Print.

201 "The Korean War." *Center for Educational Technologies (A NASA-sponsored project).* Web. 15 Jul 2010. http://www.cotf.edu/ete/modules/korea/kwar.html.

202 Matray, James I. "Review Essay – Korea's Partition: Soviet-American Pursuit of Reunification, 1945–1948." 1998. Web. 9 Feb 2010. http://www.mtholyoke.edu/acad/intrel/korpart.htm

203 "A State of Mind: North Korea and the Korean War, 1953 – Present the Aftermath." *Wideangle.* 11 Sep 2003. Web. 10 Feb 2010. http://www.pbs.org/wnet/wideangle/episodes/a-state-of-mind/north-korea-and-the-korean-war/1953-present-the-aftermath/1369/

204 "Principal Wars in Which the United States Participated: U.S. Military Personnel Serving and Casualties (Military Casualty Information, DoD Principal Wars)." *U.S. Department of Defense.* N.p., May 2008. Web. 25 Mar 2010. http://siadapp.dmdc.osd.mil/personnel/CASUALTY/WCPRINCIPAL.pdf

205 White, Matthew. "Source List and Detailed Death Tolls for the Man-made Megadeaths of the Twentieth Century." *Historical Atlas of the Twentieth Century.* N.p., Jun 2005. Web. 25 Mar 2010. http://users.erols.com/mwhite28/warstats.htm.

206 Daggett, Stephen. "CRS Report for Congress: Costs of Major U.S. Wars." *Federation of American Scientists.* Congressional Research Service: Library of Congress, 24 Jul 2008. Web. 24 Mar 2010. http://www.fas.org/sgp/crs/natsec/RS22926.pdf.

207 (It is interesting to note that the Vietnamese Declaration of Independence was "modeled nearly verbatim after the American Declaration of Independence and the French Declaration of the Rights of Man and Citizen.") Quoting "U.S.

Involvement in Indochina, End of Japanese occupation." Web. 11 Sep 2009. http://www.u-s-history.com/pages/h1888.html

208 Halsall, Paul, ed. "Modern History Sourcebook: Vietnamese Declaration of Independence, 1945." Fordham University, Internet History Sourcebooks Project, n.d. Web. 13 Jul 2010. http://www.fordham.edu/halsall/mod/1945vietnam.html.

209 Wells, Ronald A., Ed. *The Wars of America – Christian Views*. (2nd ed.) Macon, Georgia: Mercer University Press, 1991. 236. Print.

210 "The Pentagon Papers, Chapter 4, US and France in Indochina, 1950–56," Part I, A, 3 (The Line of Containment and The Domino Theory). Web. 11 Sep 2009. http://www.mtholyoke.edu/acad/intrel/pentagon/pent9.html

211 Wells, Ronald A., Ed. *The Wars of America – Christian Views*. (2nd ed.) Macon, Georgia: Mercer University Press, 1991. 259. Print.

212 Ibid., 261.

213 Ibid., 263.

214 "Gulf of Tonkin Index – 11/30/2005 and 5/30/2006." *National Security Agency/Central Security Service*. National Security Agency/Central Security Service, n.d. Web. 11 May 2010. http://www.nsa.gov/public_info/declass/gulf_of_tonkin/index.shtml.

215 Hanyok, Robert J. United States National Security Agency. *Spartans in Darkness: American SIGINT and the Indochina War, 1945–1975: Chapter 5 – Skunks, Bogies, Silent Hounds, and the Flying Fish: The Gulf of Tonkin Mystery, 2–4 August 1964*, 177. 2002. Web. 12 May 2010. http://www.fas.org/irp/nsa/spartans/index.html. [A clearer reproduction is also found at http://www.gwu.edu/~nsarchiv/NSAEBB/NSAEBB132/relea00012.pdf.]

216 Ibid., 198.

217 Ibid., 213.

218 Hanyok, Robert J. United States National Security Agency. *Spartans in Darkness: American SIGINT and the Indochina War, 1945–1975: Chapter 5 – Skunks, Bogies, Silent Hounds, and the Flying Fish: The Gulf of Tonkin Mystery, 2–4 August 1964* , 2002. Web. 12 May 2010. http://www.fas.org/irp/nsa/spartans/index.html. [a clearer reproduction is also found at http://www.gwu.edu/~nsarchiv/NSAEBB/NSAEBB132/relea00012.pdf]

219 "Vietnam Mishaps Revealed in Newly Declassified Papers." *Scott Simon, Host, with John Prados*. National Public Radio (NPR): 12 Jan 2008. Radio. Retrieved from npr.org 11 May 2009 at http://www.npr.org/templates/story/story.php?storyId=18045569

220 Prados, John, Ed. "The Gulf of Tonkin Incident, 40 Years Later" and "Tonkin Gulf Intelligence 'Skewed' According to Official History and Intercepts: Newly Declassified National Security Agency Documents Show Analysts Made 'SIGINT fit the claim' of North Vietnamese Attack." *The National Security Archive, The George Washington University.* N.p., n.d. Web. 11 May 2010. http://www. gwu.edu/~nsarchiv/NSAEBB/NSAEBB132/index.htm and http://www.gwu. edu/~nsarchiv/NSAEBB/NSAEBB132/press20051201.htm.

221 "Gulf of Tonkin Index – 11/30/2005 and 5/30/2006." *National Security Agency/Central Security Service.* National Security Agency/Central Security Service, n.d. Web. 11 May 2010. http://www.nsa.gov/public_info/declass/gulf_of_ tonkin/index.shtml.

222 Aftergood, Steven. "NSA Releases History of American SIGINT and the Vietnam War." *Secrecy News.* American Federation of Scientists, 7 Jan 2008. Web. 11 May 2010. http://www.fas.org/blog/secrecy/2008/01/nsa_releases_history_of_ americ.html

223 "Vietnam Veterans and Agent Orange Independent Study Course." *Veterans Health Initiative VHI* (March 2002 updated June 2008): 8,9,14. Web. 13 May 2010. http://www.publichealth.va.gov/docs/vhi/VHIagentorange_text508.pdf.

224 Ibid., 41.

225 Lewis, Jerry M. and Thomas R. Hensley, "The May 4 Shootings at Kent State University: The Search for Historical Accuracy." Kent State University, Department of Sociology. Web. 16 Dec 2009. http://dept.kent.edu/sociology/lewis/lewihen. htm. Web address updated on 18 Jul 2013 to http://www.kent.edu/about/history/ may4/lewihen.cfm.

226 "The Pentagon Papers, Chapter 4, US and France in Indochina, 1950–56", Part I, B, 3 (Critique), f (Costs Not Weighed). Web. 11 Sep 2009. http://www.mtholyoke.edu/acad/intrel/pentagon/pent9.htm.

227 "Principal Wars in Which the United States Participated: U.S. Military Personnel Serving and Casualties (Military Casualty Information, DoD Principal Wars)." *U.S. Department of Defense.* N.p., May 2008. Web. 25 Mar 2010. http:// siadapp.dmdc.osd.mil/personnel/CASUALTY/WCPRINCIPAL.pdf

228 White, Matthew. "Source List and Detailed Death Tolls for the Man-made Megadeaths of the Twentieth Century." *Historical Atlas of the Twentieth Century.* N.p., Jun 2005. Web. 25 Mar 2010. http://users.erols.com/mwhite28/warstats.htm.

229 Daggett, Stephen. "CRS Report for Congress: Costs of Major U.S. Wars." Federation of American Scientists. Congressional Research Service: Library of Congress, 24 Jul 2008. Web. 24 Mar 2010. http://www.fas.org/sgp/crs/natsec/ RS22926.pdf.

230 Bush, George H.W., "Public Papers – 1990 – September: Address Before a Joint Session of the Congress on the Persian Gulf Crisis and the Federal Budget Deficit, 1990-09-11," George Bush Presidential Library and Museum. 11 Sep 1990. Web. 22 Mar 2012. http://bushlibrary.tamu.edu/research/public_papers. php?id=2217&year=1990&month=9

231 Based largely on: "Excerpts from Iraqi Document on Meeting with U.S. Envoy." *The New York Times International.* 23 Sep 1990. Web. 30 Mar 2012. http:// www.chss.montclair.edu/english/furr/glaspie.html.

232 Dowd, Ann Reilly and Suneel Ratan. "How Bush Decided: He sees Saddam Hussein as another Hitler. Once the President concluded economic sanctions wouldn't work – and Iraq wouldn't back down – his only option was war." *Fortune Magazine.* CNN Money. 11 Feb 1991. Web. 31 Mar 2012. http://money.cnn.com/ magazines/fortune_archive/1991/02/11/74659/index.htm

233 Ibid.

234 Gardner, Lloyd C. *The Long Road to Baghdad: A History of U.S. Foreign Policy from the 1970s to the Present.* New York: The New Press, 2008. 82. Print. [Quoting George H.W. Bush and Brent Scowcroft, *A World Transformed.* New York: Scribner, 1997. 454. Print]

235 Dowd, Ann Reilly and Suneel Ratan. "How Bush Decided: He sees Saddam Hussein as another Hitler. Once the President concluded economic sanctions wouldn't work – and Iraq wouldn't back down – his only option was war." *Fortune Magazine.* CNN Money. 11 Feb 1991. Web. 31 Mar 2012. http://money.cnn.com/ magazines/fortune_archive/1991/02/11/74659/index.htm

236 Gardner, Lloyd C. *The Long Road to Baghdad: A History of U.S. Foreign Policy from the 1970s to the Present.* New York: The New Press, 2008. 85. Print.

237 El-Najjar, Hassan A. *The Gulf War: Overreaction & Excessiveness.* Dalton, GA: The Amazone Press, 2001. 224. Print. (Referencing Alexander Cockburn's "Back to Dropping [sic] Up Saddam," Los Angeles Times, 4 Apr 1991.)

238 El-Najjar, Hassan A. *The Gulf War: Overreaction & Excessiveness.* Dalton, GA: The Amazone Press, 2001. 227. Print.

239 Ibid., 228.

240 Ibid., 232.

241 Dowd, Ann Reilly and Suneel Ratan. "How Bush Decided: He sees Saddam Hussein as another Hitler. Once the President concluded economic sanctions wouldn't work – and Iraq wouldn't back down – his only option was war." *Fortune Magazine.* CNN Money. 11 Feb 1991. Web. 31 Mar 2012. http://money.cnn.com/ magazines/fortune_archive/1991/02/11/74659/index.htm

242 Gardner, Lloyd C. *The Long Road to Baghdad: A History of U.S. Foreign Policy from the 1970s to the Present.* New York: The New Press, 2008. 87. Print. [Referring to Rhodes' 27 Nov 1990 opinion piece, "Iraq's Atomic Red Herring," for *The New York Times.*]

243 Ibid., 83–84.

244 "How PR Sold the War in the Persian Gulf," The Center for Media and Democracy's *PR Watch.* Web. 25 May 2012. http://www.prwatch.org/books/tsigfy10.html. (Article is excerpted from: Stauber, John and Sheldon Rampton, *Toxic Sludge is Good for You: Lies, Damn Lies, and the Public Relations Industry.* Common Courage Press, 2002. Chapter 10. Print.)

245 Ibid.

246 "Excerpts from Iraqi Document on Meeting with U.S. Envoy." *The New York Times International.* 23 Sep 1990. Web. 30 Mar 2012. http://www.chss.montclair.edu/english/furr/glaspie.html.

247 Ibid.

248 Gardner, Lloyd C. *The Long Road to Baghdad: A History of U.S. Foreign Policy from the 1970s to the Present.* New York: The New Press, 2008. 90. Print.

249 "Judiciary Power and Practice – The war powers resolution." *Encyclopedia of the New American Nation.* Web. 31 Mar 2012. http://www.americanforeignnelations.com/E-N/Judiciary-Power-and-Practice-The-war-powers-resolution.html.

250 El-Najjar, Hassan A. *The Gulf War: Overreaction & Excessiveness.* Dalton, GA: The Amazone Press, 2001. 246–248. Print.

251 "Jan 12, '91 Senate Roll Call Vote #00002." *Democrats: Official news and legislative information from Democrats in the U.S. Senate.* Web. 2 Apr 2012. http://democrats.senate.gov/1991/01/page/2/

252 La Rocque, Steve. "How Congress Backed President Bush's Use of Force Against Iraq in 1991." *Washington File.* 11 Sep 2002. Web. 02 Apr 2012. http://usinfo.org/wf-archive/2002/020911/epf308.htm

253 Connelly, Joel. "In the Northwest: Bush-Cheney flip-flops cost America in blood." *The Seattle Post-Intelligencer.* 28 Sep 2004. Web. 30 Mar 2012. http://www.seattlepi.com/news/article/In-the-Northwest-Bush-Cheney-flip-flops-cost-1155271.php

254 "Costs and Consequences of War in Iraq. Fact Sheet 2." CESR (Center for Economic and Social Rights). New York. Web. 31 Mar 2012. http://www.cesr.org/downloads/Cost%20and%20Consequences%20of%20War%20in%20Iraq.pdf.

255 El-Najjar, Hassan A. *The Gulf War: Overreaction & Excessiveness.* Dalton, GA: Amazone Press, 2001. Web. 22 Mar 2012. http://www.gulfwar1991.com/Gulf%20

War%20Complete/Introductionr%20The%20Real%20Story%20of%20the%20
Gulf%20War%20By%20Hassan%20A%20El-Najjar.htm.

256 Ibid., 22.

257 "Riegle Report (1994) by the United States Senate: U.S. Senate Committee
on Banking, Housing, and Urban Affairs, United States Senate, 103d Congress, 2d
Session." Riegle Report – Wikisource. Web. 29 Mar 2012. http://en.wikisource.org/
wiki/Riegle_Report.

258 Ibid.

259 Ibid.

260 El-Najjar, Hassan A. *The Gulf War: Overreaction & Excessiveness.* Dalton, GA:
Amazone Press, 2001. 241. Print.

261 Ibid., 242.

262 Weiss, Martin A. "Iraq's Debt Relief: Procedure and Potential Implication for
International Debt Relief," *Congressional Research Service.* 29 Mar 2011. Federation of American Scientists. Web. 24 May 2012. http://www.fas.org/sgp/crs/
mideast/RL33376.pdf.

263 "Persian Gulf War – Casualty Summary." *Military Casualty Information, U.S.
Military Casualties – Persian Gulf War.* U.S. Department of Defense, 29 Jan 2010,
Web. 24 Mar 2012.
http://siadapp.dmdc.osd.mil/personnel/CASUALTY/GWSUM.pdf

264 Kelly, Jack. "U.S. News – Estimates of deaths in first war still in dispute."
Post-Gazette. 16 Feb 2003. Web. 24 Mar 2012. http://old.post-gazette.com/
nation/20030216casualty0216p5.asp

265 Ibid.

266 "Costs and Consequences of War in Iraq. Fact Sheet 2." *CESR (Center for
Economic and Social Rights).* New York. Web. 31 Mar 2012. http://www.cesr.org/
downloads/Cost%20and%20Consequences%20of%20War%20in%20Iraq.pdf

267 Daggett, Stephen. "Cost of Major U.S. Wars." *Congressional Research Service.*
29 Jun 2010. Web 30 Mar 2010. http://www.fas.org/sgp/crs/natsec/RS22926.pdf

268 "Iraq surveys show 'humanitarian emergency." *UNICEF Information News-
line.* 12 Aug 1999. Web. 29 Mar 2012. http://www.unicef.org/newsline/99pr29.
htm. ("Ms. Bellamy {UNICEF Executive Director Carol Bellamy} noted that if
the substantial reduction in child mortality throughout Iraq during the 1980s had
continued through the 1990s, there would have been half a million fewer deaths
of children under five in the country as a whole during the eight year period 1991
to 1998…. 'Even if not all suffering in Iraq can be imputed to external factors,
especially sanctions, the Iraqi people would not be undergoing such deprivations

in the absence of the prolonged measures imposed by the Security Council and the effects of war."')

269 Tucker, Richard P. and Edmund Russell, Ed. *Natural Enemy, Natural Ally: Toward an Environmental History of War*. Corvallis, Oregon: Oregon State University Press, 2004. Print.

270 Tucker, Richard P. "The World Wars and the Globalization of Timber Cutting." *Natural Enemy, Natural Ally: Toward an Environmental History of War*. Ed. Richard P. Tucker and Edmund Russell. Corvallis, Oregon: Oregon State University Press, 2004. 136. Print.

271 Ibid., 119.

272 Tucker, Richard P. "The Impact of Warfare on the Natural World: A Historical Survey." *Natural Enemy, Natural Ally: Toward an Environmental History of War*. Ed. Richard P. Tucker and Edmund Russell. Corvallis, Oregon: Oregon State University Press, 2004. 32. Print.

273 Bennett, Judith A. "Pests and Disease in the Pacific War: Crossing the Line." *Natural Enemy, Natural Ally: Toward an Environmental History of War*. Ed. Richard P. Tucker and Edmund Russell. Corvallis, Oregon: Oregon State University Press, 2004. 240. Print.

274 Tucker, Richard P. and Edmund Russell, Ed. *Natural Enemy, Natural Ally: Toward an Environmental History of War*. Corvallis, Oregon: Oregon State University Press, 2004. 33. Print.

275 Ibid., 33–34.

276 Ibid., 11.

277 Laakkonen, Simo. "War – An Ecological Alternative to Peace? Indirect Impacts of World War II on the Finnish Environment." Tucker, Richard P. and Edmund Russell, Ed. *Natural Enemy, Natural Ally: Toward an Environmental History of War*. Corvallis, Oregon: Oregon State University Press, 2004. 190–191. Print.

278 "Statistical Summary of America's Major Wars." *Home of the American Civil War*. Web. 18 Jul 2013. http://www.civilwarhome.com/warstats.htm

279 "On This Day: April 15, 1986 – U.S. Launches Air Strikes on Libya." *BBC News*. N.p., n.d. Web. 14 Jul 2010. http://news.bbc.co.uk/onthisday/hi/dates/stories/april/15/newsid_3975000/3975455.stm.

280 Zinn, Howard. "Terrorism over Tripoli," *Failure to Quit: Reflections of an Optimistic Historian*. Cambridge, MA: South End Press, 1993 and 2002. 120. Print.

281 http://www.history.navy.mil/library/online/forces.htm

282 Grimmett, Richard F. "Instances of Use of United States Armed Forces Abroad, 1798–2004." Navy Department Library. 14 Mar 2005. Department of the Navy. Web. 23 Mar 2010. http://www.history.navy.mil/library/online/forces.htm.

283 "The US's Intervention in Grenada, 1983" and "The US's Intervention in Panama, 1989" from *The Responsibility to Protect: The Report of the International Commission on Intervention and State Sovereignty.* Dec 2001. Ottawa, ON, Canada: International Development Research Centre. Web. 22 Mar 2012. http://web.idrc.ca/en/ev-28497-201-1-DO_TOPIC.html.

284 "Iraqi civilian death tally at 3,240." 11 Jun 2003. USAToday.com. Web. 29 Jan 2014. http://usatoday30.usatoday.com/news/world/iraq/2003-06-11-iraqi-toll_x.htm

285 "Off Target: The Conduct of the War and Civilian Casualties in Iraq." Human Rights Watch. 12 Dec. 2003. 6. Web. 30 Jan 2014. http://www.hrw.org/sites/default/files/reports/usa1203_sumrecs.pdf

286 Williams, Timothy [New York Times News Service]. "U.S. companies race to cash in on Iraqi oil projects." *The Oregonian,* 15 Jan 2010. A7. Print.

287 "Note on U.S. Covert Action Programs." *Foreign Relations of the United States, 1964–1968* XII. (2001). Web. 12 May 2010. http://www.fas.org/sgp/advisory/state/covert.html.

288 Ibid.

289 *The Oregonian,* Portland, Oregon. 5 Nov 2002. Print.

290 Ibid.

291 Rosenball, Mark. "A License to Kill Our Own?" *Newsweek* 15 Feb 2010. 10. Print.

292 Mock, Ron. *Loving Without Giving In: Christian Responses to Terrorism & Tyranny.* Telford, Pennsylvania: Cascadia Publishing House, 2004. 206. Print.

293 Wise, David. "The CIA, Licensed to Kill." *The Los Angeles Times.* 22 Jul 2009. Web. 8 Mar 2010. http://articles.latimes.com/2009/jul/22/opinion/oe-wise22.

294 Isikoff, Michael. "A House Is Not A Home." *Newsweek.* 16 Nov 2009. 12. Print.

295 "Video: Abu Omar, Victim of Rendition and Secret Detention." *Amnesty International.* Web. 24 Jun 2008. http://www.amnesty.org/en/news-and-updates/video-and-audio/video-abu-omar-victim-rendition-secret-detention-20080624

296 "CIA Agents Guilty of Italy Kidnap." *BBC News.* 04 Nov 2009. Web. 27 March 2010. http://news.bbc.co.uk/2/hi/8343123.stm.

297 Stone, Colonel Kathryn, United States Army. "'All Necessary Means' – Employing CIA Operatives in a Warfighting Role Alongside Special Operations

Forces." *U.S. Army War College Strategy Research Project* (2003): 11–12. Web. 12 May 2010. http://www.fas.org/irp/eprint/stone.pdf.

298 Best Jr., Richard A., and Andrew Feickert. "Special Operations Forces (SOF) and CIA." *Congressional Research Service* RS22017. (2009): 5. Web. 12 May 2010. http://www.fas.org/sgp/crs/natsec/RS22017.pdf.

299 Stone, Colonel Kathryn, United States Army. "'All Necessary Means' – Employing CIA Operatives in a Warfighting Role Alongside Special Operations Forces." *U.S. Army War College Strategy Research Project* (2003): iii. Web. 12 May 2010. http://www.fas.org/irp/eprint/stone.pdf.

300 Campbell, Alexander. "Address on War." 1848. *We Who Dared to Say No to War: American Antiwar Writing from 1812 to Now.* Murray Polner and Thomas E. Woods, Jr., Ed. New York: Basic Books (Perseus Books Group), 2008. 45–56. Print.

301 Hedges, Chris. *War is a Force That Gives Us Meaning.* Cambridge, MA: Public Affairs (The Perseus Books Group), 2002. 30–31. Print.

302 Newman, Phil. December 2012. Conversation and correspondence with the author.

303 Interview by author with veteran of U.S. Army who fought in both the Afghanistan War (2001– …) and the Iraq War (begun in 2003). Name withheld. 13 Oct 2009, Newberg, Oregon.

304 Vulliamy, Ed. "Iraq: the human toll." *The Observer.* London, 06 Jul 2003. Print. Copyright Guardian News & Media Ltd. 2003. Used by permission.

305 "Peaceful prevention of deadly conflict" is a term used by Friends Committee on National Legislation (FCNL), Washington, D.C. They have clearly and concisely put forth the steps needed to accomplish this on an international level.

306 "Creative Quotations from Abraham Maslow." *Creative Quotations.* Web. 10 Feb 2010. http://creativequotations.com/one/1838.htm.

307 Rogers, Fred. "Sometimes People Are Good." *Mister Rogers' Songbook.* New York: Random House, 1970. 24. Print.

308 Delgado. Aiden, interviewed in *The Ground Truth.* Patricia Foulkrod, Director. Focus Features/Universal Studios. Universal City, CA: Universal Studios, 2006. Film.

309 "Emergency: Meet the Staff (Interview with Dr. Gino Strada, war surgeon)." *POV, Documents With a Point of View.* PBS. 18 Mar 2009. Web. 23 Mar 2010. http://www.pbs.org/pov/afghanistanyear1380/afghanistan_year_1380_-_emerge.php.

310 Pettman, J.J. *Worlding Women: A Feminist International Politics.* London: Routledge, 1996. 89. (Pettman says: "Technological advances have vastly

increased the destructiveness of war, and blurred distinctions between civilian and combatant. In World War 1, 80 per cent of casualties were soldiers; in World War 2, only 50 per cent. In the Vietnam War some 80 per cent of casualties were civilian, and in current conflicts the estimate is 90 per cent – mainly women and children.")

311 "History of Veterans Day." Office of Public and Intergovernmental Affairs, U.S. Department of Veteran Affairs. Website. 29 Jan 2014. http://www.va.gov/opa/vetsday/vetdayhistory.asp

312 American Friends Service Committee. Exhibit.

313 Solomon, Norman. "Orwellian Logic 101 – A Few Simple Lessons." *fair.org.* Web. 15 Feb 2010. http://www.fair.org/media-beat/980827.html.

314 Chomsky, Noam. "The Journalist from Mars – How the 'War on Terror' should be reported." New York City, 22 January 2002. Address. Web. 11 Nov 2013. http://fair.org/extra-online-articles/the-journalist-from-mars/

315 "Nye Committee." *Wikipedia.* Web. 18 Dec 2009. http://en.wikipedia.org/wiki/Nye_Committee

316 "Report of the Special Committee on Investigation of the Munitions Industry (The Nye Report), U.S. Congress, Senate, 74th Congress, 2nd sess., February 24, 1936, pp. 3–13". Mount Holyoke. Web. Re-accessed 18 Jul 2013. http://www.mtholyoke.edu/acad/intrel/nye.htm

317 Ibid., p. 5 of 9.

318 Oregon PeaceWorks, Salem, Oregon. 10 Dec 2009. Letter: "According to the Center for Responsive Politics' OpenSecrets.org database, Obama was the top recipient of defense industry money in the 2008 election cycle. He received $1,029,997, far surpassing his hawkish Republican opponent Sen. John McCain's $696,948."

319 Manning, Robert J. "Oregon School Districts Look for Ways to Fill Budget Gaps." *Oregon Public Broadcasting News (Radio),* 12 Jul 2010. Web. 14 Jul 2010. http://news.opb.org/article/oregon-school-districts-look-ways-fill-budget-gaps/.

320 "Local Library." *Oregon Public Broadcasting News.* July 13, 2010. Radio.

321 Homecare Worker Orientation. Northwest Senior and Disability Services, McMinnville, Oregon. 14 Jul 2010.

322 "War, Weapons Force Pentagon Budget Ever Upward." *The Fiscal Times.* 21 Feb 2010. Web. 21 Jul 2010. http://www.thefiscaltimes.com/Issues/Budget-Impact/2010/02/21/War-Weapons-Force-Pentagon-Budget-Ever-Upward.aspx?p=1.

323 "Iraq, Afghanistan News Examined." National Public Radio. 28 Jul 2010. Radio. Web. 28 Jul 2010. http://www.npr.org/templates/story/story.php?storyId=128815043

324 American Friends Service Committee (AFSC), Philadelphia, PA. September 2009. Letter.

325 "Base Structure Report: Fiscal Year 2010 Baseline (A Summary of DoD's Real Property Inventory)." Department of Defense. Web. 2. 16 Jul 2013. http://www.acq.osd.mil/ie/download/bsr/BSR2010Baseline.pdf

326 "Base Structure Report: Fiscal Year 2008 Baseline (A Summary of DoD's Real Property Inventory)." Department of Defense. Web. 2. 16 Jul 2013. http://www.acq.osd.mil/ie/download/bsr/BSR2008Baseline.pdf

327 Lutz, Catherine. "US Bases and Empire: Global Perspectives on the Asia Pacific," *The Asia-Pacific Journal: Japan Focus*. Web. 5 Oct 2010. http://www.japan-focus.org/-Catherine_Lutz/3086.

328 Ibid.

329 "Base Structure Report: Fiscal Year 2010 Baseline (A Summary of DoD's Real Property Inventory)." Department of Defense. Web. 38-95. 16 Jul 2013. http://www.acq.osd.mil/ie/download/bsr/BSR2010Baseline.pdf

330 "List of US Military Bases." Military Travel Zone. http://militarytravelzone.com/us-military-bases.html. Web. 16 Jul 2013.

331 "Ron Paul says U.S. has military personnel in 130 nations and 900 overseas bases." Tampa Bay Times PolitiFact.com. Web. 17 Jul 2013. http://www.politifact.com/truth-o-meter/statements/2011/sep/14/ron-paul/ron-paul-says-us-has-military-personnel-130-nation/

332 Ibid.

333 Authors as traditionally attributed. *The Bible*. Translated. Ecclesiastes 3:3,8; Matthew 24:6. Print.

334 Tolstoy, Leo. *The Kingdom of God Is Within You*. (Translated by Constance Black Garnett). New York, NY: Cassell Publishing Co., 1894. (Reprinted by University of Nebraska Press, Lincoln and London, 1984.) 158. Print. [Tolstoy quoted academician Camille Doucet: "All the congresses of both hemispheres may vote against war, and against dueling too, but above all arbitrations, conventions, and legislations there will always be the personal honor of individual men, which has always demanded dueling, and the interests of nations, which will always demand war."]

335 Whittier, John Greenleaf. "Mary Garvin." *Wikisource*. wikisource.org, n.d. Web. 17 Mar 2010. http://en.wikisource.org/wiki/Mary_Garvin.

336 Bennett, Judith A. "Pests and Disease in the Pacific War: Crossing the Line." *Natural Enemy, Natural Ally: Toward an Environmental History of War.* Ed. Richard P. Tucker and Edmund Russell. Corvallis, Oregon: Oregon State University Press, 2004. 237–38. Print.

337 Rieckhoff, Paul. "More Soldiers Lost to Suicide than to Al Qaeda in January: Iraq Veterans Storm the Hill." *Huffington Post* 10 Feb 2009. Web. 13 May 2010. http://www.huffingtonpost.com/paul-rieckhoff/more-soldiers-lost-to-sui_b_165510.html.

338 Glantz, Aaron, "After Service, Veteran Deaths Surge." *The Bay Citizen.* San Francisco. 16 Oct. 2010 Web. 11 Nov. 2010. http://www.baycitizen.org/veterans/story/after-service-veteran-deaths-surge.

339 "Vietnam Veterans and Agent Orange Independent Study Course." *Veterans Health Initiative VHI* (2002 updated June 2008): 34 (referencing studies by CDC [Centers for Disease Control] and Anderson HA, Hanraham LP, Jensen M, Laurin D, Yick WY, Wiegman P. 1986b. Wisconsin Vietnam Veteran Mortality Study: Final Report. Madison: Wisconsin Division of Health.) Web. 13 May 2010. http://www.publichealth.va.gov/docs/vhi/VHIagentorange_text508.pdf.

340 Tolstoy, Leo. *The Kingdom of God Is Within You.* (Translated by Constance Black Garnett). New York, NY: Cassell Publishing Co., 1894. (Reprinted by University of Nebraska Press, Lincoln and London, 1984.) 195. Print.

341 Ibid., 332.

342 Fry, Douglas P. *Beyond War: The Human Potential for Peace.* Oxford, New York: Oxford University Press, 2007. 5. Print.

343 Ibid., xiii.

344 Harris, Evan. "Clinton Cites Rwanda, Bosnia in Rationale for Libya Intervention." *ABC News: Political Punch.* 27 Mar 2011. Web. 09 Nov 2011. http://abcnews.go.com/blogs/politics/2011/03/clinton-cites-rwanda-bosnia-in-rationale-for-libya-intervention.

345 Kenyon, Peter. "Libya's Economy Faces New Tests After Gadhafi Era." *National Public Radio.* Web. 13 Dec 2011. http://www.npr.org/2011/11/14/142289603/libyas-economy-faces-new-tests-after-gadhafi-era.

346 Goodman, Amy. "As Calls for Intervention in Syria Grow, Vijay Prashad Urges Revaluation of NATO Attack on Libya." *Democracy Now!* 21 Feb 2012. Web. 21 Feb 2012. http://www.democracynow.org/2012/2/21/as_calls_for_intervention_in_syria.

347 "Genocide." *Peace Pledge Union online.* Peace Pledge Union, n.d. Web. 14 Nov 2011. http://www.ppu.org.uk/genocide/html.

348 "PeaceBuilder, TAG ARCHIVES: Hope International Development Agency." *Eastern Mennonite University, Center for Justice and PeaceBuilding.* N.p., n.d. Web. 13 Dec 2011. http://emu.edu/now/peacebuilder/tag/hope-international-development-agency/.

349 "Who We Are: History." *Partners for Democratic Change.* N.p., n.d. Web. 13 Dec 2011. http://www.partnersglobal.org/who/history.

350 "Genocide Prevention – Practical Policy." *Changing Policy in Washington: Friends Committee on National Legislation Annual Report 2010 – 2011.* Friends Committee on National Legislation (FCNL), 2011. 6. Print.

351 "U.S. Civilian Response Corps: Third Anniversary, Fact Sheet." *U.S. Department of State.* N.p., n.d. Web. 19 Nov 2011. http://www.state.gov/r/pa/prs/ps/2011/07/168648.htm. The individuals who comprise this Corps are "made up of specially trained civilians from the Department of State, the U.S. Agency for International Development, and the Departments of Agriculture, Commerce, Energy, Health & Human Services, Homeland Security, Justice, and Transportation."

352 "President's Proposal for the FY 2011 State Department Budget." *U.S. Department of State.* N.p., n.d. Web. 19 Nov 2011. http://www.state.gov/s/dmr/former/lew/136358.htm.

353 "Peace Corps, Fast Facts." *Peace Corps.* N.p., n.d. Web. 21 Mar 2014. http://www.peacecorps.gov/about/fastfacts/

354 Personal testimony of veteran of the U.S. Marines, speaking at George Fox University, Newberg, Oregon, 2009.

355 Cornell, Tom. "America Magazine – The Chaplain's Dilemma." *America: The National Catholic Weekly.* 11 Nov 2008. Web. 20 Feb 2010. http://www.americamagazine.org/content/article.cfm?article_id=11215.

356 Tyson, Carolyn A., compiler. Naval Historical Foundation Pamphlet: "Marine Amphibious Landing in Korea, 1871." Navy Department Library, Naval Historical Center, Department of the Navy, 1966. (Quoting letter of Lieutenant Colonel McLane Tilton, USMC, to his wife Nan: 27 Jun 1871.) 05 Mar 2007. Web. 22 March 2010. http://www.history.navy.mil/library/online/marine_amphib_korea.htm. (Also in Print.)

357 Ibid., 5.

358 Ibid., 14–15.

359 Ibid., iii. (Forward)

360 Ibíd., i.

361 Ibíd., 11.

362 Tolstoy, Leo. *The Kingdom of God Is Within You.* (Translated by Constance Black Garnett). New York, NY: Cassell Publishing Co., 1894. Reprinted by University of Nebraska Press, Lincoln and London, 1984. 313–314. Print.

363 Berry, Wendell. "The Failure of War." *Making Peace: Healing a Violent World.* Carolyn McConnell and Sarah Ruth van Gelder, Eds., from *YES! A Journal of Positive Futures.* Bainbridge Island, WA: Positive Futures Network, 2003. 61.

364 Hudgens, Tom A. *L.et's A.bolish W.ar.* Revised. ed. Denver: BILR Corporation, 1986. 34. Print.

365 Ibid., 17.

366 Ibid., 33.

367 Mathews, Dylan. *War Prevention Works: 50 Stories of people resolving conflict.* Oxford, England: Oxford Research Group, 2001. 20–21.

368 Ibid., 112.

369 Ibid., 16–17. Also see: York, Steve, Dir. *Bringing Down a Dictator.* York Zimmerman, Inc.: 2001. Film.

370 Tusty, James and Maureen Castle Tusty. *The Singing Revolution.* Sky Films, Inc., docurama.com. 2008. Film.

371 Ibid., (Heinz Valk, *The Singing Revolution.* Film.)

372 Mathews, Dylan. *War Prevention Works: 50 Stories of people resolving conflict.* Oxford, England: Oxford Research Group, 2001. 28–29.

373 Ibid.

374 Ibid., 46–47.

375 Ibid., 48–49.

376 Ibid. (Also see the website www.c-r.org for more on the Guatemala Peace Process in their *Accord.*)

377 Mathews, Dylan. *War Prevention Works: 50 Stories of people resolving conflict.* Oxford, England: Oxford Research Group, 2001.

378 Fischer, Louis. The Life of Mahatma Gandhi. New York: Collier Books, 1962. 273–274. Print.

379 Ibid., 279.

380 Christian Peacemaker Teams: www.cpt.org.

381 Mathews, Dylan. *War Prevention Works: 50 Stories of people resolving conflict.* Oxford, England: Oxford Research Group, 2001. 102–103.

382 Reticker, Gini and Abigail E. Disney, Dir. *Pray the Devil Back to Hell.* 2008. Film.

383 Mogul, Jonathan and Barbara de Boinville, Ed., *Outreach/Study Guide*. 3–4. Web. Re-accessed 18 Jul 2013. http://www.aforcemorepowerful.org/films/pdfs/studyGuide-en.pdf.

384 Wording inspired by Michael Stearn's song, "Standing in Oppression's Way," *Not in My Wildest Dreams*. http://www.mikesongs.net/dreams.html

385 Shankar, Sir Ravi. "A Universal Language, Without Boundary or Prejudice," in: Ahmed, Akbar and Brian Forst, Eds. *After Terror: Promoting Dialogue Among Civilizations*. Malden, MA: Polity Press, 2005. 93. Print.

386 Fry, Douglas P. *Beyond War: The Human Potential for Peace*. Oxford, New York: Oxford University Press, 2007. xv. Print.

387 Keller, Helen. "Strike Against War" (an address to the Women's Peace Party of New York City on January 5, 1916). Quoted in: Polner, Murray, Ed. and Thomas E Woods, Jr. *We Who Dared to Say No to War: American Antiwar Writing From 1812 to Now*. New York: Basic Books (Perseus Books Group), 2008. 140. Print.

388 Fry, Douglas P. *Beyond War: The Human Potential for Peace*. Oxford, New York: Oxford University Press, 2007. 228–229. Print.

389 Mock, Ron. *Loving Without Giving In: Christian Responses to Terrorism & Tyranny*. Telford, Pennsylvania: Cascadia Publishing House. 2004. 247. Print.

390 Kristof, Nicholas. "1 Soldier or 20 Schools?" *New York Times*. 28 Jul 2010. Web. 29 Jul 2010. http://www.nytimes.com/2010/07/29/opinion/29kristof.html?ref=nicholasdkristof

391 Mathews, Dylan. *War Prevention Works: 50 Stories of People Resolving Conflict*. Oxford, England: Oxford Research Group, 2001. 24–25. Print.

392 Tad Beckwith and Virginia Olin, PeaceBike, First Expedition, 1999–2001. www.peacebike.org. Also see www.peacebikejourney.org.

393 See www.playingforchange.com.

394 Someone I love and who loves others deeply.

395 "If War is Not the Answer, What Is? Peaceful Prevention of Deadly Conflict," Friends Committee on National Legislation (FCNL), Washington DC. (Date unrecorded). 4. Booklet.

396 United States Department of Defense Quadrennial Defense Review Report, 2006. 75. Web. Re-accessed 3 Sep 2015. http://www.globalsecurity/military/library/policy/dod/qdr-2006-report.pdf

397 Kilcullen, David. "New Paradigms for 21st Century Conflict." *Small Wars Journal*. Web. 13 Feb 2010. http://smallwarsjournal.com/blog/2007/06/new-paradigms-for-21st-century/.

"Remedy the imbalance in government capability: At present, the U.S. defense budget accounts for approximately half of total global defense spending, while the U.S. armed forces employ about 1.68 million uniformed members.*(8)* By comparison, the State Department employs about 6,000 foreign service officers, while the U.S. Agency for International Development (USAID) has about 2,000.*(9)* In other words, the Department of Defense is about 210 times larger than USAID and State combined – there are substantially more people employed as musicians in Defense bands than in the entire foreign service.*(10)*"

398 Herold, Marc. "A Dossier on Civilian Victims of United States' Aerial Bombing of Afghanistan: A comprehensive Accounting [revised]." *Cursor*. Web. 15 Feb 2010. http://cursor.org/stories/civilian_deaths.htm.

399 "1996 Annual Defense Report, Part I – Defending the Nation, Chapter 1 – U.S. Defense Strategy." *U.S. Department of Defense*. Web. 24 Mar 2010. http://www.dod.mil/execsec/adr96/chapt_1.html

400 Ibid.

401 Kilcullen, David. "New Paradigms for 21st Century Conflict." *Small Wars Journal*. Web. 13 Feb 2010. http://smallwarsjournal.com/blog/2007/06/new-paradigms-for-21st-century/. (See quotation included in footnote #397.)

402 Cook, Major Gregory P., USAF. "Waging Peace: The Non-Lethal Application of Aerospace Power." *Federation of American Scientists*. Web. 24 Mar 2010. http://www.fas.org/spp/eprint/cook.htm.

403 "1996 Annual Defense Report, Part I – Defending the Nation, Chapter 1 – U.S. Defense Strategy." *U.S. Department of Defense*. Web. 24 Mar 2010. http://www.dod.mil/execsec/adr96/chapt_1.html

404 Tolstoy, Leo. *The Kingdom of God Is Within You*. (Translated by Constance Black Garnett). New York, NY: Cassell Publishing Co., 1894. (Reprinted by University of Nebraska Press, Lincoln and London, 1984.) 153. Print.

405 Weill-Greenberg, Ed. *10 Excellent Reasons Not to Join the Military*. New York: The New Press. 2006. Print.

406 Beckwith, Kathy. "America's Unfinished Sentence Syndrome." 2013. Print Article.

407 Beckwith, Kathy. *Corremos*. (Author's "mas o menos" translation):

To understand the life of others,
Going and seeing, is what we need.
But if we're stuck without a plane,
Let's run to books, and read and read!

408 Roosevelt, Franklin D. "Undelivered Jefferson Day Address, Scheduled for April 14, 1945," GeorgiaInfo. Web. 27 Apr 2010. http://georgiainfo.galileo.usg.edu/FDRspeeches/FDRspeech45-1.htm.

409 Horgan, John. *The End of War.* San Francisco: McSweeney's Books, 2012. 168. Print.

410 Ibid., 169.

411 Fuller, Millard. "Quotations – Quotes, Change." *Managers Forum.* Available from http://www.managersforum.com/quotes/QuoteDetail.asp?Type=CHANGE. Web. 13 Feb 2010.

412 Swanson, David. *When the World Outlawed War.* davidswanson.org, 2011. 155. Print

Suggested Reading/Viewing

Author's Note: The following books and films are my recommendation for beginning a personal study of America's history of war and the need to question war. Each raises issues and explores details of the past and present that I have found to be useful resources in some way. However, their inclusion in this list does not signify full agreement with content nor endorsement; in fact, some disagreement is hereby noted. Those books that include Christian perspectives are purposefully included because of the quality of the work and applicability to the subject at hand, rather than to highlight any one faith, its stance on war, or to indicate a concurrence with any specific content.

To get your toes wet

Buchheit, Paul, Ed., *American Wars: Illusions and Realities.* Atlanta, GA: Clarity Press, 2008. Print.

Strada, Gino. *Green Parrots: A War Surgeon's Diary.* English ed. Milan: Edizioni Charta, 2004. Print. (This book has been bumped up on the list after a new friend, who grew up in Algeria, France, and Belgium, asked if I wanted to know what many Europeans say about why Americans find it so easy to go to war. "Yes," I answered. She said, "Because you haven't seen war here in America and you don't know what it's really like." Gino Strada helps fill the gap.)

War Made Easy. Loretta Alper and Jeremy Earp, Directors. Media Education Foundation, Northampton, MA: 2007. Film.

Wells, Ronald A., Ed., *The Wars of America: Christian Views.* Macon, GA: Mercer University Press, 1991. Print.

www.ericachenoweth.com

www.worldbeyondwar.org: World Beyond War: A Global Movement to End All Wars, 2014. Website. (Start with www.worldbeyondwar.org/quotes, and then explore the rest of the site for reasons to end war and how it can be done.)

Zinn, Howard. "Just and Unjust Wars," *Failure to Quit: Reflections of an Optimistic Historian.* Cambridge, MA: South End Press. 1993/2002. 99–115. Print.

To launch the study

A Force More Powerful: A Century of Nonviolent Conflict. York, Steve, Director, Films for the Humanities, York Zimmerman Inc. & WETA-TV, 2000. Film.

Andreas, Joel. *Addicted to War: Why the U.S. Can't Kick Militarism.* Oakland: AK Press, 2004. Print.

Beebe, Ralph. *Cousins at War: A Civil War Novel.* Bloomington, IN: iUniverse. 2013. Print.

Beckham, Stephen Dow. *Oregon Indians: Voices from Two Centuries.* Corvallis, OR: Oregon State University Press. 2006.

Benjamin, Medea and Jodie Evans, Ed. *Stop the Next War Now.* Maui, HI: Inner Ocean Publishing, Inc. 2005. Print. Don't overlook the following contributions:

Mejia, Camilo. "Regaining My Humanity." 8–10.

Almon, Joan. "The Challenge of Educating for Peace." 46–49.

Benjamin, Medea. "A Life in the Movement: An Interview with Frida Berrigan." 60–65.

Goodman, Amy. "The Power of Dissent." 128–130.

Schroeder, Patricia Scott. "On Not Passing the Buck." 146–147.

Woolsey, Lynn. "Get SMarT: A Better Response to Terrorism." 153–155.

Klein, Naomi. "Bring Halliburton Home." 191–193.

Benjamin, Medea. *Drone Warfare, Killing By Remote Control.* New York, London: OR Books. 2012. Print.

Bringing Down a Dictator. York, Steve, Director, Martin Sheen, Narrator. Washington, D.C.: York Zimmerman, Inc., 2001. Film.

Chapter 10: Bush and Obama: Age of Terror, The Untold History of the United States. Stone, Oliver, Director, and Peter J. Kuznick, Matt Graham. 2012. Film.

Costs and Consequences of War in Iraq. Fact Sheet 2. CESR (Center for Economic and Social Rights). New York. 2 pages. Web. 31 Mar 2012. http://www.cesr.org/downloads/Cost%20and%20Consequences%20of%20War%20in%20Iraq.pdf.

Fry, Douglas P. *Beyond War: The Human Potential for Peace.* Oxford, New York: Oxford University Press, 2007. Print.

Harris, Jonathan. *Hiroshima: A Study in Science, Politics, and the Ethics of War.* Menlo Park, CA: Addison-Wesley Publishing Co., 1970. Print.

Hawaii's Last Queen: The Embattled Reign of Queen Lili'uokalani. Vivian Ducat, Producer. PBS American Experience Series, Narr. Anna Deavere Smith. Boston: WGBH, 1997. Film.

Hedges, Chris. *War is a Force That Gives Us Meaning.* Cambridge, MA: Public Affairs (The Perseus Books Group), 2002. Print. (Author's note: Hedges' story of Fadil Fejzic's cow [pages 50–53] is worth the price of the book or the trip to the library.)

Herold, Marc. *A Dossier on Civilian Victims of United States' Aerial Bombing of Afghanistan: A comprehensive Accounting [revised].* Cursor. Web. 15 Feb 2010. http://cursor.org/stories/civilian_deaths.htm.

Horgan, John. *The End of War.* San Francisco: McSweeney's Books, 2012. Print.

Joyeux Noel. Christian Carion, Director. Sony Pictures: 2005. Film.

Mathews, Dylan. *War Prevention Works: 50 Stories of People Resolving Conflict.* Oxford, England: Oxford Research Group, 2001. Print.

Mock, Ron. *Loving Without Giving In: Christian Responses to Terrorism & Tyranny.* Telford, PA: Cascadia Publishing House, 2004. Print.

Mortenson, Greg and David Oliver Relin. *Three Cups of Tea.* New York: Penguin Books, 2006. Print.

O'Donnell, Terence. *An Arrow in the Earth: General Joel Palmer and the Indians of Oregon.* Portland, OR: Oregon Historical Society Press, 1991. Print.

Perkins, John. *The Secret History of the American Empire.* New York: Penguin Group, 2007. Print.

Polner, Murray, Ed., and Thomas E. Woods, Jr., Ed. *We Who Dared to Say No to War: American Antiwar Writing from 1812 to Now.* New York: Basic Books (A Member of the Perseus Books Group), 2008. Print.

Roy, Arundhati. "Come September," *War Talk.* Cambridge, MA: South End Press, 2003. Print. (After reading "Come September," I suspect you will want to start over and read the entire book.)

Salbi, Zainab. *The Other Side of War: Women's Stories of Survival & Hope.* Washington, D.C.: National Geographic Society. 2006. Print.

Swanson, David. *When the World Outlawed War.* www.davidswanson.org, 2011. Print.

Swanson, David. *War No More: The Case for Abolition.* Charlottesville, VA: www.davidswanson.org, 2013. Print.

The Ground Truth. Patricia Foulkrod, Director. Focus Features/Universal Studios, Universal City, CA: 2006. Film.

The Most Dangerous Man in America: Daniel Ellsberg & the Pentagon Papers. Ehrlich, Judith and Rick Goldsmith, Producers. Daniel Ellsberg, Narrator. Kovno Communication & Insight Communication. 2010. Film.

The Singing Revolution. Tusty, James and Maureen Castle Tusty. 2008. Sky Films, Inc. docurama.com. Film.

Tucker, Richard P., Ed., and Edmund Russell, Ed. *Natural Enemy, Natural Ally: Toward an Environmental History of Warfare.* Corvallis, Oregon: Oregon State University Press, 2004. Print.

Ury, William L. *Getting to Peace: Transforming Conflict at Home, at Work, and in the World.* New York: Viking Penguin, 1999. Print.

Weill-Greenberg, Elizabeth. Ed. *10 Excellent Reasons Not to Join the Military.* New York: The New Press, 2006. Print.

Zinn, Howard. *A People's History of the United States.* New York: Harper & Row, Publishers, Inc., 1980. Print.

To continue the study

Baldwin, Barbara, Amber Baldwin D'Amico, and Heather Baldwin Duff. *Dear Soldier: Heartfelt Letters from America's Children.* Franklin, TN: Integrity Publishers, 2006. Print. [Included to offer a sample of what children learn about war at a very young age.]

Buckley, Ian. "Australia's Foreign Wars: Origins, Costs, Future?!" *The British Empire.* Stephen Luscombe. Web. 21 Aug 2009. http://www.britishempire.co.uk/article/australiaswars1.htm.

El-Najjar, Hassan A. *The Gulf War: Overreaction & Excessiveness.* Dalton, GA: Amazone Press, 2001. Print.

Freeman, Joseph, and Scott Nearing. *Dollar Diplomacy: A Study in American Imperialism.* New York: Monthly Review Press, 1925. Print.

Ferguson, Niall. *The Pity of War.* New York: Penguin Press, 1998. Print.

Fisher, Louis. "The Mexican War and Lincoln's 'Spot Resolutions.'" The Law Library of Congress, 18 Aug 2009. Web. 10 Mar 2010. http://loc.gov/law/help/usconlaw/pdf/Mexican.war.pdf.

Gardner, Lloyd C. *The Long Road to Baghdad: A History of U.S. Foreign Policy from the 1970s to the Present.* New York: The New Press, 2008. Print.

Hoover, Herbert, and Hugh Gibson. *The Problems of Lasting Peace.* Rev. ed., 1943. New York: Doubleday, Doran and Company, Inc., 1942. Print.

Jaspers, Karl. *The Question of German Guilt.* Translated by E.B. Ashton. New York: The Dial Press, 1947. Print.

Kentta, Robert. *A Siletz History.* 2000. Siletz Tribal Newspaper (Parts 1 – 15). Print. Also located on the website of the Confederated Tribes of Siletz Indians at: http://www.ctsi.nsn.us/chinook-indian-tribe-siletz-heritage/our-history/part-i.

Link, Arthur Stanley. *Wilson the Diplomatist: A Look at His Major Foreign Policies.* Baltimore: Johns Hopkins Press, 1957. Print.

Mackenzie, Angus. *Secrets: The CIA's War at Home.* Berkeley: University of California Press, 1997. Print.

McEnroe, Sean. "Painting the Philippines with an American Brush: Visions of Race and National Mission among the Oregon Volunteers in the Philippine Wars of 1898 and 1899." *Oregon Historical Quarterly* 104.1 (2003): 60 pars. 7 May 2010. http://www.historycooperative. org/journals/ohq/104.1/mcenroe.html.

Meinecke, Friedrich. *The German Catastrophe: Reflections and Recollections.* First published in 1950 by Harvard University Press; translated by Sidney B. Fay. Boston: Beacon Press, 1963. Print.

Morgan, H. Wayne. *America's Road to Empire: The War with Spain and Overseas Expansion.* New York: John Wiley & Sons, Inc., 1965. Print.

Sharp, Gene. *The Politics of Nonviolent Action: Parts One, Two, and Three.* Boston: Extending Horizons Books, Porter Sargent Publishers, 1973. Print.

Small, Melvin. *Was War Necessary? National Security and U.S. Entry Into War.* Beverly Hills, CA: Sage Publications, Inc., 1980.

Stewart, Gail B. *The Revolutionary War* (America's Wars series). San Diego, CA: Lucent Books, 1991. Print.

Tolstoy, Leo. *The Kingdom of God Is Within You.* (Translated by Constance Black Garnett). New York, NY: Cassell Publishing Co., 1894. (Reprinted by University of Nebraska Press, Lincoln and London, 1984.) Print.

Wink, Walter. *Jesus and Nonviolence: A Third Way.* Minneapolis: Fortress Press, 2003. Print.

A Starter List of Picture Books to Share With Children

Asch, Frank. *Bread and Honey.* New York: Parents Magazine Press, 1981. Print.

Beckwith, Kathy and Lea Lyon, Ill. *Playing War.* Gardiner, ME: Tilbury House, 2005. Print.

Beckwith, Kathy and Carol Henderson, Ill. *If You Choose Not to Hit.* Minneapolis: Educational Media Corp., 2001. Print.

Bregoli, Jane. *The Goat Lady.* Gardiner, ME: Tilbury House, 2004. Print.

Bromley, Anne C. *The Lunch Thief.* Gardiner, ME: Tilbury House, 2011. Print.

Bruchac, Joseph, and S.D. Nelson, Ill. *Crazy Horse's Vision.* New York: Lee & Low Books Inc., 2000. Print.

Fleisher, Robbin, and Ati Forberg, Ill. *Quilts in the Attic.* New York: Macmillan Publishing Co., Inc., 1978. Print.

Gikow, Louise and Joe Mathieu, Ill. *Red Hat! Green Hat!* New York: Golden Books Publishing Co., Inc., 2000. Print.

Hesse, Karen, and Wendy Watson, Ill. *The Cats in Krasinski Square.* New York: Scholastic Press, 2004. Print.

Hines, Anna Grossnickle. *Come to the Meadow.* New York: Clarion Books/ Ticknor & Fields, 1984. Print.

Jaques, Florence Page and Laura McGee Kvasnosky, Ill.. *There Once Was a Puffin.* New York: Dutton Children's Books, 1995. Print.

Judge, Lita. *One Thousand Tracings: Healing the Wounds of World War II.* New York: Hyperion Books for Children, 2007. Print.

Kent, Jack. *The Wizard of Wallaby Wallow.* New York: Parents' Magazine Press, 1971. Print.

Leaf, Munro, and Robert Lawson, Ill. *The Story of Ferdinand.* New York: Puffin Books, 1977. (Originally published by Viking Press, 1936). Print.

Lionni, Leo. *Swimmy.* New York: Dragonfly Books, Alfred A. Knopf, 1963. Print.

Martin Jr., Bill, John Archambault, and Ted Rand, Ill. *Knots on a Counting Rope*. New York: Henry Holt and Company, 1987. Print.

McCain, Becky Ray and Todd Leonardo, Ill. *Nobody Knew What to Do: A Story About Bullying*. Morton Grove, IL: Albert Whitman & Company, 2001. Print.

Milord, Sue and Jerry. *Maggie and the Goodbye Gift*. New York: Lothrop, Lee & Shepard Books, 1979. Print.

Moss, Peggy and Lea Lyon, Ill. *Say Something*. Gardiner, ME: Tilbury House, 2005. Print.

Moss, Peggy and Penny Weber, Ill. *One of Us*. Gardiner, ME: Tilbury House, 2010. Print.

Munson, Derek and Tara Calahan King, Ill. *Enemy Pie*. San Francisco: Chronicle Books, 2000. Print.

Muth, Jon J. (Retold and Ill.) *Stone Soup*. New York: Scholastic, Inc., 2003. Print.

Muth, Jon J. *The Three Questions* (Based on a story by Leo Tolstoy). New York: Scholastic, Inc., 2002. Print.

Scholes, Katherine, and Robert Ingpen, Ill. *Peace Begins with You*. San Francisco: Sierra Club Books, 1990. Print.

Silverman, Erica, and S.D. Schindler, Ill. *Don't Fidget a Feather!* New York: Simon & Schuster Books for Young Readers, 1994. Print.

Trivizas, Eugene, and Helen Oxenbury, Ill. *The Three Little Wolves and the Big Bad Pig*. New York: Margaret K. McElderry Books (Simon & Schuster Children's Publishing Division), 1993. Print.

Willems, Mo. *Can I Play Too?* (An Elephant & Piggie Book). New York: Hyperion Books for Children, 2010. Print.

Book Club – Reading Group Discussion Questions

1) What surprised you most in reading this book?

2) What memories or teachings about America's wars do you recall that were challenged here?

3) At the close of the historical review of America's wars (see page 153), Kathy relates the *London Observer's* article about the use of bones to manure the fields of England. She concludes: "Surely we can question manure." Yet she had acknowledged in the opening chapter that questioning takes real courage. What do you feel is hardest about questioning your nation's pattern of war, or a specific war, or the need for war?

4) Ed Vulliamy of the *London Observer* gave a heart-breaking report of war in Iraq (Chapter 3). The stories of the doctor in Vietnam and the soldiers in Iraq told what it was like up close for them. How did these stories impact you? How important is it that we know such details?

5) There are seven reasons listed in Chapter 4 that explain why war sells – taking away the other's humanity, naming ourselves as the good guys who do no wrong, using fancy words, pomp & fanfare, seeing it all from our own viewpoint, making money by making war, and not feeling the money spent is real. What personal experience of yours sheds light on any one of these reasons? How did the experience influence your thoughts about war? Is there an "On the other hand..." that you're feeling about the issues raised?

6) Which of the "People say..." quotations on page 185 have you been most likely to use in the past? What is your reaction to the counter-proposal Kathy gives for that saying?

7) Did you grow up learning stories of national and international nonviolent conflict resolution? What stories had an impact on you?

8) How are you personally involved in peace-building or problem-solving through nonviolent ways? What have you learned there that you think could apply on a national or international level?

9) What do you think is most needed in order for governments to rely more on nonviolent resolution of international conflict and less on the use of war?

10) Are you one who has experienced war up close? Has it been easy or difficult to tell others about it? Do people seem eager or reluctant to know more about war?

11) How did you react to Kathy's proposal (page 246) that we begin personally by communicating better, learning something new and asking for an opinion on it, and then stop doing or saying one thing? Have you tried it?

12) If you feel that change is needed, what will be your first step to act and do something? Will you try to do it with others or solo?

13) What else would you like to say?

About the Author

Kathy Beckwith is a mediation trainer from Dayton, Oregon, working with schools (K-12) and community mediation programs. She is a mediator in parent/teen, victim/offender, and neighborhood mediation, and volunteers as a school mediation coach. Kathy became concerned about America's strong reliance on war as a means of resolving international conflict. That concern led to research and study, and finally to this book. She discovered that she had, indeed, missed some things in U.S. History class.

Kathy is also the author of the picture book *Playing War;* a young adult novel, *Critical Mass,* dealing with sexual abuse in the lives of teens; and two books related to problem-solving, *If You Choose Not to Hit,* and *Don't Shoot! We May Both Be on the Same Side.*

Kathy is a graduate of Northwest Nazarene University, Nampa, Idaho. She has been a Peace Corps volunteer, caregiver in a residential treatment home for boys, secretary for a geological exploration office, teacher at an international school in South India, and host parent for exchange students, in addition to living and playing with her family on a small farm where wild blackberries abound.

More Dignity Press books related to peace building and peace education
Order at www.dignitypress.org

Ada Aharoni
Rare Flower
Life, Love and Peace Poems
326 pages, hardcover, 29.00 US-$
ISBN 978-1-937570-10-1

Francisco C. Gomes de Matc
Dignity Multidimensional

144 pages, hardcover, 16.00 US-$
ISBN 978-1-937570-37-8

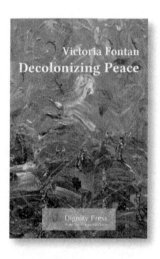

Victoria Fontan
Decolonizing Peace

220 pages, softcover, 16.00 US-$
ISBN 978-1-937570-15-6

Pierre-Amal Kana
Afghanistan - Le rêve
pashtoun et la voie de la paix
French, 332 pages, softcover, 18.00 US
ISBN 978-1-937570-18-7

More Dignity Press books related to peace building and peace education
Order at www.dignitypress.org

Hilary Roseman
Generating Forgiveness

432 pages, softcover, 20.00 US-$
ISBN 978-1-937570-48-4

Hayal Köksal
Çekirdekten Yetiştirme
(Catch them Young)
Turkish, 164 pages, 11.90 US-$
ISBN 978-1-937570-57-6

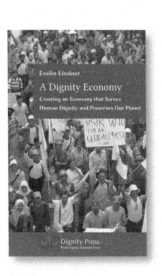

Evelin Lindner
A Dignity Economy

460 pages, 28.00 US-$
ISBN 978-1-937570-03-3

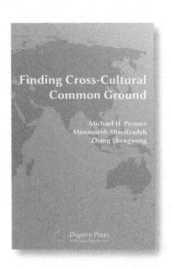

Michael H. Prosser
Finding Cross-Cultural
Common Ground
511 pages, 22.00 US-$
ISBN 978-1-937570-25-5

CPSIA information can be obtained
at www.ICGtesting.com
Printed in the USA
FSOW04n0446291215
14885FS